Philosophy and an African culture

Philosophy and
an African culture

KWASI WIREDU

Professor of Philosophy
University of Ghana, Legon

CAMBRIDGE UNIVERSITY PRESS

CAMBRIDGE

LONDON   NEW YORK   NEW ROCHELLE

MELBOURNE   SYDNEY

Published by the Press Syndicate of the University of Cambridge
The Pitt Building, Trumpington Street, Cambridge CB2 1RP
32 East 57th Street, New York, NY 10022, USA
296 Beaconsfield Parade, Middle Park, Melbourne 3206, Australia

First published 1980

Set, printed and bound in Great Britain by
Fakenham Press Limited,
Fakenham, Norfolk

ISBN 0 521 22794 1 hard covers
ISBN 0 521 29647 1 paperback

Library of Congress Cataloguing in Publication Data
Wiredu, Kwasi.
Philosophy and an African culture.
Includes index.
1. Philosophy, African—Addresses, essays, lectures.
2. Philosophy—Addresses, essays, lectures. I. Title.
B5305.W57 199'.6 79–19805
ISBN 0 521 22794 1 hard covers
ISBN 0 521 29647 1 paperback

Contents

For Adwoa and the Children

Acknowledgments

I wish to express my sincere thanks to Dr Jeremy Mynott of CUP for valuable advice on revising the essays contained in this book and working them into a unified volume. I am indebted also to Mr Sinclair-Wilson for his editorial assistance. Special thanks are due to Dr John Skorupski who read the entire manuscript and made very useful comments and criticisms from which, I believe, the book has benefited immensely. This applies particularly to the final chapter, which has not been previously published. Had I been able to accept all his criticisms my views on the concept of truth as expressed in the book would, perhaps, have sounded less strange than they are likely to do. Certainly without those criticisms they would have sounded more obscure. I thank also my colleague Professor Gyekye for reading the manuscript and making useful suggestions. To the publishers of the previous versions of the essays are due thanks for permission to use them here. Finally there is my younger brother and colleague in the Department of Philosophy at Legon, Mr M. A. Kissi. Among brothers, according to my understanding of our culture, no thanks are due. But I would like to mention his unfailing help in this as in all my philosophical writing.

Introduction

The essays in this volume fall into three main groups. The first four deal directly with the idea of African philosophy. I discuss the problem of what a contemporary African philosopher is to make of his African background of traditional thought in trying to fashion a philosophy cognisant of intellectual developments in the modern world. Among the distinctions made in this group of essays I stress the distinction between African philosophy as folk thought preserved in oral traditions and African philosophy as critical, individual reflection, using modern logical and conceptual techniques. I emphasise the importance of not using the term 'African philosophy' to mean just African traditional folk thought and point out some unfortunate consequences of doing so. In 'How not to compare African traditional thought with Western thought' (chapter 3),[1] in particular, I try to show that these ill-effects do not bear only on philosophy in Africa but also adversely affect the whole process of modernisation in Africa. 'Philosophy and an African culture' (chapter 1) is even less narrowly philosophical. In it I take a critical look at Ghanaian traditional culture, analysing it philosophically and attempting to distinguish those aspects worthy of being preserved and fostered from those it would be better to abandon.

The importance of a serious study of African traditional philosophy by philosophers in Africa is now very widely appreciated. But there is need for careful thought as to the aims of such a study. It is not enough simply to collect information about what our ancestors

---

[1] In view of persistent misunderstanding I should point out that the argument of this chapter is not that no comparisons should be made, but only that a certain type of comparison ought not to be made.

said or thought; we must try to interpret, clarify, analyse and, where appropriate and after a critical evaluation, assimilate and develop the resulting body of thought. This last mentioned part of the enterprise, namely, the critical evaluation of our traditional philosophies, ought to be both theoretically and practically motivated. The theoretical aspect of the matter requires little or no comment as it is obvious that any philosophical investigation involves a quest for pure understanding. But the practical side is in danger of being overlooked. Contemporary Africa is in the middle of the transition from a *traditional* to a *modern* society. This process of modernisation entails changes not only in the physical environment but also in the mental outlook of our peoples, manifested both in their explicit beliefs and in their customs and their ordinary daily habits and pursuits. Since the fundamental rationale behind any changes in a world outlook is principally a philosophical matter, it is plain that the philosophical evaluation of our traditional thought is of very considerable relevance to the process of modernisation on our continent. Accordingly, we need to approach African traditional philosophy with an alert awareness of this particular kind of interplay between thought and action. This standpoint informs the remaining two essays of the first set, namely, 'On an African orientation in philosophy' (chapter 2), and 'What can philosophy do for Africa?' (chapter 4), as thoroughly as the essays already mentioned.

The test of a contemporary African philosopher's conception of African philosophy is whether it enables him to engage fruitfully in the activity of modern philosophising with an African conscience. If African philosophy means *traditional* African philosophy, as surprisingly many people seem to think, then we can forget any pretence of modern philosophising. In most parts of Africa we would have, in that case, to abstain from such disciplines as symbolic logic and its philosophical interpretation; the philosophy of mathematics and of the natural and social sciences, the theory of knowledge associated with the foregoing disciplines and the moral, political and social philosophy which has arisen as a response to the needs of modern times. We would have to regard all such disciplines as *un-African* and content ourselves with repeating the proverbs and folk conceptions of our forefathers. Or, should we be moved by some quirk of the spirit to dabble in those modern disciplines, we should have to represent ourselves as venturing into un-African domains.

The point of view of this whole volume stands in very definite contrast to such a conception. There is a traditional African philosophy, and there is an emerging modern African philosophy.[2] A modern African philosophy will appropriate whatever there is of value in the disciplines above and domesticate them, and it will seek also to make contributions to them. The contemporary African can do all this without ignoring his own background of traditional African thought. Nor should he be oblivious to the resources of his indigenous language as an aid to philosophical reflection. Though for historical reasons he writes in English or French, there is no reason why in his philosophical meditations he should not test formulations in those languages against intuitions in his own language. This point is enlarged upon in chapter 2 (pp. 34–6). I believe that it is a point worthy of the closest attention of African philosophers.

All the remaining essays – apart, that is, from the first four – are devoted to tackling philosophical issues in the manner in which I think modern African philosophising might proceed. At present a lot of time is given by philosophers in Africa to talking *about* African philosophy as distinct from actually doing it. There are good reasons for this. The search for the correct conception of African philosophy is part of the post-colonial African quest for identity. But it is necessary at this stage to balance this concern with Meta-African Philosophy with a readiness to get along with the task itself of modern philosophical thinking; that is the only

[2] There is a school of thought in contemporary Africa which sees ancient Egyptian philosophy as the *classical* phase of African philosophy. According to this line of thought ancient Egyptian thought was the head and spring of ancient Greek philosophy and, through it, of Western philosophy as a whole. (See, for example, L. Keita 'The African Philosophical Tradition' and H. Olela, 'The African Foundations of Greek Philosophy' in Richard A. Wright (ed.), *African Philosophy: An Introduction*, University Press of America, 1977.) On this reasoning an African pursuing philosophy as it has been developed in the West today can see himself as merely resuming a tradition which was started by his own peoples in ancient times. If this soothes his African conscience in his modern philosophical pursuits, well and good. But in view of the possible historical and even conceptual problems in this way of looking at the history of thought, it is good to note that the justification of the cultivation of modern philosophy in Africa need not involve this exercise in genealogy, however intriguing it may be in itself.

way in which the establishment of a modern African philosophical tradition can be advanced.

Two of the essays referred to in the last paragraph fall naturally into one group. They are 'Marxism, philosophy and ideology' (chapter 5) and 'In praise of utopianism' (chapter 6). These two essays are a critique of Marxism from the point of view of a libertarian socialism. The importance of Marxist socialism in Africa can hardly be denied, and the time is overdue for a serious philosophical examination of it in African philosophical circles.

The next group of essays, which constitutes the last part of this volume, has one central preoccupation: the concept of truth. The question of the meaning of truth is, I believe, one of both a theoretical and a practical interest. It emerges earlier, in connection with relatively more practical concerns, in chapters 4, 5 and 6, and in the third group of essays it is foreshadowed in chapter 7, 'Philosophy, mysticism, and rationality', an essay which examines mystical experience as a mode of *knowing*. The view proposed in the essays dealing directly with the concept of truth is that truth is nothing over and above opinion. As I know from experience, it is a highly controversial view, and I have tried to argue it as clearly as I can.

My view of truth bears some resemblance to the view advanced in 1927 by the English philosopher and logician Frank Ramsey according to which there is no problem of truth separate from the problem of assertion; though in chapter 8 (page 120) I note what seems to me to be a defect in this view, which is usually known as the Redundancy theory of truth. My own strongest sense of affinity is with John Dewey's theory of truth according to which truth is the same as warranted assertibility. I first state my view in 'Truth as opinion' (chapter 8), taking note of some likely objections. Then in a substantial section of 'What is philosophy?' (chapter 10, section III, 'The theory of truth', pp. 153–61) I place the view in the context of the three main theories of truth traditional[3] in Western philosophy, namely, the Correspondence, Pragmatic and Coherence theories. In this I expand on the general conception of philos-

---

[3] Note the difference in the connotation of the word 'traditional' as it occurs in the phrases 'traditional African philosophy' and 'traditional Western philosophy'.

ophy which underlies the conception of African philosophy expounded in the first four essays of the book. I try to give expression to the over-all practical orientation of my conception of philosophy. It is, I think, worth emphasising that a practical orientation is fully compatible with the highest level of theoretical and technical elaboration in philosophy. In the intervening chapter, declaring itself in its title, 'To be is to be known', I argue a position about knowledge and existence which is presupposed by my view of truth.

A philosophical thesis is usually expressible quite briefly, witness the following historic examples: To be is to be perceived; Matter is the permanent possibility of sensation; Reality is systematic coherence; The meaning of a proposition is its method of verification; Mind is prior to Matter; Matter is prior to Mind; Things in themselves are unknowable, only appearances can be objects of knowledge; Space and time are forms of intuition; Pleasure is the only thing good in itself. The elaboration of such theses beyond the stage of preliminary clarification consists, as a rule, in the forestalling of anticipated misunderstandings. This is hardly ever adequate. It is generally in response to criticisms that a philosopher begins to attain anything approaching an adequate sharpening of exposition. Thus philosophical discourse is essentially a dialogue, either proleptic, anticipating objections, or disputational, replying to criticisms.

The career of the thesis that truth is nothing but opinion has been no exception and in chapter 11 ('In defence of opinion') I confront a published criticism of my view by Dr Odera Oruka, a vigorous Kenyan philosopher. In chapter 12 ('Truth, a dialogue') I take up some unpublished criticisms with which I have been confronted, and anticipate others in the hope that I might throw some light on what may otherwise remain obscure in my conception. It is in the form of a dialogue in which PROPONENT, in my own person, responds to a series of objections from CRITIC. A full understanding of my view is unlikely to be reached without the reading of chapters 8, 9, 10 (section III 'The theory of truth'), and both chapters 11 and 12.

These essays have been written in such a way as to interest both philosophers and general readers in Africa and outside Africa. Unexplained technicalities have been purposely left out. The essays in the three main parts of the volume hang together closely, as I have indicated above. I hope that as a whole they furnish an adequate characterisation and a good example of one type of modern African philosophy. For African philosophy generally my hope is that a hundred flowers will bloom.

I

Philosophy and an African culture

The study of African culture has, as a rule, been undertaken from an anthropological point of view. It cannot be denied that this has provided important insights, but amid the exigencies of the cultural transition that is taking place in contemporary Africa there is a need for critical and constructive analysis. Philosophy has obvious responsibilities in this connection, and in the present chapter I attempt a philosophical treatment of a particular African culture, the Ghanaian. Different aspects of this same subject will occupy us in the next three chapters.

I wish to start by calling attention to three complaints which can afflict a society. They are anachronism, authoritarianism and supernaturalism. Let me quickly explain how I am going to construe these '-isms', which may at first sight appear either obscure or ambiguous, as well as inelegant. My use of the word 'anachronism' here is a fairly straightforward extension of the ordinary use. I propose to call anything anachronistic which outlasts its suitability. Anachronism then becomes the failure to perceive anachronistic things for what they are and to discard or modify them as the case may require. Various habits of thought and practice can become anachronistic within the context of the development of a given society; but an entire society too can become anachronistic within the context of the whole world if the ways of life within it are predominantly anachronistic. In the latter case, of course, there is no discarding the society; what you do is to *modernise* it. Probably every society suffers from some degree of anachronism, but the implication of calling a society 'under-developed', or, in the suppositious synonym, 'developing', is that it suffers from this malady in both ways. I shall be concerned with anachronism *within* a society, rather than *of* that society; even though the same things may be anachronistic in each case, the contrasts made give the discussion a different focus.

Authoritarianism is somewhat harder to define. In talking of authoritarianism here I do not simply have political matters in mind; the political aspect of social life is only one aspect, and that not the most basic. The really fundamental aspects of social life are those which relate to personal interaction, to which I will return in due course. What I mean by authoritarianism may be stated in a preliminary way as follows: Any human arrangement is authoritarian if it entails any person being made to do or suffer something against his will, or if it leads to any person being hindered in the development of his own will. This definition is likely to be felt to be too broad. It might be objected that no orderly society is possible without some sort of constituted authority which can override a refractory individual will. Anybody wishing to elaborate on this kind of objection has a rich tradition of both Western and non-Western philosophical thought to draw upon. Let me here cut the matter short by making a concession. We might now say that what is authoritarian is the *unjustified* overriding of an individual's will. This qualification is suggestive at least in this way: there is implied in it a certain sense of the primary value and importance of the human will, for the onus of justification is placed on anyone who would interfere with it. I suggest that the more rigorously one thinks about the possible basis of any such justification the more important the requirement of the unimpeded development of the individual's will implied in our preliminary definition becomes; for may it not be that what we call a refractory will is, after all, frequently a will whose development has been hampered by early social conditions? A consideration which grows in importance when one reflects that it is quite conceivable for a Brave-New-World type of society to exist in which no one is made to do or suffer anything against their will; and yet such a society would be seen to be revoltingly authoritarian in as much as a person's will would usually be the result of manipulation by others.

There is, even in conventional wisdom, a distinction which reflects awareness of the foregoing point. People are accustomed to distinguish between education and indoctrination. Education is the kind of training of the mind that enables people to make deliberate rational choices. Indoctrination, on the other hand, is the kind of moulding of the mind which leads to built-in choices. It is in the first kind of case that the concept of free will applies. An indoctrinated mind can make 'free' choices, but only in a superficial sense. The will in this case is the result of external scheming.

This distinction between education and indoctrination has implications which are anything but conventional. Any training intended to enable people to make deliberate rational choices must aim at enabling them to perceive, in relation to any given issue, as many as possible of the relevant alternatives; for there is no choice in the absence of perceived alternatives, and the omission or concealment of a relevant alternative extinguishes a potential choice. Now, if we measure existing practices by this yardstick, we must admit that we fall far short of this requirement, and what we call education, especially in early life, should more appropriately be described, if not as indoctrination, then by some intermediate term. Consider, for example, how we forestall the future choices of children by baptising them into our own religious persuasions and filling their young minds with sermons that accord a low priority, if any at all, to the discussion of alternatives or even to the rational justification of the one given alternative.[1]

In the particular matter of the education of infants there are, I concede, limiting natural circumstances. A mind too raw to grasp anything like relevant alternatives still needs to be led, at least, away from danger. The point, however, is that even when alternatives can begin to be understood, we still deliberately, even self-righteously, permit only one. Nor is this restricted to the education of children or even formal education in general. The very atmosphere we breathe in many areas of life in our society seems to be suffused with an authoritarian odour; though, if our noses have been acclimatised to it through long conditioning we may possibly not find the odour offensive, or even remark on it in the first place. To take an example, anyone who inquires after the reason behind some established procedure at a government ministry in this country is lucky if he is not met with some such rebuff as: 'That is how it has always been done. I don't want any argument.' Reason is what ought to decide between alternatives, and the disinclination to entertain questions about the reasons behind an established

[1] It is not suggested here that this kind of thing is peculiar to our society.

practice or institution is a sure mark of the authoritarian mentality. This attitude is deeply ingrained in our society. Political authoritarianism is only an unsurprising reflection of this grassroots authoritarianism.

Was there anything in our traditional culture of this nature? I believe that the answer is yes. Our traditional society was deeply authoritarian. Our social arrangements were shot through and through with the principle of unquestioning obedience to superiors, which often meant elders. Hardly any premium was placed on curiosity in those of tender age, or independence of thought in those of more considerable years. Our traditional culture is famous for an abundance of proverbs – those concentrations of practical wisdom which have a marvellous power when quoted at the right moment to clinch a point of argument or reinforce a moral reflection. But it is rare to come across ones which extol the virtues of originality and independence of thought.[2]

It is important to place what has just been said in a historical perspective. That our traditional culture was authoritarian is a distinctly modern comment. It is a comment made from an intellectual milieu very different from that of traditional times. Traditional society was founded on a community of shared beliefs in the wisdom of age, the sanctity of chieftaincy and the binding force of the customs and usages of our ancestors. It cannot be assumed, therefore, that traditional systems of authority, both formal and informal, must have been felt to be authoritarian within the traditional milieu itself. But the influence of this outlook has waned markedly, particularly in our urban areas,[3] while the old manners of authority persist in various shapes and forms. It is in these changed circumstances that the traditional culture is increasingly felt to be authoritarian. It may be said, thus, that the particular phenomenon of authoritarianism touched upon in the foregoing remarks is also an instance of an anachronism. We may take it also

[2] There is, of course, no suggestion here that our forefathers totally lacked the spirit of inquiry. I know, for example, of the Akan symbol of inquiry. (See Kofi Antubam, *Ghana's Heritage of Culture*, Koehler & Amelang, Leipzig, 1963, pp. 158, 159.) There is also the saying '*ohwehwe asem mu a na wo hu mu*' (you only find out about a matter if you investigate it). See also J. B. Danquah, *The Akan Doctrine of God*, second edition, edited by Kwesi A. Dickson, Frank Cass and Co. 1968, p. 190 maxim numbered 1196.

[3] See further pp. 29–31.

that, in general, cultural anachronism needs to be approached with a certain measure of *practical* relativism.

Paradoxically the authoritarianism mentioned above is closely connected with one of the strongest points of our culture, namely, the great value it places on what we might call communal belonging. To my mind one of the greatest problems facing anyone who would like to see a judicious adaptation of our traditional culture to modern conditions is how to preserve this feature while eliminating the negative aspects, such as the authoritarianism just mentioned, which seems to be intertwined with it. It is important – at any rate, that is the belief which motivates this discussion – to try to see what contributions philosophical thinking can make towards the solution of a problem of this kind.

It is now time to consider the third of the three evils which I mentioned at the start, namely, supernaturalism. By supernaturalism I do not mean the belief in the existence of supernatural beings. If there are such beings, it can hardly be suggested that belief in their existence is an evil. Whether or not there are such beings seems to me to be a factual question, given some, not necessarily simple, preliminary conceptual clarification. But associated with any such belief or system of beliefs *may* be an outlook potentially harmful to humanity, as is evident in the tendency to seek the basis of morality in some supernatural source. This outlook is what I mean by supernaturalism. Its opposite is humanism, the point of view according to which morality is founded exclusively on considerations of human well-being. When rules, policies and actions are based on people's appreciation of the conditions of human well-being there is, indeed, no absolute guarantee that consequences will always actually be in accord with humane ideals, human understanding being limited. But it is altogether a different thing when standards of good and evil are derived from a supernatural source. In that case it becomes quite possible for policies which lead manifestly to human suffering to be advocated or pursued with a sense of piety and rectitude. Let me give an example. Suppose it comes to be believed that it is the will of God that the number of human beings should multiply without any artificial control. Suppose, further, that the will of God is held to define what is morally good or morally evil, and, lastly, that it can be shown that unless artificially controlled the increasing numbers of our species will lead to human misery. Still it would be wrong by this supernatural morality to seek to control our numbers by artificial devices; and it would, indeed, be pious to say so.

It has often been said that our traditional outlook was intensely humanistic. It seems to me that, as far as the basis of the traditional ethic is concerned, this claim is abundantly justified. Traditional thinking about the foundations of morality is refreshingly non-supernaturalist. Not that one can find in traditional sources elaborate theories of humanism. But anyone who reflects on our traditional ways of speaking about morality is bound to be struck by the preoccupation with human welfare: What is morally good is what befits a human being; it is what is decent for man – what brings dignity, respect, contentment, prosperity, joy, to man and his community. And what is morally bad is what brings misery, misfortune, and disgrace. Of course, immoral conduct is held to be hateful to God, the Supreme Being, and even to the lesser gods. But the thought is not that something is good because God approves of it but rather that God approves of it because it is good in the first place – a distinction which, as Socrates[4] noted in the context of a different culture, does not come easily to every pious mind.

There is an aesthetic strain in our traditional ethical thought which is worthy of special mention in this connection. As noted already, what is good is conceived to be what is fitting (*nea efata*, in Akan); and what is fitting is what is beautiful (*nea εyε fε*). There are, indeed, aesthetic analogies in the moral language of other cultures. But aesthetic analogies are taken very much more seriously and have more extensive moral relevance in our traditional thought. This aesthetic orientation of our tradition is obviously of a piece with its non-supernaturalism. I believe that this freedom from supernaturalism in our traditional ethic is an aspect of our culture which we ought to cherish and protect from countervailing influences from abroad.

I have spoken repeatedly of *our* traditional culture. This is not because I wish to pretend that the whole of Ghana (or, even more incredibly, the whole of Africa) has one homogeneous traditional culture. There are in Ghana a variety of ethnic groups with traditional cultures that differ in some respects. Nevertheless, there

4 In Plato's *Euthyphro*.

are deep underlying affinities running through these cultures which justify speaking of a Ghanaian traditional culture. Indeed, for the same reason one might speak of the traditional culture of Africa, though with a more considerable attenuation of content. In his little known book, *Ghana's Heritage of Culture*, the late Kofi Antubam, combining the intuition of an artist of genius with an intense anthropological enthusiasm for the culture of his mother-land, attempted an inventory of the basic common elements in terms of which an overall Ghanaian culture might be defined. As a sort of preliminary he gave a list of what he calls 'some of the common aspects of African life and culture' in which he mentions the African's strong belief in the existence and power of a hierarchy of spiritual beings headed by an omnipotent God; his belief in life after death; his 'communalistic' custom of holding land and property in general in common with relatives; his spontaneity and sincerity of expression, his tendency 'to clothe all his cherished ideas in verbal and graphic symbols' and generally to attach meanings to artistic forms; his love of colour and capacity for long suffering; his tendency to equate age with wisdom; his habit of giving impersonal representation of persons in art and, finally, 'his possession and use of talking drums in his music which is largely featured with rich expression of variations of rhythms' (p. 23).

Apart from its rather idiosyncratic phrasing, which is only slightly reflected in the above paraphrase but more amply illustrated in the quotation to be given below, Antubam's list is probably an uncontroversial one. But when he turns specifically to Ghana he becomes a trifle indiscriminate. In reproducing his list here, I take slight liberties with the ordering though not with the wording. 'The Ghanaian of today,' he declares,

> is confronted with the traditions of a culture which upholds among many others the values contained in the following beliefs and practices:
> (1) the idea of the existence of One Great God as an integral member of society as distinct from the Western and Christian idea of God staying aloof in Heaven in the community of good spirits, looking down on the evil ones in Hell, and yet seeking to govern a mixture of the sinners and the righteous on earth;

(2) the belief in the perpetual existence of life, in which there is a cycle of pregnancy, life, death and a period of waiting in a universal pool of spiritual existence with a subsequent state of reincarnation, by which it is possible to change one's lot for better or for worse;

(3) the belief in the sanctity of man as opposed to woman in society;

(4) the belief in the idea that man is born free from sin and the idea that he remains so until he becomes involved in some polluting circumstances in life, as opposed to the Jewish and Christian idea of man born with original sin which he is said to have inherited from his ancestors Adam and Eve;

(5) the idea of beauty of thought, speech, action and appearance as a basic and necessary prerequisite for appointment to the high office of state;

(6) the ability to produce a child as a necessary factor for the continuance of marriage;

(7) the importance of marriage as a criterion of social status;

(8) the principle of age as a vital criterion of wisdom;

(9) the tendency to stress, in all forms of art, the quality of significance as a criterion of beauty and virtue as opposed to the eternal emphasis on the slogan art for art's sake, which is tending to render human life in modern Europe so grossly pointless and not different from that of the beast of the field;

(10) spontaneity of self-expression [the lack of] which is the greatest weakness of modern Western diplomacy;

(11) the peculiar conception that it is improper and obscene to say thanks soon after one has been offered food by a neighbour.

So far, the list seems to be substantially unexceptionable, though Antubam's own way of giving life to an idea does at times make for exaggeration. For example, his suggestion that Ghanaians traditionally believed in 'the sanctity of man as opposed to woman' is a curious exaggeration of the traditional idea that it is spiritually inauspicious to have contact with women in some circumstances. Again, surely, it is too strong to say that the ability to produce a child is a necessary condition for the continuance of marriage in traditional Ghanaian society. Divorce may standardly be conceded where it is lacking, but it is not mandatory. In the matter of his contrasts, it is obvious, for example, that the remark that the notion of art for art's sake is rendering life in modern Europe so grossly pointless that it is not different from that of the beast of the field must be put down to the idiosyncrasies of a restless genius. Still, with appropriate allowances, the foregoing list gives a reasonably authentic impression of some aspects of the over-all culture of Ghana.

Antubam, however, goes on to enumerate items of doubtful universality in Ghana. He mentions such things as the association of the right hand with the opposite sex and with impropriety generally; the sharp intolerance on the part of males of spirited language from females; the custom of inheriting taboos patriline-ally and property matrilineally; the use of a seven day week and a forty day month calendar and the conception of society in terms of seven clans (*ibid.*, pp. 28–9). Though these ideas and usages are not quite universal in Ghana, they are of relevance in the present context as they are most certainly operative among a large majority of Ghanaians.

Referring to Antubam's list the Ghanaian sociologist E. H. Mends in a highly interesting paper entitled 'Some Basic Elements in the Culture of Ghana'[5] comments: 'Whilst Antubam deserves to be praised for detailing these points, I would suggest that some of these features are spurious and others are specifically applicable to the Akan and cannot be generalised for the other component ethnic groups.' In that paper Mends does not pursue this comment in detail but he has indicated in conversation that he would be in basic agreement with the remarks I have made above.

Mends has proposed his own list of Ghanaian cultural charac-teristics. It contains six items of which the last two are reproduc-tions, with due acknowledgement, of elements in Antubam's list. I now quote from Mends:

(1) The stress or importance that is attached to group life.

(2) The importance of kinship as represented in the institu-

[5] Presented at a conference on Ghanaian Culture organised jointly by the Minis-try of Education and Culture, the Institute of African Studies and the Department of Philosophy both of the University of Ghana at Legon in April 1975.

tional form of the extended family system irrespective of the differences of descent systems.

(3) Chiefship and its symbolic significance.
(4) The pervasiveness and stress on ceremony and ritual in many aspects of social life.
(5) The idea of beauty of speech, thought, action and appearance as a prerequisite for appointment to high office.
(6) The tendency to stress, in all forms of art, the quality of significance as a criterion of beauty and virtue.

In comparison with Antubam's list this is clearly more sober. It is somewhat austere in its economy but, nevertheless, more comprehensive in scope. Both lists, however, have a certain merit in common which I would like to highlight. They both display a sense of the wide ranging character of culture. They show an awareness that culture means more than art, song and dance. It might antecedently have been thought that this was obvious enough. But in Africa today, certainly in Ghana, this truism is in danger of being forgotten, and there is, consequently, ample justification for canvassing it rather earnestly. The culture of a people is their total way of life, and this is seen as well in their work and recreation as in their worship and courtship;[6] it is seen also in their ways of investigating nature and utilising its possibilities and in their ways of viewing themselves and interpreting their place in nature. Nor is that all. To gain an adequate idea of the culture of a people, one has to take account of the manner in which they house and clothe themselves; their method of conducting war and arranging peace; their systems of statecraft, of education, of rewards and punishment and the way they regulate personal relations generally. One has also to understand the ideas underlying their institutions and practices. All this and, perhaps, more are relevant when one talks of a culture. Yet in this country it is common to think only of drums and dancing when culture is mentioned. Any cultural policy based on such an impoverished conception of culture is not likely to be of very much use since drumming and dancing are not the things in which our culture particularly needs to be improved.

If we now return, with an enlarged conception of culture, to the lists of Antubam and Mends, there are a few things that we might

[6] If the juxtaposition of worship and courtship sounds unexpected, please note that courtship is, after all, a kind of worship, only not metaphysical.

add, partly in elaboration and partly in supplementation, though we will still not be able, in view of our limited purpose in this discussion, to attain anything like adequate comprehensiveness. We might add (in random order) such things as kindness to strangers, reverence for ancestors and other departed relatives who are believed to be able to affect the living; elaborate rituals of mourning;[7] the belief in the existence and influence of lesser gods as agents of the one Supreme God, and in witchcraft and a variety of spirits, fetishes and powers, both good and bad; the notion that human beings are born into the world with an unalterable destiny bestowed in advance by God; the tendency to stress, not just in forms of art but in sundry other practices, the quality of significance; the institution of polygamy and the high esteem for large families; the strong sense of rhythm as manifested not only in music and dance but also, for example, in the gait of women; the emphasis on the beauty and correctness of speech as a condition not only of high office of state but also of general social respectability; the influence of myths, totemism and taboos in thought and action; the attachment of a religious significance to the office of a chief,[8] with reverence for and complete obedience to his authority, except where that is undermined by his own wickedness or malpractice; the high premium placed on consensus in group endeavour and a great capacity for reconciliation after even the bitterest conflict or dissension; the education of children through the informal processes of day-to-day upbringing rather than through formal institutions; the dependence on oral rather than written records.

Closely connected with this last is perhaps the most important addition of all yet to be made. It concerns our traditional mode of understanding, utilising and controlling external nature and of interpreting the place of man within it. That mode is common not only to the peoples of Ghana but also to the whole African race. It is the intuitive, essentially unanalytic, unscientific mode. Senghor

[7] The lively survival of this cultural practice in present-day Ghanaian life is an anachronism with some quite unhappy economic consequences. See chapter 3, pp. 44–5 for a discussion of this matter.

[8] It ought to be noted, though, that chieftaincy was not always a feature of the culture of certain of the peoples of the northern part of Ghana, notably the Kokomba. See for example, Tait's contribution in J. Middleton and D. Tait, *Tribes without Rulers*, Kegan Paul (1958).

has been criticised for repeatedly pointing this out. On the bare fact of this attitude of mind, he is, I think, not open to criticism. However, he has tended to exaggerate the role of emotion in the thinking of Africans, and he has even seemed inclined to postulate a biological foundation for the alleged differentiating characteristics of the African outlook in a manner that does little credit to his great learning. It is almost as if he has been trying to exemplify in his own thought and discourse the lack of the analytical habit which he has attributed to the biology of the African. Most seriously of all, Senghor has celebrated the fact that our (traditional) mind is of a non-analytical bent; which is very unfortunate, seeing that this mental attribute is more of a limitation than anything else.

Admittedly, there is a place for intuition and emotion in life. Life is not all logic. But this kind of point is often covertly taken as an excuse for being unmindful of logic and rational procedures generally; as if from the fact that life is not all logic it follows that it is not logic in any part at all. On the contrary, it is as true in Africa as anywhere else that logical, mathematical, analytical, experimental procedures are essential in the quest for the knowledge of, and control over, nature and, therefore, in any endeavour to improve the condition of man. Our traditional culture was somewhat wanting in this respect and this is largely responsible for the weaknesses of traditional technology, warfare, architecture, medicine, etc. There can be little doubt that many of the hardships of traditional life were, and still are, traceable to this cause.

Take traditional medicine, for instance. Our ancestors must have been gifted with penetrating perception, which, had it been combined with an analytical and experimental inclination, might conceivably have put us in the forefront of medical knowledge, in particular, and of science and technology in general. I am inclined almost to a kind of ancestor worship when I consider how effective traditional medicine can be, sometimes in extremely difficult cases where even modern medicine is unsuccessful. Yet traditional medicine is terribly weak in diagnosis and weaker still in pharmacology. Instead of a sober inquiry into the causes of disease whether of the mind or of the body or both, our medicine men launch into stories of malevolent witchcraft and necromancy. Meanwhile, both children and adults, the children in greater numbers, die or are incapacitated through the administration of scientifically unresearched prescriptions. In this situation any inclination to glorify the unanalytical cast of mind is not just retrograde; it is tragic.

Consider another way in which our unanalytical heritage serves us poorly in our contemporary circumstances. All African nations have implicitly or explicitly made a choice in favour of modernisation through literacy, science and industrialisation. But industrial activities, to take only this aspect of the matter, often involve the use and therefore the repair and maintenance of machines, and this usually requires precision measurement and systematic analysis of cause and effect. Yet our culturally ingrained, intuitive attitudes frequently deter us from just these procedures.

Take a comparatively simple illustration. The gap at the contact breaker point in the distributor of a car, the contraption which effects the distribution of electrical currents to the spark plugs, is of the utmost importance for the functioning of the engine at all, in the first place, and its smooth running, in the second place. The gap, which varies only slightly from one make of car to another, is measured in thousandths of an inch or fractions of a millimetre. For example, for a Volkswagen 1200 it is 0.016 of an inch or 0.4 millimetres. A gap of this narrowness cannot be accurately set by the unaided eye; so car manufacturers have made feeler gauges for the purpose. However, without some form of persuasion, a Ghanaian mechanic will often not use a feeler gauge in adjusting the contact breaker point. When a Ghanaian mechanic works under a European supervisor in a company workshop he will set such gaps with perfection using a feeler gauge and generally do a fine job of engine maintenance. Let the same mechanic establish his own workshop; he will promptly return to the unaided powers of the eye, and an engine newly tuned up by him will immediately stall. I have often tried in the politest manner to convince Ghanaian mechanics of the importance of precision in measurement and therefore of the necessity of using gauges and other such aids. Frequently I have only managed to annoy them. I would discount any suggestion that this habit of our mechanics is due to laziness or stupidity or ill-will. It is due, I believe, to their having been brought up in a culture that places no special value on exact measurement. There are many other ways in which the effects of our traditional culture are manifested in our dealings with technology. The result is ruined machines, shaky constructional works and delayed projects.

I have already mentioned the belief in witchcraft as an element of our culture. This belief is not peculiar to Ghana or to Africa. But the strength and spread of this type of belief in a country is inversely proportional to the strength and spread of the scientific orientation within its boundaries. The virtues of our extended family system are often praised, and rightly. It is possible to see in it the seeds of a humane society. Unfortunately, as of now, the family is the witches' acknowledged domain of operation. Witches are rarely credited with good works. Evil is their speciality; and this evil they are supposed to visit exclusively on kith and kin within their own (extended) families.[9] I would be surprised indeed if the number of families in this country completely untouched by fears of witches in their midst is more than a very few, even allowing that there are any at all. Not unexpectedly, there is tension, suspicion and ill-feeling, often concealed by public shows of solidarity and harmony, in well-nigh every family. Suppose an individual suffers a series of misfortunes or illnesses. Then clearly, some old woman in the family is a witch, and it is she who is responsible for all his woes. It may be a distant aunt or a close one; it may be a grand-mother or even the actual mother of the supposed victim, depend-ing on the verdict of the medicine man consulted. Many of our latter-day spiritual priests and prophets are fast gaining fame and income as consultants and deliverers in competition with the tra-ditional fetish authorities. The cultural continuity is, however, obvious.

From time to time there are calls from public figures, sometimes government leaders, occasionally traditional rulers, for the aboli-tion or reform of 'outmoded' customs. We should be grateful for whatever good might come out of such exhortations. But we must not be too sanguine. And this for two reasons. First, these calls usually relate only to the more grotesque customs. Secondly, they are of an *ad hoc* character, not being based on any thorough and fundamental appraisal of the cultural foundations of the particular practices that happen to be being deplored. A philosophical

---

[9] One of the most frequent uses of a very popular adage which says 'The insect that bites you comes from your own clothing' (*Aboa bi bɛ ka wo a na ofi wo ntoma mu*) is to reinforce allegations of witchcraft against close relatives.

approach to our culture is the kind that probes fundamentals. If we consider the matters discussed in the previous four paragraphs, namely, those relating to the limitations of traditional medicine, our unhappy attempts at industrialisation and the belief in witchcraft, it becomes apparent that at the base of them all is the unanalytical, unscientific attitude of mind, probably the most basic and pervasive anachronism afflicting our society. It stands to reason to suppose that were the opposite of this mentality to be cultivated by sufficient of our people (one cannot hope to change the mental habits of an entire population; even in the scientifically and technologically developed countries you will meet individuals espousing all manner of superstition), were there to be such a change in mental habits, nothing short of a cultural revolution would ensue in our country. Not only would our traditional medicine or our handling of machines or our interpretation of unaccountable ill-fortune be affected for the better but also a whole host of poorly supported beliefs about man and external nature and the customs associated with them would die off.

However, such changes in outlook do not come about overnight. Nothing is apparently more difficult than to change habits of thought hardened for us into customs by the long-standing practice of our forefathers. The desired change will be a long process. Its principal agency will be education, but not just any type of education. It cannot be pretended that our system of education has hitherto been efficacious in propagating the rational, analytical, scientific orientation. At best it has tended to develop only a veneer of enlightenment. How thin this veneer is becomes clear at the onset of any misfortune that does not easily yield to explanation. Superstition quickly comes into its own. My suggestion is that, starting from fairly early stages, our education needs to be given a considerable methodological component. Our children should be initiated early in life into the discipline of formal and informal logic and into the methodology of rational thinking. One is not envisaging here the mere furnishing of minds with facts from the sciences. That would not necessarily meet the case. What is wanted is a certain kind of training in method, the kind of training that will produce minds eager and able to test claims and theories against observed facts and adjust beliefs to the evidence, minds capable of logical analysis and fully aware of the nature and value of exact measurement. Such a training is not only likely to discourage superstition; it would also tend to undermine that authoritarianism on which I commented earlier. A generation steeped in the procedures of rational investigation is unlikely to be unkind to inquiries for the reasons for a practice or institution.

There is another, more direct way in which philosophy can be of service in the reform, adaptation and development of our traditional culture. The culture itself is highly philosophical, a fact which is indirectly recognised by both Antubam and Mends when they speak in their lists of 'the tendency to stress in all forms of art the quality of significance as a criterion of beauty and virtue'. As I have already pointed out, this stress on significance in our traditional culture is not only in art but in very many aspects of life down, indeed, to some very minute details. Traditional life in our country is guided at many points by conceptions of the sort that might broadly be called philosophical. A fact about philosophy in a traditional society, particularly worthy of emphasis, is that it is alive in day-to-day existence. When philosophy becomes academic and highly technical it can easily lose this quality. It is, of course, not necessary that this should happen. Though technicality and a high degree of complexity are inevitable in any serious and sustained philosophical inquiry, the best philosophers are always conscious of the ultimate relevance of their thinking to the practical concerns of life. To return to traditional philosophy: the closeness of the relation between traditional philosophy and practical life makes a thorough examination of traditional philosophical ideas imperative. We are living in a transitional epoch in which our actions and habits of mind are governed, frequently unconsciously, by inherited traditional conceptions in combination with ideas and attitudes coming to us from foreign lands. It is saying the obvious to remark that the combination is often riddled with confusion in both parts. We might as well begin to try to get clear about our own traditional side of the combination. It would be good if clarity could begin at home.

Let me, then, touch very briefly on a notion that is very deep and pervasive indeed in our traditional thought, namely, the notion of fate or destiny. Within the limits of the present discussion it will only serve as an illustration. As indicated in my supplementary list of Ghanaian cultural characteristics, it is traditionally believed that each man comes into this world with a specific and unalterable destiny apportioned to him by the Supreme God. This belief naturally affects conduct and the way a man regards himself. A successful man is likely to regard himself as being blessed with a good destiny and be so regarded by others. The thought may stimulate him to more exertions and greater success. A man encountering difficulties and reverses in his life can, still, if he is generally highly motivated, take comfort in the traditional maxim: 'If poverty overtakes you, do not give up life, better days will come' (*Ehia wo a enwu na da pa bɛ ba*).[10] In moments of deep depression he may be constrained to wonder whether, perhaps, his appointed destiny is not an unhappy one. But he may derive strength by reminding himself of the maxim and be thereby enabled to shake off the creeping metaphysical pessimism. And who knows? His way may eventually meet with success. On the other hand, adversity may lead a man to resignation. This happens everywhere and in all cultures. But in our culture the notions about destiny just mentioned are apt to facilitate the resignation of a despairing soul. He may reason as follows with a certain appearance of cultural appropriateness: 'My destiny is obviously a gloomy one. However hard I may try I will never succeed, for no one can change the destiny that was fixed for him by God.' After this kind of meditation we should not be surprised if he tries less and less till he becomes a dependant of his family. Such people ought to reflect that there is at least one bright spot on the dark canvass of their destiny. The fact is that the same culture that furnishes them with the metaphysical excuse for defeatism also provides a compensating family system. In another culture they might find themselves quite destitute.

Some do not even need to wait on adversity. In the way of excuses a lazy or wayward person in our society has a rich set of options. He can, of course, blame witchcraft by a member of his family. Witness the soliloquy of the habitual drunkard, immortalised in song by Kwaw Mensah:[11] 'My relatives have placed an alcohol receptacle in my belly; I will die a straw man' (*Mabusuafo de*

---

[10] Incidentally there is a beautiful Twi poem by Professor J. H. Nketia, Director of the Institute of African Studies, University of Ghana, Legon, on this theme which evinces and communicates an indescribable depth of feeling.

[11] Kwaw Mensah is a well-known Ghanaian traditional guitarist and band leader.

grawa asi me yɛm, menam saa na mawu). More cosmically, he can
trace everything to an unkind fate. When exhorted to do better, he
might retort 'What better can I do when I am saddled with a
wretched destiny?' Moreover, there is a saying which he might well
quote: 'You have an unlucky fate and do you suppose that you can
ever pay your debts?' (*Wuti nyɛ wose mereko me ka*). (These sayings
are in Akan but I have verified that they are easily duplicated in
common maxims among our other peoples.)

Bad fate attributed to people can sometimes provoke harsh
treatment from others. It is, for example, not unknown for a man to
divorce his wife on the grounds that she is a woman of bad fate. His
argument, that since he married her disaster has consistently dog-
ged his steps, would traditionally be considered perfectly sound.

Our culture is not unique in entertaining notions of predestina-
tion. But our traditional philosophy is probably highly remarkable
in the personal directness and individual immediacy of the doctrine
of fate and, further, in the sincerity and practical seriousness with
which it is entertained in the day-to-day life of our people. One
might recall here the saying, 'I saw God and took leave of him
before coming' (*Mihuu Nyame na medraa no ansa na mereba*). God is
not just supposed to arrange destinies generally and impersonally.
He actually hands to each individual the 'message' of his destiny in
a face-to-face meeting.

How valid, then, is the doctrine? On raising a question of this
sort one is immediately faced with difficulties of interpretation.
For example, how comprehensive is the message of destiny? Does
it determine every single detail in the entire life of a person? Some
elders, expert in our traditional philosophy, give a negative answer.
A man's destiny, they say, only determines the broad outlines of his
life, not its minute details. They are particularly anxious to insist
on this when the question of free will and punishment is in view.
The institution of praise and blame, reward and punishment seems
to presuppose the freedom of the will; and the problem of how a
person can be said to make a free choice, if every detail of his life is
externally pre-appointed, does not escape these elders. But
although their solution is plausible for some patterns of life, it is
problematic in others. If you take a case such as one in which a man
is supposed to be broadly destined to be, say, a philosopher, it
seems quite plausible to suggest that he still retains free will and

accountability in that it is still open to him whether he shall be, say, an idealist or a materialist or something else altogether. This satisfies the idea of free will because choice based on deliberate rational reflection is certainly a paradigm case of free will. However, consider a case in which a man is supposed to be destined, equally broadly, to become a confirmed drunkard. It would surely be a poor assurance of free will to point out that it is still open to him whether he will drink 'akpeteshie'[12] or beer, or that he can very well choose which bars to frequent.

This is possibly not an insoluble difficulty. It is conceivable that what our traditional philosophy of man implies is not that man as such has free will but only that man is, in principle, capable of attaining free will. Such a view does have a rational flexibility lacking in the blanket postulation of free will for man. There is, however, a very much more intractable difficulty which emerges when we ask the question why it comes to be supposed in the first place that man has an unalterable pre-appointed destiny. A question of this sort is of the first importance in the assessment of a philosophy, for the real meaning of a philosophical thesis remains more or less hidden until the reasoning behind it is known. One argument known to me maintains that certain events just do appear to seek out particular individuals. Imagine the following story, of a man's death in a bus crash, actually occurred. When he originally tried to get on to the bus, it was already filled to capacity with passengers, but just as he decides to postpone his journey and is turning to go a seat is vacated; one of the passengers, for some reason or other, has to get off in a hurry. So he gets on. His destination is the very first stop of the bus, and he is, in fact, the passenger travelling the shortest distance. But, just one mile from his destination the calamity occurs: a puncture and the bus crashes. Unbelievably, everyone on board escapes with minor bruises except one. Alone of fifty passengers our traveller dies. Would we not all agree that that must all the time have been his fate? Nothing could have prevented it. Or to put it in another tense, what will be will be. Nor, so the argument goes, can this be supposed to apply to our tragic character alone. Those who were saved must have been going to be saved; that was their destiny. So, then, everyone has his appointed destiny which nothing can change. As the traditional

---

[12] Akpeteshie is a notorious local gin.

saying goes, there is no avoiding the destiny appointed to man by God (*Onyame nkrabea nni kwatibea*).

Confronted with patterns of tragedy such as that of our hypothetical traveller, the human mind, not just the Ghanaian traditional mind, turns to such fatalistic reflections. In approximate logical form the core of the argument boils down to: What will happen will happen, by whatever means; therefore whatever happens, happens of necessity. It can be shown symbolically, using the resources of modern logic, to be fallacious. But even without symbolic logic a little thinking should suffice to cast doubt on its validity. It is obvious that the life of any individual will consist of a series of events of one kind or another. To say that the events will necessarily be what they will be is to utter a tautology. But to say of any one event that it is unavoidable is to make an empirical claim about that particular event which can be justified, if justifiable, only by reference to the character of its antecedents together with any relevant empirical laws. Such a claim could never be a logical consequence of a tautology since a tautology cannot say anything in particular about any particular thing.

The argument for the traditional doctrine of fate which we have been considering is not a good argument, but the doctrine also has a theological component, and there may well be independent theological arguments that can be marshalled in its favour. Possibly also, other types of arguments may be developed. If a particular argument for a certain conclusion is shown to be invalid, its conclusion is not *ipso facto* shown to be false. Nevertheless, if an argument for a belief is shown to be invalid, then we have no rational right to maintain it in the absence of other known arguments that are valid. In the present case I doubt that any such arguments exist, though I cannot be dogmatic. I would, however, like to remark that in view of its effects in our society the demise of the traditional doctrine of fate, if it could be brought about through legitimate causes, would be a highly desirable riddance.

It is a function, indeed a duty, of philosophy in any society to examine the intellectual foundations of its culture. For any such examination to be of any real use it should take the form of reasoned criticism and, where possible, reconstruction. No other way to philosophical progress is known than through criticism and adaptation. Those who seem to think that the criticism of African traditional philosophy by an African is something akin to betrayal are actually more conservative than those among our elders who are real thinkers as distinct from mere repositories of traditional ideas. If you talk to some of them you soon discover that they are not afraid to criticise, reject, modify or add to traditional philosophical ideas.

If we quickly run through what remains of the lists of cultural characteristics mentioned earlier on in this discussion, we will find, I think, that the most important is the great value placed on communal fellowship in our traditional society. Mends notes this in his list by speaking, in his very first item, of 'the stress or importance attached to group life'. The stress on group life would, of course, be pointless if it was not matched on the part of individuals by a sense of fellowship which extends sympathy to people beyond one's own immediate blood relations. The extended family, I believe, is the breeding ground of this extended sense of communal fellowship. And so, when Mends mentions, in his second item, 'the importance of kinship as represented in the institutional form of the extended family system irrespective of differences in the descent systems', he is pointing to a closely complementary element of the greatest importance.

The sense of solidarity and fellowship which, as it were, spills over from the extended family to the larger community and the well-known spontaneity of our people mentioned by Antubam, combine to infuse our social life with a pervasive humanity and fullness of life which visitors to our land have always been quick to remark. This quality of our culture is obviously one which we must not only preserve but positively develop and deepen. It would profit us little to gain all the technology in the world and lose the humanist essence of our culture. If we look carefully at those societies in which technology has been developed to a high degree and in which, consequently, the very form of life has been transformed by industrialisation, we find that there is a tendency for the qualities of spontaneity and fellow feeling to be eclipsed.

This is not specially difficult to understand. An industrialism propelled by large machines and motivated by a single-minded calculation of profitability whether to private industrialists and businessmen, as in capitalism, or to the state, as in socialism, tends to create large towns and cities in which people live for the most part as strangers, with relationships regulated by the formal rules of state law rather than the informal rules of face-to-face communal living. Social life thus becomes more formal, sympathies more restricted, and, amidst the gradual withering away of the tradition of communal caring, many individuals begin to lose their sense of human security. It is a palpable fact that our culture is suffering from the creeping onset of such conditions.

It must be stressed, however, that it is not technology or industrialisation in itself that is responsible for the undesirable developments. It is the unrestrained urbanisation which accompanies a narrowly oriented industrialism. It is quite clear to me that unrestricted industrial urbanisation is contrary to any humane culture; it is certainly contrary to our own. Our best hope lies in the development of smaller centres of industry spread through the countryside and carefully integrated with communal life and its values. In this way we can hope to unite the deep fellow-feeling of rural community life with the ethic of the industrial work place and thus reverse the morally unedifying situation in which many people live and work in a more or less Hobbesian milieu in the towns and cities and can only renew contact with genuine communal feeling when visiting their villages in rare moments of respite from work. There is another consideration closely allied to this. At present one of the powerful strains on our extended family system is the very extensive poverty which oppresses our rural population. Owing to this, people working in the towns and cities are constantly burdened with the financial needs of rural relatives which they usually cannot entirely satisfy. The result is ill-feeling, sometimes even recrimination. An intelligent programme of rural oriented industrialisation would not only help to improve the conditions of life of the large mass of our peoples – this is probably realised by many – but also, what is probably not generally realised, help in the preservation of the better parts of our culture.

However, even such a programme cannot solve all the problems which industrialisation poses for our culture. Given even the best type of rural development there still will be some cities, however modest in size, and there still will be the need in various spheres of life for central institutions where people from all parts of the country will work together. Here it would seem that we have to create a delicate balance, and carefully limit the stress on family and kinship communality, which we have seen to be so potentially valuable. It is essential that new foundations of communal feeling be created in the urban areas to humanise the conditions of life. There are doubtless various ways in which this might be achieved. There ought, for example, to be a conscious effort at building a sense of neighbourhood fellowship within manageable areas of our towns and cities.

From the philosophical point of view a very basic consideration in this connection relates to our ethical attitudes. There is what one might call a certain home-town orientation in our traditional thinking which is, I think, a consequence of the emphasis on family and kinship relations. Villagers are proverbially indulgent in judging the sharp practices of one of their number in some far-off city, provided that the conduct brings advantage to their particular village. Those who hold high public positions of responsibility can testify to the constant, insistent pressure from relations and the people of their home towns for help and favours regardless of the claims of other people. As is well-known, such nepotism is an evil that often occurs in public life.

This orientation of our people is not an altogether simple matter. It is not that they are without a sense of fairness. Of course they are not. What is more, they are famous for goodwill and hospitality to strangers to their villages. It seems to me, then, that the undue power which kinship considerations seem to have in the thinking of the more traditionally minded in the sort of way just mentioned is an anachronism which, with the different consequences it has today, no longer possesses the same moral character. We may note, at the very least, that the phenomenon of belonging at once to two worlds, namely, the world of the modern urban industrial centre and that of the traditional rural home, was unknown when this ethic evolved. Little wonder if the new dualism causes a kind of ethical schizophrenia in some spheres of conduct.

Dr Danquah in his *Akan Doctrine of God* seems to note what I have called the home-town orientation of our traditional morality when he remarks, speaking specifically of the Akans, 'that they hold the family to be the supreme good' (p. xxviii). 'The family, the neighbours,' according to him, were 'those of the blood, the group held together by community of origin and obligation to a common ancestor, Nana. It was for this group [he adds] that morality was of value.' Soon, however, he goes on so to enlarge the significance of the concept of the Akan family that it comes to 'embrace not only the Akan but the entire race of [man], the manlike family of humanity' (p. xxix). In this Dr Danquah, I think, mixes figurative with literal meaning. There can be little doubt that it was the more literal concept of the family as defined by Danquah in the first quotation that was immediately influential in the traditional moral outlook. The traditional family, as we have previously noted, indeed offers a natural bridge to a wider community, but it is obvious that Danquah's unlimited extension of the concept of family must be accompanied by significant reductions in moral fervour. Here, then, in the kinship orientation of traditional morality, is a problem that we must recognise and face up to. It is one of the most subtle problems of anachronism in our present day society.

There are other problems of anachronism, somewhat less subtle but no less important. I will here note three of them, barely mentioning, without discussing, them. There is, in the words of Mends, 'the pervasiveness and stress on ceremony and ritual in many aspects of social life' which, however important previously, should now be kept in more reasonable bounds. There is again what Antubam calls 'the principle of age as a vital criterion of wisdom'. In a time of computers such a principle is apt to lead to serious distortions in social relations. Knowledge is, indeed, not identical with wisdom. On the other hand, the wisdom of uninstructed longevity is unlikely to prove extensively applicable in the complex environments of modern life. Finally, let me mention the importance attached to fertility. It is hardly necessary to remark that when children are produced without regard to the means of upkeep and upbringing the consequences can be serious for them and the society. One safeguard against anachronisms such as these is the cultivation of a philosophical cast of mind, so that our institutions and practices may be reviewed in the light of first principles.

In drawing this discussion to a close I would like to return to some of the more positive aspects of our culture. I have had occasion to remark that art, song and dance are not the whole of culture. But without a doubt they are a most important part of it. Man is pre-eminently an aesthetic animal; and our traditional culture, as should be evident from Antubam's list and his book, more extensively, is a pre-eminently aesthetic culture. Thanks largely to the work of Professor Nketia, the virtues of our music are now widely known. Not only that. Our music is being preserved and developed with the aid of borrowed techniques and insights in a manner which should provide a model of cultural adaptation generally. What remains is to strengthen the aesthetic component of cultural education in our schools, colleges and universities.

I have not discussed every single Ghanaian cultural characteristic mentioned in one or other of the lists considered at the beginning of this discussion but I hope I have done enough, not necessarily in my specific conclusions, but in my general manner, to illustrate the character of a philosophical approach to our culture.

When one has talked of a philosophical approach to our culture the question must naturally arise: How should a contemporary African approach the discipline of philosophy itself?[13] The next chapter is devoted to this question.

---

[13] On the question of the nature of philosophy in general see chapter 10.

2

On an African orientation in philosophy

A department of physics or engineering in an African university is unlikely to be asked to teach African physics or African engineering. What they may legitimately be asked to do is to apply the disciplines to African conditions. African physicists and engineers can be expected to accept with no loss of self-respect that the future in these disciplines for Africans does not lie in trying to create distinctively African sciences, but in seeking to master and advance a body of knowledge and techniques which has already been developed, and particularly in seeking to apply tried methods to the solution of relevant problems in Africa. The sensible African will, in other words, try to develop a particular orientation not in the disciplines themselves but in their application.

In general this attitude can be adopted by African students of the natural and mathematical sciences and some, even, of the social sciences. Indeed, for the time being, a good number of the subjects comprised in the humanities may be pursued in a similar spirit without absurdity. An African student of history must acquire his historical training in ways that cannot be called peculiarly African before he can profitably apply himself to the study of African history. Even more remarkable is the fact that the academic study of the English and French languages and their literatures by African students has been a major factor in the emergence of a crop of gifted African writers keenly aware of the relevance of their origins to their calling. The African writer or artist is in a specially favourable position, for when he turns from the study of the literature and other artistic productions of foreign cultures, he can apply his technical expertise to an extremely rich artistic heritage.

The question now is: can the African student approach the pursuit of philosophy in a similar spirit? No simple answer seems possible. Suppose an African student of philosophy were to reason as follows: 'Just as my fellows in physics need to master the discipline of physics before they can be in a position to apply their knowledge and skills to their African situation, so also must I acquire my philosophical training through instruction in techniques of thinking already developed by other peoples before applying myself to my African background of thought.' It can be expected that this outlook would be criticised on grounds such as these: In physics one can speak of fairly well established knowledge to be mastered. In philosophy there is no such thing. Even if our would-be African philosopher – let us call him the universalist – already shows a certain awareness of this point by omitting any reference to philosophical *knowledge*, it might still be pointed out that, in mentioning techniques of thinking in philosophy, he begs the question rather fundamentally. For one thing, it is not possible in principle to separate technique in any absolute manner from doctrine as far as philosophy is concerned. How, for example, does one distinguish between Kant's method of transcendental analysis and the content of his critical philosophy? It used to be said by Wittgenstein and his followers that philosophy is not a body of doctrine but a method of clarification. But the opposition which this outlook on philosophy encountered among philosophers of different persuasions should serve to underline the tendentious character of the Wittgensteinian disclaimer. For another thing, there is no generally accepted technique of philosophising. When one takes account of cultural factors the position becomes even worse. What have British empiricists and Oriental spiritual philosophers in common? The analogy with physics recedes far into the distance. It might, accordingly, be held that the attitude of the African universalist boils down simply to an unthinking willingness to submit himself to instruction in the philosophies of other cultures before attending to those of his own. Why may he not reverse the order?

The anti-universalist line – let us name it the nationalist approach, it being understood that such labels are mainly for convenience – might be reinforced by a brief review of what the universalist might actually get in the way of a philosophical training. A student taking an honours course at a Western-oriented University in Africa may expect to be instructed in the logic of

Aristotle and its traditional modifications, in the algebraic logic of Boole and in the symbolic logics of Frege, Russell, Quine, etc. In other branches of philosophy he will very probably read and discuss the Pre-Socratics, Plato and Aristotle, the European rationalists, the British empiricists, Kant . . . In contemporary philosophy, attention can be expected to centre around British and American analytic philosophy. Why, the nationalist might ask, should an African be philosophically brought up in a manner that seems to suggest that his own race is totally innocent of philosophy? And why, in any case, should philosophical traditions of such long standing as those of India, China and of the Arab peoples be ignored in favour of European philosophy, and one particular style at that?

The nationalist case is a just one – in principle. Our peoples have their own traditional philosophies – the accumulated wisdom of what might be called the collective mind of our societies, handed down through traditions both verbal and behavioural, including aspects of art, ritual and ceremonial. Certainly traditional African philosophies should command the highest interest in their conception of man and society, their ideas of law and government, their doctrines of God and of the Good. It comes out clearly, for example, in Professor Abraham's *The Mind of Africa* (Weidenfeld, paper edition, 1966) that in theoretical sweep and practical bearing traditional African philosophies concede nothing to the world views of European philosophy. Why, then, should the African philosophy student not be steeped in his own heritage of philosophy before looking elsewhere?

When we consider this question seriously and objectively, however, certain limitations become apparent in the nationalist case. One difficulty arises from the fact that the African philosophies as they are available today are folk philosophies. They generally consist of what 'elders' said or are said to have said. Although our philosophers of old must have had elaborate and persuasive reasons for their doctrines, such justifications are often no longer evident, and the contemporary inquirer has to depend on the reconstructions of the wise men of the tribe. All this, admittedly, should provide exciting challenges to the dedicated researcher but the resulting material could hardly provide the basis for the main part of a modern course in philosophy.

Very much more serious is the consideration that traditional philosophies are pre-scientific. In order to forestall any misunderstandings that might be occasioned by this statement, I hasten to point out that this remark is not restricted to traditional African philosophies. Every traditional philosophy is essentially pre-scientific; and every people has its own traditional philosophy, a stock of originally unwritten proverbs, maxims, usages, etc., passed on through successive generations from times when societies were simpler and organised science was as yet unknown. No doubt some enlarged sense of the term 'scientific' could be specified in which every such philosophy might be called scientific; but in this way essential contrasts between modern and aboriginal times are lost. An inescapable fact of the contemporary world is the influence of science or its consequences in the lives of a large and rapidly increasing proportion of mankind. To us in Africa this influence with its concomitants has come in ways that we cannot cherish – it has come through colonialism. Nevertheless, its implications have been far reaching.

Industrialisation, barely started in colonial times and intensified since African independence, has changed the face of our societies in various important ways. The development of large urban centres which has attended it has dislocated the structure of traditional family life, and the exigencies of urban life are in agonising tension with the communal orientation of the rural and still relatively 'unmodernised' areas. In consequence, the traditional ethic has lost a large part of its hold on a significant section of the peoples of Africa, as was bound to happen. Traditional codes of conduct evolved in the context of less complicated societies, in which extensive family and neighbourhood connections facilitated the development of a sense of communal fellowship and responsibility. The societies were of a type in which the elders were rightly considered custodians of knowledge and wisdom. They were societies in which education was not formal but acquired through every aspect of a person's upbringing, and in which his moral outlook was fortified by an unquestioning faith in the religion of his ancestors.

For good or ill that milieu is no more. Education has, for most, become institutionalised and formal in approach and, in content, less parochial. Longevity is naturally no longer the only route to knowledge. Scientific education, for all that it is in general rudimentary in our schools and junior colleges, conflicts with aspects of traditional religion and medicine. Even more radical, perhaps, are the instabilities introduced by fundamentalist Christianity, an import from other cultures. (It ought always to be remembered that the Christianity which was brought to our peoples was, and virtually remains, fundamentalist.) Christianity, a comprehensive metaphysic with an associated ethic, has itself been in historic conflict with science. In the intellectual outlook of those peoples whose evangelists carried it into our lands it usually survives in co-existence with the scientific temper only by making accommodations of varying degrees of subtlety and candour. Thus the African, converted to Christianity but with some roots in his own past, or born into a 'converted' family, as a rule has been inculcated with elements of traditional religion and world view, the teachings of fundamentalist Christianity, and smatterings of science or bits of vaguely science-orientated information. These elements persist in mutual incompatibility, and become selectively operative in the various circumstances of life.

One consequence of this is an unthinking scepticism and cynicism which may increasingly pose a threat to our societies. As the impact of science becomes more and more felt not only at the level of material life through the effects of industrialisation, but also at the deeper level of intellectual habits, philosophy becomes more and more a matter of individual responsibility. The African youth, more or less bereft of the security of traditional orthodoxies, stands in need of a new philosophy. And because, dazzled by the prospect of wealth, the semi-detribalised African may (alas, he already frequently does!), yield to the temptation to abandon his scruples for the principle of 'Grab what you can get, no holds barred', this is an urgent desideratum. But what philosophy should the modern African live by? (I am here thinking principally of the educated African, for it is he who experiences the moral and intellectual tensions arising from the impact of science, industry and foreign religions in their highest intensity; and it is he who must become the creator of a new outlook upon the world.)

It should be clear from the foregoing reflections that traditional conceptions of things just cannot provide an adequate basis for a contemporary philosophy. Again, I wish to stress that it is not in

Africa alone that this is so. The 'advanced' nations too have their own heritage of traditional philosophy, though, of course, they do not teach it in their philosophy departments, and for the same reason – to avoid anachronism. Nor, probably, do they investigate it in their departments of sociology and anthropology, presumably being too deeply engrossed in the study of 'primitive' societies, although I am inclined to recommend it as a subject for serious research. I venture to suggest that such a study might have the welcome effect of discouraging people from too readily declaring this or that aspect of traditional African philosophy to be peculiarly African.[1]

Let us, however, return to the question of a philosophy for the contemporary African. If, as contended above, philosophical salvation does not lie in our traditional background of thought, does it follow that the African must look to Europe, or America, or India, or China? The question is wrongly put. Unless he be a son of a country such as Egypt which has a long tradition of *written* philosophy – a tradition longer than those of European countries – history has ensured that the question should rather be what he shall do with British or French or, perhaps, German philosophy. But this very realisation should be the basis of his particular orientation in the study of philosophy. If he is fully aware that it is by some manner of historical accident that his education has come to be concerned with a certain set of foreign philosophies, he will understand at once that he ought to adopt a highly critical approach to his studies, and, as a corollary, a comparative method. He should try to acquaint himself with the different philosophies of the different cultures of the world, not to be encyclopaedic or eclectic, but with the aim of trying to see how far issues and concepts of universal relevance can be disentangled from the contingencies of culture. The available time, especially at university, is, however, short, and there are severe limits to how far an undergraduate programme can go in this direction.[2] Nevertheless, it is good to keep the ideal clearly in mind.

[1] Another welcome by-product would be to undermine certain erroneous ways of comparing African thought with Western thought which are criticised in the next chapter.

[2] A practical step that African departments of philosophy can take in this direction, if they have not already done so, is to introduce courses in comparative philosophy to cover our own traditional philosophies, as well as the philosophies,

Two assumptions underlie this discussion which I must now explicitly acknowledge. First, for my part, I take science to be the crucial factor in the transition from the traditional to the modern world. All developing nations are endeavouring to improve their living standards through the application of science, and any philosophy not thoroughly imbued with the spirit of science cannot hope to reflect this. It is not, of course, incumbent on the African philosopher, or indeed any philosopher, to become a scientist. The sort of awareness of science which is required, indeed indispensable here, is broadly methodological. The habits of exactness and rigour in thinking, the pursuit of systematic coherence and the experimental approach so characteristic of science are attributes of mind which we in Africa urgently need to cultivate not just because they are in themselves intellectual virtues but also because they are necessary conditions of rapid modernisation. At any rate, my own observation of the character of many of the difficulties and confusions, failures and crises that afflict the attempt at modernisation in my own country[3] leaves me no alternative conclusion. If, then, a scientific outlook is an urgent necessity at the practical level of national life, it is hardly reasonable to exempt the philosopher from the need to evince similar qualities in his abstract meditations. On the contrary, it is for the philosopher to precipitate the desired revolution in intellectual habits. I am under no illusion that abstract philosophy has the power to make an immediate and dramatic impact on the mental habits of the mass of men, but neither – to say the least – am I convinced that philosophy is condemned to eternal futility.

The reader will have noticed how the connotation of the word 'philosophy' as I have employed it in this discussion has oscillated from the broad sense of the word in which philosophy is, so to speak, a guide to the living of life, to the narrower concept of philosophy as a theoretical discipline devoted to detailed and complicated argument.[4] This has been deliberate. Whether or not

---

both traditional and modern, of other cultures. Naturally such coverage is bound to be sketchy at undergraduate level; but valuable work in this field can be done at the research level. Far-sighted authorities of higher education in Africa should endow their philosophy departments with Research Fellowships in Comparative Philosophy. There is here an opportunity for an African contribution to world philosophy.

[3] Recall the specific examples given in the previous chapter, pp. 12–14.

[4] See chapter 10, p. 142.

technical philosophy can have a significant impact on the generality of mankind, it certainly ought directly to affect the outlook on life of the philosopher himself. In other words, both concepts of philosophy should be operative in his life.

The bearing of my remarks concerning the need for a scientific outlook on the type of training suitable for the modern African student of philosophy should be obvious. Given that the traditional philosophies are inadequate, the African may, with good sense but subject to the rider already entered and another soon to be urged, acquire a training in methods of scientifically orientated philosophical thinking of the type evolved where scientific and technological advance has been greatest. This brings me to my second assumption.

I assume that philosophy *can* be universal. Here again, I do not pretend to describe what is at present the case; I only project an ideal. In actuality philosophy is, and has been, culture-relative in various subtle ways, which justifies to some extent the unease of the nationalist at the uncritical assimilation by an African of the philosophical traditions of other nations. Two respects in which philosophy is culture bound deserve to be mentioned: the type of concern or issue that excites inquiry, and the content of the philosophical theses that emerge. Now, it is obvious that good reasons could be put forward for a measure of relativism in the first sense. There is no reason why the philosophical preoccupations of African philosophers should be in every way identical with those of thinkers elsewhere. One of the hallmarks of an African orientation in philosophy must surely be a sensitivity to what is specific to the African situation. In the second sense, however (i.e. as regards the content of philosophical theses), conscious relativism is not a rationally defensible policy. Some philosophical positions must be nearer the truth than others, irrespective of origin. For instance, the truth value of a proposition to the effect that God is Three in One or just One in One, or identical with the Null class, should be arguable on grounds other than the question of who propounded it, provided that acceptable definitions are available for the crucial terms. It is true, of course, that some philosophical issues framed formally as issues of truth or falsity may turn out really to be normative. As there would seem to be no reason why all societies should have the same norms, cultural factors may seem to explain why a number of philosophical theses are adopted. Careful analysis, however, will reveal the real character of such questions.

There is a further, more pertinent way in which cultural considerations may be relevant to – though not determinants of – philosophical theories. I refer to the effect of language on philosophical thinking. The nature of a given philosophical position may be influenced by the structure and other characteristics of the language in which it is formulated, and may derive plausibility from the form itself of the expression. Here is a good reason for extra vigilance on the part of an African who studies foreign philosophies in foreign languages. When we learn a new natural language we also, to a certain extent, learn a philosophy. For the most part, this goes on unconsciously. But it is part of the function of philosophers to elicit the general conceptions buried under the forms and turnings of a given language for critical examination. For this, a certain degree of linguistic detachment is obviously needful though not easily attained. Such detachment may, perhaps, come more easily to foreign speakers of a language than to natives, so that the African student may be able to avoid the philosophical pulls of English which native speakers of that language may resist only with difficulty or not at all. An African student is in quite a strong position in this respect. Not having conducted his philosophical studies in his own language, he may the more easily maintain a critical perspective on the philosophical intimations of his own language. He can, moreover, check the philosophical presuppositions of, say, the English language against those of his own. The balance that is likely to accrue should be an aid to sober reflection.

To make this more concrete, consider the following contrast between the English language and Twi, the language of the Akans of Ghana. The former has a superabundance of abstract nouns; the latter dispenses almost completely with that grammatical category, expressing abstractions by means of gerunds and various periphrastic expedients. Not surprisingly, one can say such a thing as *universals are a species of objects* with a considerable show of plausibility in English. Translate it into Twi, and it fails even of a preliminary plausibility. This consideration is not by itself decisive either way. It would be uncommonly absurd to make the peculiarities of any language a reflection of philosophic truths or of the reverse. I happen to think that the particular richness of the English language alluded to above is a mixed blessing. While it makes for economy and elegance in the formulation of complicated ideas, it can lead to ontological fantasies. But if so, the point ought, on the appropriate occasion, to be demonstrable in the English language itself and on independent grounds.[5] It is important, moreover, to note that, in this matter, language can only incline, not necessitate; so there is no lack of English philosophers who are able to resist the ontological suggestiveness of their own vocabulary. In all this, what is chiefly to be emphasised is that, by taking philosophical cognisance of his own language, an African philosopher might bring an added dimension to his theoretical considerations.[6]

It should be observed also that even in the individual African's reference to his language in his philosophical investigations, a certain sense of discrimination is called for. While his language is likely to be of help in the more speculative aspects of his subject, he might well find resort to his vernacular not the same boon in the more formal, technical, parts. Thus I shudder to think what lengths of periphrasis one would have to go in order to make out in, say, Twi, the outline, let alone the details, of a relatively uncomplicated result of advanced logic such as Henkin's completeness proof for the Functional Calculus of the First Order. For reasons of culture or environment or both, formal logic did not, with few exceptions, engage the attention of our forefathers. It is not to be wondered at, therefore, that the language we have inherited is not immediately ideal for the sort of formal studies just mentioned. But language is flexible without limit; and any language can be adapted to any conceivable needs of communication. It will one day be

---

[5] I have occupied myself with a task of this sort in my series of four articles on 'Logic and Ontology' in *Second Order: An African Journal of Philosophy*, vol. II, nos. 1 and 2, January and July 1973, vol. III, no. 2, July 1974, and vol. IV, no. 1 January 1975.

[6] In case this should move anybody to question why African departments of philosophy should not teach the subject in their own languages, I would advise caution. Until enough unity is achieved in Africa to make it possible to realise the idea of a continental *lingua franca*, Africans will have to temper their sense of the importance of their own languages with a dose of international realism. To exchange English and French for a chorus of national languages would be to build barriers to philosophical communication not only between Africa and the world beyond but also between the peoples themselves of Africa.

opportune perhaps to bend some African language to the purpose of expressing all things not just in the field of philosophy but also in the whole gamut of human knowledge. It is implicit in sundry remarks already made in this paper that it is a particular (though not exclusive) responsibility of African philosophers to research into the traditional background of their philosophical thought. There is the need to record, reconstruct, and interpret, and above all to correct false interpretations. But it should be clear also that there is a need, possibly more urgent, to fashion philosophies based upon contemporary African experience with its many-sidedness. From this point of view, one might suggest without being whimsical that the term 'African philosophy' should be reserved for the results of that enterprise. African philosophy, as distinct from African *traditional world-views*, is the philosophy that is being produced by contemporary African philosophers. It is still in the making.

Suppose now that a critic should attribute what I have written to my particular educational background; I am bound to concede as much. In a certain obvious sense we are all children of our circumstances. But were the existence of such 'bias' proof of falsity, universal silence would be obligatory on all mankind. I should like to conclude with the hope that my remarks will provoke critical discussion from which I too shall come away more enlightened.

3

How not to compare African traditional thought with Western thought

In the last chapter a distinction was made between two senses of the term 'philosophy'. For African philosophy the distinction may be formulated as being between the varieties of folk world-view and philosophy as the results of the work of individual Africans using the intellectual resources of the modern world to grapple with philosophical problems. There is a third possible sense in which one might refer to the thought of a class of individuals in traditional African societies who, though unaffected by modern intellectual influences, are capable of critical and original philosophical reflection as distinct from repetitions of the folk ideas of their peoples. Because the fruits of such reflection are generally not perpetuated in print they tend to be swamped in the pool of communal thought, leaving, if anything at all, only faint traces.[1] Griaule's *Conversations with Ogotemmelli* (Oxford University Press, 1965) might have been a rare exception if it had not been so ethnographic in conception. The recording and critical study of the thought of individual indigenous thinkers is worthy of the most serious attention of contemporary African philosophers.

When one has the first sense in mind one ought more strictly to speak of African *traditional* philosophy. A reference to British philosophy is unlikely to be interpreted as alluding to the communal *weltanschauung* of, say, British rural communities. Indeed, even when one speaks of *traditional* British philosophy this will be taken not in an anthropological sense, but to refer to the line of British empiricists stemming from Bacon. On the other hand, African philosophy is usually taken in the sense of the traditional, folk thought of Africa. To an extent this is understandable. Con-

[1] Recall in this connection the remarks in chapter 1, p. 21. See also chapter 10, p. 143.

temporary African societies are still largely traditional in the anthropological sense. Nevertheless, it is important for the future that the significance of the current processes of modernisation in Africa should be realised not only in terms of material changes, but also in terms of intellectual development. From this more forward-looking point of view, it is a mistake to continue to think of African philosophy in the old way. In interpreting the term 'African philosophy' one ought to take cognisance of contemporary philosophical efforts on this continent, and one must even begin to envisage the time when, with the growth of this effort, the term will come to have the type of non-anthropological reference that terms like 'European philosophy', 'Soviet philosophy', etc., have (see p. 36). Meanwhile, the old way of regarding African philosophy persists, and in this chapter I shall be concerned with various misleading comparisons of African thought with Western thought which it inspires.

Many Western anthropologists and even non-anthropologists have often been puzzled by the ubiquity of references to gods and all sorts of spirits in traditional African explanations of things. Robin Horton has suggested that this failure of understanding is partly attributable to the fact that many Western anthropologists 'have been unfamiliar with the theoretical thinking of their own culture'.[2] I suggest that a very much more crucial reason is that they have also apparently been unfamiliar with the folk thought of their own culture.

Western societies too have passed through a stage where explanations of phenomena likewise relied on the agency of spirits. Indeed, significant residues of this tradition remain a basic part of the mental make-up of a large mass of the not-so-sophisticated sections of Western populations, and more importantly, elements are, in fact, deeply embedded in the philosophical thought of many contemporary Westerners – philosophers and even scientists.

Obviously it is of prime philosophical importance to distinguish between traditional, pre-scientific thought, and modern, scientific thought by means of a clearly articulated criterion, or set of criteria.

[2] Robin Horton: 'African Traditional Thought and Western Science', reprinted in *Rationality*, edited by Bryan Wilson (Oxford, Basil Blackwell) from *Africa*, vol. XXXVII, nos. 1 and 2, 1967. Horton's philosophically sophisticated account of African traditional thought *vis-à-vis* modern scientific thought is, while controversial, probably the most interesting and worthwhile of its kind.

Indeed one of the most influential and fruitful movements in recent Western philosophy, namely, logical positivism, may be said to have been motivated by the quest for just such a criterion. With that distinction made it is of importance to try to understand how each mode of thought, and especially the traditional, functions in the total context of its society. Since African societies are among the closest approximations in the modern world to societies in the pre-scientific stage of development, the interest which anthropologists have shown in African thought is largely understandable. However, instead of seeing the basic non-scientific characteristics of African traditional thought as typifying traditional thought in general, Western anthropologists and others besides have mistakenly tended to take them as defining a peculiarly African way of thinking, with unfortunate effects.

One such effect is that the really interesting cross-cultural comparisons of modes of thought have rarely been made. If one starts with the recognition that each nation has some background of traditional thought – and remember by *traditional* thought that here I mean pre-scientific thought of the type that tends to construct explanations of natural phenomena in terms of the activities of gods and spirits – then the interesting and anthropologically illuminating comparison will be to see in what different ways the belief in spirits is employed by various peoples in the attempt to achieve a coherent view of the world. In such specific differences will consist the real peculiarities of African traditional thought in contradistinction to, say, Western traditional thought. Such comparisons may well turn out to hold less exotic excitement for the Western anthropologist than present practice would seem to suggest. In the absence of any such realisation, what has generally happened is that not only the genuine distinguishing features of African traditional thought but also its basic non-scientific tendencies have been taken as a basis for contrasting Africans and Western peoples. One consequence is that many Westerners have gone about with an exaggerated notion of the differences in nature between Africans and the people of the West. I am not implying that this has necessarily led to anti-African racism. Nevertheless, since in some obvious and important respects traditional thought cannot match modern, science-oriented thought, some Western liberals appear to have had to think hard not to conceive of Africans as their intellectual inferiors.

Another ill-effect relates to the self-images of Africans themselves. Partly through the influence of Western anthropology and partly through insufficient critical reflection on the contemporary African situation, many very well-placed Africans are apt to identify African thought with *traditional* African thought. The result has not advanced the cause of modernisation, usually championed by the very same class of Africans. The mechanics of this interplay of attitudes is somewhat subtle. To begin with, such people have been in the habit of calling loudly, even stridently, for the cultivation of an authentic African personality; a call which, when not merely a political slogan, is usually motivated by a genuine desire to preserve the indigenous culture of peoples whose confidence in themselves has been undermined by colonialism. But it was a pervasive trait of this indigenous culture that enabled sparse groups of Europeans to subjugate much larger numbers of Africans and keep them in colonial subjection for many years, and which even now makes them a prey to neo-colonialism. I refer to the traditional and non-literate[3] character of the culture, with its associated technological underdevelopment. Being traditional is, of course, not synonymous with being non-literate. A culture can

---

[3] It is a paradox of cultural history that the traditional Ghanaians, for example, did not develop writing, for, as can be seen from our previous observations on Ghanaian culture in chapter 1, that culture was very highly symbolic; it was a culture that placed special emphasis on the significance of *symbols*. Indeed it has sometimes been suggested that the Akans of Ghana actually had their own indigenous script. However, what the evidence seems to show is that they had symbolic constructs similar but not actually identical with a script. Besides, if they had a script, it would be a mystery why so historically and philosophically minded a people as the Akans did not commit their history and philosophy, if not anything else, to script. It would be difficult, moreover, to understand why Ashanti Kings should have hired Moslem secretaries to keep records of trade transactions in Arabic. Although in other parts of West Africa a variety of indigenous scripts are known to have been invented around the middle of the nineteenth century such as those of the Vai of Liberia, the Mende of Sierra Leone, the Nsibidi of Eastern Nigeria, the Bamoun of the Camerouns and others, writing, unfortunately, never became culturally effective among any of these peoples. Certainly none of them seems to have built up a tradition of written indigenous philosophy. (Prof. S. I. A. Kotei of the Department of Library and Archival Studies at the University of Ghana has discussed these scripts in his article on 'The West African Autochthonous Alphabets: An Exercise in Comparative Palaeography', *Ghana Social Science Journal*, vol. 2, no. 1, May 1972.)

be literate and yet remain traditional, i.e. non-scientific, as the case of India proves. India has a long tradition of written literature, yet it was not until comparatively recent times that the scientific spirit made any appreciable inroads into the Indian way of life. But, of course, a culture cannot be both scientific and non-literate, for the scientific method can flourish only where there can be recordings of precise measurements, calculations and, generally, of observational data. If a culture is both non-scientific and non-literate, then it is handicapped in some important respects. We shall in due course note the bearing of the non-literate nature of traditional African culture on the question of just what African philosophy is.

What is immediately pertinent is to remark that uncritical exhortations to Africans to preserve their indigenous culture are not particularly useful – indeed, they can be counter-productive. There is an urgent need in Africa today for the kind of analysis that would identify and separate the backward aspects of our culture from those aspects worth keeping. That such desirable aspects exist is beyond question, and undoubtedly this motivates many African political and intellectual leaders. Yet the analytical dimension seems to be lacking in their enthusiasm. So we have, among other distressing things, the spectacle of otherwise enlightened Africans pouring libations to the spirits of their ancestors under the impression that in so doing they are demonstrating their faith in African culture.

In fact, many traditional African institutions and cultural practices such as the ones just mentioned are based on superstition. By 'superstition' I mean a rationally unsupported belief in entities of any sort. The attribute of being superstitious attaches not to the content of a belief but to its relation to other beliefs. Purely in respect of content the belief, for example, in abstract entities common among many philosophers in the West is no better than the traditional African belief in ancestor spirits. But these philosophers are given to arguing for their beliefs, and while I happen to think their arguments for abstract entities wrong-headed,[4] it is not open to me to accuse them of superstition. When, however, we come to the traditional African belief in ancestor

---

[4] My reasons for this remark will be found in my series of articles on 'Logic and Ontology' in *Second Order: An African Journal of Philosophy*, vol. II, nos. 1 and 2, January and July 1973, vol. II, no. 2, July 1974 and vol. IV, no. 1, January 1975.

spirits – and this, I would contend, applies to folk beliefs everywhere – the position is different. That our departed ancestors continue to hover around in some rarefied form ready now and then to take a sip of the ceremonial schnapps is a proposition that I have never heard rationally defended. Indeed, if one were to ask a traditional elder, 'unspoilt' by the scientific orientation, for the rational justification of such a belief, one's curiosity would promptly be put down to intellectual arrogance acquired through a Western education.

Yet the principle that one is not entitled to accept a proposition as true in the absence of any evidential support is not intrinsically Western of course. The Western world is merely the place where this principle has received its most sustained and successful application in certain spheres of thought, notably in the natural sciences and mathematics. But even in the Western world there are some important areas of belief wherein the principle does not hold sway. In the West just as anywhere else the realms of religion, morals and politics remain strongholds of irrationality. Even Western scientists, fully convinced of the universal reign of law in natural phenomena, may pray to a supernatural being for rain and a good harvest. Those who are tempted to see in such a thing as witchcraft the key to specifically *African* thought – there is no lack of such people elsewhere as well as in Africa – ought to be reminded that there are numbers of white men in London today who proudly proclaim themselves to be witches. Moreover, if they read, for example, Trevor-Roper's historical essay on 'Witches and Witchcraft'[5] they might come to doubt whether witchcraft in Africa has ever attained the heights to which it reached in Europe in the sixteenth and seventeenth centuries.

It should be noted, conversely, that the principle of rational evidence is not entirely absent from the thinking of the traditional African. Indeed, no society could survive for any length of time without basing a large part of its daily activities on beliefs derived from the evidence. You cannot farm without some rationally based knowledge of soils, seeds and climate; and no society can achieve any reasonable degree of harmony in human relations without the basic ability to assess claims and allegations by the method of objective investigation. The truth, then, is that rational knowledge

[5] *Encounter*, vol. XXVIII, Nos. 5 and 6, May and June 1967.

is not the preserve of the modern West[6] nor is superstition a peculiarity of the African.

Nevertheless, it is a fact that Africa lags behind the West in the cultivation of rational inquiry. One illuminating (because fundamental) way of approaching the concept of 'development' is to measure it by the degree to which rational methods have penetrated thought habits. In this sense, of course, one cannot compare the development of different peoples in absolute terms. The Western world is 'developed', but only relatively. Technological sophistication is only an aspect, and that not the core, of development. The conquest of the religious, moral and political spheres by the spirit of rational inquiry remains, as noted earlier, a thing of the future even in the West. From this point of view the West may be said to be still underdeveloped. The quest for development, then, should be viewed as a continuing world-historical process in which all peoples, Western and non-Western alike, are engaged.

There are at least two important advantages in looking at development in this way. The first is that it becomes possible to see the movement towards modernisation in Africa not as essentially a process in which Africans are unthinkingly jettisoning their own heritage of thought in the pursuit of Western ways of life, but rather as one in which Africans in common with all other peoples seek to attain a specifically human destiny – a thought that should assuage the qualms of those among thoughtful Africans who see modernisation as a foreign invasion. The relation between the concepts of development and modernisation ought to be obvious. Modernisation is the application of the results of modern science for the improvement of the conditions of human life. It is only the more visible side of development; it is the side that is more immediately associated with the use of advanced technology, and novel techniques in various areas of life such as agriculture, health, education and recreation. Because modernisation is not the whole of development there is a need to view it always in a wider human perspective. Man should link the modernisation of the conditions of his life with the modernisation of all aspects of his thinking. It is just the failure to do this that is responsible for the more unlovable features of life in the West. Moreover, the same failure bedevils

[6] Note that 'the West' and 'Western' are used in a cultural, rather than ideological, sense in this discussion.

attempts at development in Africa. Rulers and leaders of opinion in Africa have tended to think of development in terms of the visible aspects of modernisation – in terms of large buildings and complex machines, to the neglect of the more intellectual foundations of modernity. It is true that African nations spend every year huge sums of money on institutional education. But it has not been appreciated that education ought to lead to the cultivation of a rational[7] outlook on the world on the part of the educated and, through them, the population as a whole. So, even while calling for modernisation, influential Africans can still be seen to encourage superstitious practices in the belief that in this kind of way they can achieve development without losing their Africanness. The second advantage of seeing development in the way suggested above is that the futility of any such approach becomes evident. To develop in any serious sense, we in Africa must break with our old uncritical habits of thought; that is to say, we must advance past the stage of traditional thinking.

Lest these remarks appear rather abstract, let us consider a concrete situation: the institution of funerals in Ghana. Owing to all sorts of superstitions about the supposed career of the spirits of departed relatives, the mourning of the dead takes the form of elaborate, and, consequently, expensive and time consuming social ceremonies. When a person dies there has first to be a burial ceremony on the third day; then on the eighth day there is a funeral celebration at which customary rites are performed; then forty days afterwards there is a fortieth day celebration (*adaduanan*). Strictly, that is not the end. There are such occasions as the eightieth day and first anniversary celebrations, and all these are large gatherings. Contrary to what one might be tempted to think, the embracing of Christianity by large sections of the Ghanaian population has not simplified funeral celebrations; on the contrary, it has brought new complications. Christianity too teaches of a whole hierarchy of spirits, starting from the Supreme Threefold

[7] I am aware that my insistence on the overriding value of rationality will be found jarring by those Westerners who feel that the claims of rationality have been pushed too far in their countries and that the time is overdue for a return to 'Nature' and the exultation in feeling, intuition and immediacy. No doubt the harsh individualism of Western living might seem to lend support to this point of view. But in my opinion the trouble is due to too little rather than too much rationality in social organisation. This, however, is too large a topic to enter into here.

Spirit down to angels and the lesser spirits of the dead. Besides, conversion to Christianity in our lands has generally not meant the exchange of the indigenous religion for the new one, but rather an amalgamation of the two, made the more possible by their common belief in spirits. So, in addition to all the traditional celebrations, there is nowadays the neo-Christian Memorial Service, replete with church services and extended refreshments, a particularly expensive phase of the funeral process. The upshot is that if a close relation of a man dies, then unless he happens to be rich, he is in for very hard financial times indeed. He has to take several days off work, and he has to borrow respectable sums of money to defray the inevitable expenses.

The extent of the havoc that these funeral habits have wrought on the national economy of Ghana has not been calculated, but it has become obvious to public leaders that it is enormous and that something needs urgently to be done about it. However, the best that these leaders have seemed capable of doing so far has been to exhort the people to reform their traditional institutions in general and cut down on funeral expenses in particular. These appeals have gone unheeded; which is not surprising, if one recalls that these leaders themselves are often to be seen ostentatiously taking part in ceremonies based on the same sort of beliefs as those which lie behind the funeral practices. It has so far apparently been lost upon our influential men that while the underlying beliefs retain their hold, any verbal appeals are wasted on the populace.

The ideal way to reform backward customs in Africa must, surely, be to undermine their foundations in superstition by fostering in the people – at all events, in the new generation of educated Africans – the spirit of rational inquiry in all spheres of thought and belief. Even if the backward beliefs in question were *peculiarly* African, it would be necessary to work for their eradication. But my point is that they are not African in any intrinsic, inseparable sense; and the least that African philosophers and foreign well-wishers can do in this connection is to refrain, in this day and age, from serving up the usual congeries of unargued conceptions about gods, ghosts and witches in the name of African philosophy. Such a description is highly unfortunate. If at all deserving of the name 'philosophy', these ideas should be regarded not as a part of African philosophy simply, but rather as a part of *traditional* African philosophy.

Nor is this just to cavil. The habit of talking of African philosophy as if all African philosophy were *traditional* carries the implication, probably not always intended, that modern Africans have not been trying, or worse still, ought not to try, to philosophise in a manner that takes account of developments in logic, mathematics, science, and the humanities. Various causes have combined to motivate this attitude. African nationalists in search of an African identity, Afro-Americans in search of their African roots and foreigners in search of exotic diversion – all demand an African philosophy fundamentally different from Western philosophy, even if it means the familiar witches' brew. Obviously, the work of contemporary African philosophers trying to grapple with the modern philosophical situation cannot satisfy such a demand.

The African philosopher writing today has no long-standing tradition of written philosophy in his continent[8] to draw upon. In this respect, his plight is very much unlike that of, say, the contemporary Indian philosopher, who can draw on the insights contained in a long heritage of written philosophical meditations; he has what he might legitimately call *classical* Indian philosophers to investigate and profit by. And if he is broad-minded, he will also study Western philosophy and try in his own philosophising to take cognisance of the intellectual developments that have shaped the modern world. Besides all this, he has, as every people has, a background of unwritten folk philosophy which he might examine for whatever it may be worth. Notice that we have here three levels of philosophy: we have spoken of a folk philosophy, a written traditional[9] philosophy and a modern philosophy. Where long standing written sources are available folk philosophy tends not to be made much of. It remains in the background as a diffuse, immanent component of community thought habits whose effects on the thinking of the working philosopher is largely unconscious.[10] Such a fund of community thought is not the creation of

[8] The Arab portions of Africa and also Ethiopia are, of course, an exception.

[9] 'Traditional' here still has the pre-scientific connotation. Of course, if one should speak of *traditional* British empiricism, for example, that connotation would, as noted previously, be absent.

[10] Since such effects do, in fact, occur, this threefold stratification should not be taken as watertight.

any specifiable set of philosophers; it is the common property of all and sundry, thinker and non-thinker alike, and it is called a *philosophy* at all only on a generous understanding of the term. Folk thought, as a rule, consists of bald assertions without supportive arguments, but philosophy in the narrower sense must contain not just theses. Without argument and clarification, there is, strictly, no philosophy.

Folk thought can be comprehensive and interesting on its own account, but its non-discursiveness remains a drawback. For example, according to the conception of a person found among the Akans of Ghana (the ethnic group to which the present writer belongs), a person is constituted by *nipadua* (a body) and a combination of the following entities conceived as spiritual substances:[11] (1) *okra* (soul, approximately), that whose departure from a man means death, (2) *sunsum*, that which gives rise to a man's character, (3) *ntoro*, something passed on from the father which is the basis of inherited characteristics and, finally, (4) *mogya*, something passed on from the mother which determines a man's clan identity and which at death becomes the *saman* (ghost). This last entity seems to be the one that is closest to the material aspect of a person: literally, *mogya* means blood. Now, in the abstract, all this sounds more interesting, certainly more imaginative, than the thesis of some Western philosophers that a person consists of a soul and a body. The crucial difference, however, is that the Western philosopher argues for his thesis, clarifying his meaning and answering objections, known or anticipated; whereas the believer in folk conceptions merely says: 'This is what our ancestors said.'[12] For this reason folk conceptions tend not to develop with time. Please note that this is as true in the West and elsewhere as it is in Africa.

But in Africa, where we do not have even a written traditional philosophy, anthropologists have fastened on our folk world-views and elevated them to the status of a continental philosophy. They have then compared this 'philosophy' with Western (written) philosophy. In other parts of the world, if you want to know the philosophy of the given people, you do not go to aged peasants or

[11] See, for example, W. E. Abraham, *The Mind of Africa*, Weidenfeld and Nicolson, 1962, paperback edition, 1967.

[12] However, the circumstance that in Africa, for example, our traditional thought tends not to be elaborately argumentative should not be attributed to an absence of the discursive spirit but rather to the fact that the thoughts were not written down.

fetish priests or court personalities; but to the individual thinkers, in person or in print, who as individuals are bound to differ, and to present a variety of theories and doctrines, possibly but not necessarily displaying substantial affinities. Since the alternative has been the only one that has seemed possible to anthropologists, it is not surprising that misleading comparisons between African traditional thought and Western scientific thought have resulted. My contention, which I have earlier hinted at, is that African traditional thought should in the first place only be compared with Western folk thought. For this purpose, of course, Western anthropologists will first have to learn in detail about the folk thought of their own peoples. African folk thought may be compared with Western philosophy only in the same spirit in which Western folk thought may be compared also with Western philosophy, that is, only in order to find out the marks which distinguish folk thought in general from individualised philosophising. Those concerned to compare African philosophy with Western philosophy will have to look at the philosophy that Africans are producing today.

Naturally Western anthropologists are not generally interested in contemporary African philosophy. Present-day African philosophers have been trained in the Western tradition, in the continental or Anglo-American style, depending on their colonial history. Their thinking, therefore, is unlikely to hold many peculiarly African novelties for anyone knowledgeable in Western philosophy. For this very same reason, African militants and our Afro-American brothers are often disappointed with the sort of philosophy syllabus that is taught at a typical modern department of philosophy in Africa. They find such a department mainly immersed in the study of logic, epistemology, metaphysics, ethics, political philosophy, etc., as these have been developed in the West, and they question why Africans should be so engrossed in the philosophy of their erstwhile colonial oppressors.

The attentive reader of this discussion should know the answer by now: The African philosopher has no choice but to conduct his philosophical inquiries in relation to the philosophical writings of other peoples, for his own ancestors left him no heritage of philosophical writings. He must of necessity study the written philosophies of other lands, because it would be extremely injudicious for him to try to philosophise in self-imposed isolation from all modern currents of thought. In the ideal, he must acquaint himself with philosophy from all parts of the world, compare, contrast, critically assess them and make use of whatever he may find in them of value. In this way it can be hoped that a tradition of philosophy as a discursive discipline will eventually come to be established in Africa which future Africans and others too can utilise. In practice the contemporary African philosopher will find that it is the philosophies of the West that will occupy him most, for it is in that part of the world that modern developments in human knowledge have gone farthest and where, consequently, philosophy is in closest touch with the conditions of the modernisation which he urgently desires for his continent.

The African philosopher cannot, of course, take the sort of cultural pride in the philosophical achievements of Aristotle, Hume, Kant, Marx or Frege, which the Western student of philosophy may permit himself. Indeed an African needs a certain level-headedness to deal with some of these thinkers at all. Neither Hume,[13] nor Marx,[14] displayed much respect for the black man, so whatever partiality the African philosopher may develop for these thinkers must rest mostly on considerations of the truth of their philosophical thought.

As regards his own background of folk thought, there is a good reason why the African philosopher should pay more attention to it than would seem warranted in other places. Some foreigners have not even been willing to concede that Africans as a traditional

[13] Hume was able to say in his *Essays* (London, George Routledge & Sons Ltd), footnote on pp. 152 and 153 in the course of the essay on 'National Characters': 'I am apt to suspect the Negroes to be naturally inferior to the Whites. There scarcely ever was a civilised nation of that complexion, nor ever any individual, eminent either in action or speculation ... In Jamaica, indeed they talk of one Negro as a man of parts and learning; but it is likely that he is admired for slender accomplishments, like a parrot who speaks a few words plainly.' Considerable maturity is required in the African to be able to contemplate impartially Hume's disrespect for Negroes and his philosophical insights, deploring the former and acknowledging and assimilating the latter.

[14] Marx is known once, in a burst of personal abuse of Lassalle in a letter to Engels, to have animadverted: 'This combination of Jewry and Germany with a fundamental Negro streak ... The fellow's self assertiveness is Negro too.' Quoted in J. Hampden Jackson, *Marx, Proudhon and European Socialism* (London, English Universities Press, 1951), p. 144. For even more striking instances of racist sentiment in Marx (and also Engels) see Ladimeji, 'Nationalism, Alienation and the Crisis of Ideology', *Transition*, vol. 46, October/December 1974, p. 40.

people were capable of any sort of coherent world-view.[15] Those who had the good sense and the patience and industry to settle down and study traditional African thought were often, especially in the nineteenth and early twentieth centuries, colonial anthropologists whose attempts to understand our forebears were for the benefit of the colonial government.[16] Although some brilliant insights were obtained, there were also misinterpretations and straightforward errors. Africans cannot leave the task of correction to foreign researchers alone. Besides, particularly in the field of morality, there are conceptions not based on superstition from which the modern Westerner may well have something to learn.[17] The exposition of such aspects of African traditional thought specially befits the contemporary African philosopher.

Yet, in treating of their traditional thought, African philosophers should be careful not to make hasty comparisons.[18] Also they should approach their material critically. This last suggestion is particularly important since all peoples who have made any breakthrough in the quest for modernisation have done so by going beyond folk thinking. It is unlikely to be otherwise in Africa. I should like to repeat, however, that the process of sifting the elements of our traditional thought and culture calls for a good measure of analytical circumspection lest we exchange the good as well as the bad in our traditional ways of life for dubious cultural imports.

It should be clear from the foregoing discussion that the question of how African thought may appropriately be compared with Western thought is not just an academic issue but also one of great existential urgency.

---

[15] Coherent thought is not necessarily scientific thought. Traditional thought can display a high degree of coherence; and certainly African traditional thought is not lacking in coherence.

[16] R. S. Rattray, for example, one of the most hard-working and famous of the European anthropologists in Ghana during this period, was employed officially as Gold Coast Government Anthropologist.

[17] See, for example, chapter 1, pp. 5–6.

[18] I ought perhaps to point out that the kind of comparison between African thought and Western thought that has been criticised in this discussion is of a sort that seeks to characterise the given varieties of thinking as wholes in a certain way. In particular, my remarks do not affect the comparison of specific propositions.

4

What can philosophy do for Africa?

It should be clear from the last two chapters that the question of the right orientation for pursuing philosophy in Africa is of the most practical importance. On the basis of the views already put forward I would now like to tackle the question 'What can philosophy do for Africa?' This question will probably trigger off another question, namely, 'What can philosophy do for society, any society?' I do not propose to discuss this latter question at any length. I take it as axiomatic that action – by an individual or group of individuals – needs to be guided by ideas and that philosophy attempts to elucidate the most fundamental of such ideas. But man lives and moves in a complex world, and this world must be understood, at all events in some measure, in philosophy's characteristically fundamental ways before informed guidance can be offered. This task, the task of understanding the world, is difficult and, from all indications, unfinishable; but some attempt at it is essential, and any attempt is likely to be prolonged. Thus it is that throughout history philosophers have been largely engaged in trying to understand the world. They have never, if they were any good, forgotten that the understanding is not an end in itself but is for the practical good of man. In so far as Marx in his now hackneyed apophthegm 'The philosophers have only *interpreted* the world in various ways; the point, however, is to *change* it' seems to suggest that the importance, even the urgency, of changing the world had escaped philosophers (before him) in their preoccupation with the quest for understanding, he is simply wrong – one is tempted to say, inexcusably wrong. All the major philosophers of the world have tried in one way or another, successfully or unsuccessfully, to change the world for the better.

Indeed Marx himself is a shining example of a philosopher who sought to base his prescriptions for society on a philosophical understanding of the world.[1] Marx lived in revolutionary times. In such times it is always tempting for people to offer, and the populace to accept, or at any rate, to appear to accept, half baked ideas for the improvement of society. In Africa today we live in times that are not dissimilar to Marx's in this respect, and I would suggest that Marx's example is one which we should all take to heart.

In some ways our situation in Africa today is more deeply revolutionary than the Europe of the time of Marx. We are not only seeking modes of political and social organisation best suited to the requirements of rapid development but also engaged in reappraising, changing and adapting our traditional culture under the pressure of modern conditions, under the pressure, more specifically, of a foreign influence that came to us first in the form of colonialism, against which another type of revolution still continues violently in parts of Africa.

Even so brief and vague a characterisation of our situation in Africa today is sufficient to indicate certain important functions for the African philosopher. He must let his voice be heard on the question of what mode of social and political organisation is best suited to our conditions, and he must take active part, indeed, he must lead, in the reappraisal of our traditional culture. Obviously the two enterprises are inter-related, and in both he must reveal the basic principles on which to proceed.

Consider the problem of the choice (or discovery) of a social and political system. There is at the present time in Africa a vocal and perhaps widespread belief in the desirability and effectiveness of ideology in national life. This on the face of it is an invitation to the philosopher, for it appears to indicate that people are anxious to listen to him. An ideology is, in the best sense of this highly ambiguous word, a set of ideas about what form the good society should take, and any such set of ideas needs a basis in first principles, which is where philosophy enters. But, on account of the ambiguity in the meaning of the word 'ideology', a preliminary clarification is necessary when considering this matter.

---

[1] Ironically, he himself spent so much time analysing and trying to understand the world of capitalism that he was only able to leave sketchy and ambiguous prescriptions for the practical reconstruction of society.

It turns out that frequently the call for ideology is a cryptically expressed call for a particular ideology, namely, socialism. This, however, is not what gives rise to problems, for, of course, there is nothing wrong with advocating socialism. The fact is that usually such calls for ideology are a demand for a ready made set of ideas meant to be adopted by governments as the *exclusive* basis for the political organisation of society. In this sense an ideology is a set of dogmas to be imposed by the government, with force if necessary. This sense is, of course, not openly avowed, and can only be gathered from circumstantial evidence. In Ghana in the early sixties, for example, this is what ideology amounted to in actual practice, notwithstanding the official praise for humanism. It would be hard to forget the atmosphere of intellectual strangulation in Ghana in those days when it was taken almost to be subversion to express publicly any doubts about dialectical materialism. But I must not digress. The immediate reason for calling attention to this other meaning of 'ideology' is to point out that much of the current controversy on the question of ideology in Africa today is at cross-purposes. It may reasonably be presumed that those, at any rate some of those, who would have no truck with 'ideology', interpret the term in the second sense. Meanwhile, because of the existence of the first sense, the proponents of ideology can point to the absurdity of the suggestion that society can be expected to move in the right direction without people having any coherent idea as to its ideal destiny. The point, however, is that to oppose ideology in the second sense is not necessarily to deny it in the first sense.

In this matter the philosopher's role is not just to clarify the semantics of ideological talk; he must positively oppose the emergence in Africa of ideology in the second, I would say degenerate, sense. Let us, for the time being, understand the word 'ideology' in just this degenerate sense. Then, it seems to me to be the case not only that ideology is the negation of philosophy, but also that it is a bar to development. As already pointed out in the preceding chapter, development does not mean merely the acquisition of sophisticated technology with its associated material benefits; it means also the securing of such conditions as shall permit the self-realisation of men as rational beings. I am tempted to re-echo here the question as to what it would profit a man if he were to gain all the world and lose his soul.

One way in which a man can lose his soul is by being prevented from trying to think for himself or, even more terribly, by being rendered unable to think for himself. In Africa nowadays people have learnt all sorts of euphemisms for anti-humanism. Where they may say that we need an ideology to mobilise the population for rapid development they are likely to mean in actual fact that they want to force their pet preconceptions down the throats of their countrymen in order, among other things, that their actions might seem to have the support of the 'masses'. The essential anti-humanism of this kind of procedure is more easily masked by the circumstance that forms of speech are apt to make personal opinions look like independent realities. While likely to be ashamed to be seen to be forcing others to accept their own opinions, people are perfectly able to do just this with a sense of righteousness when these opinions are recommended not merely as their own but as the Truth. If some people through pig-headedness, obtuseness, or pure wilfulness are not immediately ready to embrace the things that are true and good especially in matters affecting a whole nation, may it not seem legitimate to apply some pressure?

I cannot forbear to relate in this connection a conversation I once had with a friend who obviously had a sense of mission, many years ago when we were both studying abroad. He was a citizen of one of our sister West African countries where the authorities were not very particular about such things as putting a political opponent on trial before putting him in jail. He had finished his training and was returning to his country with one ambition: to win political power and set things right. In our parting conversation he assured me that when he got into power, as he thought he inevitably would, he would never detain his opponents without trial. Everybody, he said, would be absolutely free to organise or join whatever party they pleased without the fear of arbitrary arrest and detention. But he set one small condition: Unlike the evil-minded politicians, he would summarily detain only people whose actions were really incompatible with the good of his dear country. It had apparently not occurred to him that it was just conceivable that the evil politicians had been detaining only those people whose actions struck *them* as really incompatible with the good of their own country. The impression has since grown on me that this kind of illogicality is one of the most fundamental causes of inhumanity in Africa as, of course, elsewhere.

Truth is personal,[2] and so, even more obviously, are goodness and beauty. Or, not to seem to be begging philosophical questions, I will put it in this way: Let truth, beauty and goodness – I have used small letters but whoever is given to talking of the Eternal Verities is welcome to capitals – let this trinity be of whatever metaphysical nature they may be, still that something is true, good or beautiful is a personal affirmation. If I punish another for not adhering to the true, the good, the beautiful, the penalty he pays is a result of his not adopting *my* opinions, attitudes and preferences. I have previously defined ideology, in what I called the best sense of the word, as a set of ideas as to what the good society should be like; a more naked characterisation is that an ideology is a set of personal opinions and preferences in the matter of alternative social arrangements. I venture the psychological observation that anybody who grasps this and keeps it steadfastly in mind is unlikely to feel entitled forcibly to impose his ideology on others.

Let me quickly note the standard objection to suggestions like those just put forward. Such views, it would be said, amount to subjectivism and the degrading of truth, goodness and beauty. I have always been intrigued by this kind of response, for it creates the following paradox: Tell a person that in practice truth, say, is nothing more than opinion, and he is instantly scandalised. He will not stand for any attempt to render truth worthless. But try, in the first place, to suggest to him that his opinion on some important matter is worthless and he will be equally outraged, for his opinion is, of course, precious. Which seems to suggest that in the affair of defining truth, wisdom comes in trying to eat your cake and have it.

As regards the idea of the good even greater indignation will be provoked by the suggestion that such a thing as a system of values is nothing over and above the system of human preferences. It would be a remarkable show of modesty if this reaction were an indication of someone's diffidence about their own moral convictions. But one

---

[2] On this remark and the remarks relating to the concept of truth in the next paragraph see, further, chapters 8, 9, 10, 11, and especially pp. 216–18.

soon discovers that this reaction is only a reflection of the low opinion that people have of the preferences of others. Their own preferences are apparently well considered and rational.[3] If so, logical impartiality would seem to compel at least the following conclusion: The preferences of men generally are not necessarily the same as arbitrary whims. From which it would also follow that to see human values as a system of human preferences is not necessarily to downgrade them; on the contrary, it may mean upgrading human nature. Morality, at any rate humanistic morality, is founded upon the pursuit of human well-being. The specifically *moral* preferences of human beings are those that seek to harmonise the conditions of the well-being of particular individuals with those of the well-being of society at large. It is this intentional relation between the preferences of an individual and a larger common end that makes possible the inter-personal appraisal of moral convictions. Admittedly, to decide the actual way in which particular actions, feelings and tendencies stand with this ideal of human well-being can be complicated to a high degree. Indeed, the interpretation of the notion of human well-being itself in a concrete enough form for the practical guidance of life encounters deep difficulties – two facts which account for the perplexities of the philosophical study of morals. Nevertheless, nothing is gained by seeking the foundation of human values beyond human nature.

The fear of subjectivity is at the root of this flight from human nature in many cases. But subjectivity itself is frequently misconceived. There is nothing subjective about human desires, preferences or even tastes. The taste of sourness, for example, is as complete an existence as the tongue that feels it. What may be said to constitute subjectivity is the dependence of a judgment about any of these things – about anything, for that matter – upon the peculiarities of an individual or group. For example, to an average citizen of the United States of America the possession of an automobile is a pressing need, whereas to a rural dweller in one of our villages without access to even clean water the position is quite different. One might say in this case that whether an automobile is a pressing need or not is a subjective matter. Here what is subjec-

---

[3] An analogous attitude is discussed in connection with the problem of the meaning of truth in chapter 8, pp. 117–18.

tive is not the pure state of feeling of the American or the rural Ghanaian but the associated judgment. In general, it is a judgment rather than a state that can be said to be subjective. Correspondingly, objectivity consists not in absolute independence of the subject *as such* but only in independence of the peculiarities of the individual. Human beings have a substantial communality of needs, desires, feelings, capabilities, etc., but they also have peculiarities. The former is the basis of objectivity, the latter of subjectivity.

There is a certain flexibility – from the point of view of a philosopher, one might say looseness – in the use of the notion of subjectivity in ordinary discourse. Sometimes it is not just dependence on the peculiarities of an individual or group that constitutes subjectivity but only that species of such dependence for which no explanation in terms of regular laws exists. When a man (literally) looks at objects through tainted glasses the disparity between the way he sees their colours and that of those enjoying unmediated vision is not attributed to subjectivity. Why? Because the variation is in accord with known optical laws. Even when differences in colour discriminations are due to more innate peculiarities such as colour blindness, the temptation to talk of subjectivity is held in check since knowledge of the explanation enables both the subject and the observer to make inter-personal adjustments. In the present usage it is only when the differences in judgment occasioned by individual peculiarities prove recalcitrant to a law-like account that one speaks of subjectivity.

The notion of subjectivity does, on occasion, have a more immediately ethical meaning. We frequently speak of a person as being subjective in his views when we notice that in his scheme of preferences and objectives considerations regarding his individual well-being or the well-being of a restricted group of which he is a member tend to eclipse thoughts of the well-being of society as a whole. Subjectivity in this sense still involves the dependence of judgment on the singular characteristics of the individual or group; it is the kind of dependence that (tacitly) involves maxims that cannot be universalised.

One can also point to a psycho-epistemological sense of subjectivity: If a man departs sufficiently from the acknowledged canons of reasoning then the degree of subjectivity attributed to him escalates to the point where he is regarded as mentally ill.[4]

In none of these senses of subjectivity can the notion of human preferences be held automatically to imply subjectivity.

It will be noticed that I have veered from discussing what philosophy can do about the danger of ideology in the bad sense to expressing views on the concept of truth and some of its conceptual associates. I have not tried to *argue* my philosophical position fully here; I have merely hinted at it. And my aim is simply to bring out how abstract issues, such as the question of the meaning of truth, lie at the root of more practical issues, such as the question of the relation between ideology and development. Given this realisation, it becomes easy to appreciate, for example, that the best approach open to a philosopher wishing to fight ideology in the second sense is not simply to protest but to try to get people to think critically about the abstract notions which lie at the base of ideological discourse. I will return to this point in a moment. Meanwhile, it seems obvious that if the philosopher has a duty to combat ideology in the bad sense, he also has a duty to promote ideology in the good sense.

How best may he do this? There is a common temptation in this connection to expect the philosopher to issue social prescriptions. This he may do; but it is a consequence of the point made in the previous paragraph that it would be a mistake to try to do this too hastily. If you look around Africa today, you will find that it is the politician rather than the philosopher who has tended to propound an ideology. But just because such efforts have lacked conceptual preparation and analysis, they have had no real impact upon basic thought habits. It is not surprising that such ideologies have tended to degenerate into instruments of coercion. The really enduring effects of philosophy on the thinking of the majority of men are the result of a rather slow process, and are probably always of an

---

[4] There is, distinct from all these, a usage of the word 'subjective' which almost makes it a different word from the one discussed above. It is the sense that is under consideration when by means of the word one calls attention to a mental phenomenon such as a belief, a feeling, an attitude, in its status purely as a state of the subject without regard to its relation to anything beyond itself. This is what one has in mind when one talks of viewing one's thoughts and experiences *subjectively*. It is a very neutral sense of the expression which is not quite relevant to the problem of subjectivity discussed above. Note, though, that even here what is subjective is not the state of the subject but the manner of viewing it.

indirect character. In Africa the effect is bound to be doubly slow and doubly indirect.

The explanation for this is to be found in a remark I made earlier. We are engaged not only in social and economic reconstruction but also in cultural reconstruction. What we ought to do, what we are in any case compelled by modern developments to do, is to speed up that process. This implies the admission that our culture is less than ideal in some important respects and that we have to introduce new elements into it, elements that will sometimes derive from alien sources.[5] This, if you consider the matter frankly, is what is meant by that *modernisation* which many people, high and low, say they want in Africa. That our culture – and by our culture I mean our traditional, indigenous culture – is not what it might be has always been an unpleasant thought, and very unwelcome to those engaged in the enterprise of trying to infuse a sense of racial self-respect in the African masses. This is understandable, but the thinker, whether he be a philosopher or trained in some other discipline, must rise above the common level of insight. It is, in fact, only the African who is free of a racial inferiority complex who can look critically at our culture and acknowledge its shortcomings. The period of colonial struggle was also a period of cultural affirmation. It was necessary to restore in ourselves our previous confidence which had been so seriously eroded by colonialism. We are still, admittedly, even in post-colonial times, in an era of cultural self-affirmation. The inferiority complex which colonialism induced in many of our people was responsible for a certain undiscriminating racial self-deprecation which went with an uncritical over-valuation of things and ideas originating with our erstwhile colonisers. It takes little wisdom to see that such a state of affairs ought to be reversed. But the process of reversal has some potential pitfalls. An uncontrolled nationalistic enthusiasm, such as politicians are apt to whip up in the masses, could lead to a wholesale cultural recrudescence which would in the long-run prove to be self-defeating. It is quite a subtle job to balance the enthusiasm for cultural revivalism with a spirit of forward-looking self-criticism. The initiative in this direction will not come from the people at large; it must come from their thinkers.

[5] I have discussed specific respects in which our culture needs reform in the previous chapters, particularly, in chapters 1 and 3.

I might point out further that to borrow from another culture does not necessarily imply a belief in the over-all superiority of that culture. In fact, it can be said, even on purely *a priori* grounds, that no culture in the world is perfect; so that a culture from which another culture has made a borrowing may – to be sure, will – itself be in need of reformation in some other respects. It ought always to be remembered that the history of human civilisation is a history of mutual borrowings among nations, peoples and races. We in Africa at this historic juncture have to borrow, for example, technology – appropriate technology, let us add – from the West; but this cannot be interpreted as an admission that our culture is generally inferior to Western culture. Indeed, in regard to a certain quite wide-ranging class of cultural matters it is not quite appropriate to make comparisons of this sort. For example, in Akan society if one has occasion to greet a group of people, one always proceeds from right to left. To go in the reverse order is considered a sign of deplorable cultural ignorance. I have not observed that any particular order is insisted upon in this matter in English circles, for instance. Is the one practice superior to the other? The question has little to recommend it. If a particular way of greeting suits one people and a different way happens to suit another people, we simply take note of the fact, and there is an end of the matter. Sometimes, however, an old cultural practice among a people may be found in, say, changed circumstances to stand in the way of human well-being. Then, one might sensibly compare it with a corresponding practice in another culture, *if need be*. Of course, attempts at cultural reformation need not rely on foreign comparisons. What is chiefly to be emphasised is that rational reflection on consequences is the most worthy motivation for cultural reformation. Such a critique of culture is indispensable in our present circumstances in Africa.

There is another score on which dissatisfaction might be felt with the critical sentiments I have expressed about our culture. Those who are in closest touch with our heritage of art, and have derived inspiration from that source in their creative work, know first hand the intrinsic worth of our tradition, and no philosopher can shake their conviction. Nor should any philosopher try to do that. Let us then distinguish two sides of culture: There is what one might call the aesthetic, and there is also, what I wish to call, for lack of a better word, the pragmatic side to any culture. The latter comprehends all modes of thought and practice having to do with man's utilisation of his environment – his quest for understanding and control of his environment – while the former relates to his appreciation and expressive enjoyment of the world. I do not say that these two aspects are separate, only that they are separable in thought. When the word 'culture' is mentioned the first thing that usually comes to mind is this aesthetic aspect of man's existence. In regard to this aspect of culture, an African has, of course, every reason to be proud of his inheritance.

But in regard to the pragmatic aspect of his culture the African, who asks himself why it came about that everywhere on his continent other peoples were able so easily to put his people in bondage, is bound to realise that the trouble lies not in our stars nor in our biology but in certain aspects of our culture. The trouble can, I think, be put down to the lack of a developed scientific method, broadly speaking. Our societies are being rapidly changed by industrialisation, and if we wish to understand this change and control its direction, we must adopt new ways of thinking, a new outlook upon man, society and nature. The philosopher can, and must, spearhead this endeavour. But his intellectual productions are bound to be largely alien to most of his people. For his thinking has to take cognisance of developments in human knowledge unknown to his fellows, which, added to the fact that abstract and critical thinking about the foundations of human thought and practice is alien to the common man anywhere, suggests how remote the contemporary philosopher will be from their comprehension.

But we must not exaggerate. Contemporary African populations consist of urban dwellers as well as rural folks. The experience of the mass of town dwellers has been influenced in varying degrees of intensity by modern trends. The officials who man our administrative services, the journalists who daily bombard us with propaganda, the politicians who solicit our votes, the soldiers who plan and bring off military coups every now and then – all have assimilated modern influences in one way or another. To them, some at least of the thoughts of the present-day philosopher in Africa will not seem totally alien. In any case, moreover, the philosopher usually has intermediaries; his influence will seep through to the general public through the work of less abstract thinkers who have themselves been influenced by him.

I would like to stress the importance of technical studies in the field of philosophy. It is only the philosopher who has attained competence in technical research and is at home in the most abstract regions of his subject who can speak with the clearest voice to the non-specialist public when the time comes. Philosophical issues have a habit of getting intertwined with one another. Thus although a devotion to such a question as the nature of meaning or entailment may not seem immediately relevant to any human concerns, any thorough-going attempt to construct, say, a moral theory is apt sooner than later to come up against a problem of that sort. Therefore the African philosopher need not let superficial calls for immediate relevance divert him from his studies. So long as he understands the basic practical motivation of his discipline, he is well advised to seek enlightenment in the most abstruse researches.

I would say, then, that what the African philosopher can do for his society is in principle no different from what philosophers in other cultures can do for their societies. The function of philosophy everywhere is to examine the intellectual foundations of our life, using the best available modes of knowledge and reflection for human well-being.

5

Marxism, philosophy and ideology

Marxism is one of the most influential theories of social organisation in Africa today. African philosophers ought not to leave the discussion of this doctrine to political propagandists alone.

Though not myself a Marxist, I regard Karl Marx as one of the great philosophers. If I am going to be engaged largely in criticism of his philosophy in this chapter, it is because I believe that philosophical greatness has nothing to do with infallibility. Besides, if I may speak in a manner somewhat reminiscent of the Marxists, philosophy is a *dialectic* of individual viewpoints, and criticism is its very life blood. I take it as a presupposition of any rational discussion that no one person or group of persons has exclusive possession of the truth.

Indeed, it is one of the cardinal tenets of the Marxist philosophy that *absolute* truth is a chimerical notion. On this view truth is intrinsically provisional. For my part, I regard this contention about truth as an insight whose importance can scarcely be exaggerated. Apart from other considerations, it seems to me reasonably clear that if, *per contra*, truth were thought of as absolute, then human beings would either have to lay claim to infallibility, which would be absurd – has it not been said that to err is human? – or otherwise abandon themselves to absolute scepticism.

Friedrich Engels expresses this conception of truth with characteristic vigour and lucidity in his essay entitled *Feuerbach and the End of Classical German Philosophy*, and I would like to quote him at some length. In the course of a favourable exposition of a certain aspect of the philosophy of Hegel, he writes: '*Truth, the cognition of which is the business of philosophy*, was in the hands of Hegel no longer an aggregate of finished dogmatic statements, which once discovered had merely to be learnt by heart. Truth lay now in the process of cognition itself, in the long historical development of science which mounts from lower to ever higher levels of knowledge without ever reaching, by discovering so-called absolute truth, a point at which it can proceed no further . . . And what holds good for the realm of philosophical knowledge holds also good for that of every kind of knowledge and also for practical affairs' (p. 328 Karl Marx and Friedrich Engels; *Selected works*, Moscow, 1951, vol. II). In writing this, Engels is, I believe, in conformity with Marx's standpoint as adumbrated, for example, in the second of his (i.e. Marx's) *Theses on Feuerbach*. (See next chapter, p. 98 n. 8, where this thesis is quoted in full.)

To return to Engels – and we frequently have to go to Engels because he was largely responsible for the elaboration though, perhaps, not often for the origination, of the abstract contentions of Marxism – we note that later in the same discourse on Feuerbach he declares that upon the adoption of this philosophical point of view 'the demand for final solutions and eternal truths ceases once for all; one is always conscious of the necessary limitation of all acquired knowledge, of the fact that it is conditioned by the circumstances in which it was acquired' (*ibid.*, p. 351).

Viewing this quotation from Engels together with the one that has gone before, I would like to call attention to five points: (1) The cognition of truth is recognised by Engels as the business of philosophy; (2) What is denied is absolute truth, not truth as such;[1] (3) The belief, so finely expressed, in the progressive character of truth; (4) Engels speaks of this process of cognition as the 'development of science'. I do not think that it is by accident that Engels without further ado apparently equates the cognition of truth to the development of science and also the cultivation of philosophical knowledge. He and Marx held all genuine knowledge

---

[1] In the next sentence, however, Engels proceeds to make an unfortunate remark, foreboding a 'dialectical' paralogic untouched by the fear of contradictions: 'On the other hand, one no longer permits oneself to be imposed upon by the antitheses, insuperable for the still common old metaphysics, between true and false, good and bad, identical and different, necessary and accidental. One knows that these antitheses have only a relative validity; that which is recognised now as true has also its latent false side which will later manifest itself.' It does not seem to have occurred to Engels to ask himself whether this latent false side also has its latent true side having its own latent false side boasting in turn of a latent true side which also has its latent false side which . . . (See, further, chapter 11, pp. 180–1.)

to be scientific; and it was for this reason that they were so emphatic on the scientific character of their own outlook.

It is, I think, of the utmost importance to understand that when it is said that all knowledge, particularly philosophical knowledge, is scientific, it is not thereby being claimed that every case of knowing is the result of controlled experiments involving all manner of apparatus. On such reasoning, much of the taxonomy in science would have, absurdly, to be dismissed as pseudo-scientific. At all events, what is essential to scientific knowledge is the commitment to a method which starts as a matter of necessity from premises *derived from experience* and constructs judgments which are in principle refutable or otherwise confirmable by the joint processes of observation, conceptual analysis and logical deduction. (On scientific method see further chapter 10 pp. 144–5.)

We may say, therefore, that the claim of the Marxists that their philosophy is scientific is, in principle – but mark that I only say *in principle* – altogether unexceptionable. Marx believed, rightly, as it seems to me, in common with certain philosophers before him (and also after him) that many grand systems of philosophy are radically and irredeemably undermined by any critique mounted from the platform of scientific method in the fundamental sense just explained.

The remaining point, (5), is that Engels in the second passage quoted above asserts that a consciousness of limitation is a necessary element in all acquired knowledge; which limitation consists in 'the fact that it is *conditioned by the circumstances in which it was acquired*' (my italics). Engels obviously does not consider that this inescapable dependence upon circumstances vitiates the process or outcome of cognition in any way. On the contrary, indeed, the boot, as far as Engels is concerned, is on the opposite epistemological foot. Absolutist claims to truth are vitiated specifically by the disavowal of that limitation.

It is necessary to point out, moreover, that the determination by circumstances which Engels refers to is to be taken in a strictly epistemological sense (that is to say, in a sense relating only to the logical conditions of knowing). So, for example, if a man should try to engage in serious and profound discourse shortly after a fierce argument with his wife, he is likely to talk nonsense. That is a kind of determination by circumstances; but it is one which

we ought carefully to distinguish from Engels' type of determination. His wife's anger affects only one specific exercise in the
pursuit of truth and wisdom; whereas Engels' factor has to do
with knowing *in general*. For the same reason, the food one eats, the
hairstyle one adopts, the amount of money one has, the power one
wields – all these and such like circumstances are irrelevant from an
epistemological point of view, although any of them might affect
the success or failure of some specific cognitive endeavour.

The kind of circumstances which Engels can sensibly be alluding
to, in view of his reference to the long historical development of
science, etc., must be such things as the nature of the evidence
available to the most determined research, the existing background
of accepted knowledge and the degree of development of experimental and logical techniques. If we class all these and all similar
considerations under the heading, 'epistemological point of view',
or, for short, simply 'point of view' (the appropriate context being
easily determined), then we may epitomise this point about the
nature of truth, which I think is a valid one, in the maxim that truth
logically presupposes a point of view.[2]

But since a rather different kind of mental determination will
later be found to play a role in the Marxist philosophy, I must ask
the reader to note that the determinism which I have expounded
with approval involves only an epistemological determination by
circumstances.

The conception of truth we have been studying is a beautifully
humanistic one, at any rate, in theory. Recognition that truth
necessarily involves a point of view should lead one to reflect that
the 'truths' which one happens to espouse are not ineluctable and
final, and that opposite points of view celebrating opposite 'truths'
are in themselves neither evidence of insincerity nor proof of
stupidity. To be sure, one is not saying that antithetic points of
view are all to be embraced as 'true'. What is implied is that, no one
'truth' being finally self-validating, persuasion is the only rational
method of resolving such opposition. Furthermore, there is a
chance that eschewing self-justifications by reference to such a
huge, transcendent, abstraction as 'The Truth' might prove bene-

---

[2] On the role of the concept of point of view in the definition of truth see chapter
8, p. 115 and chapter 11, pp. 185–7.

ficial to human relations. If a man is able clearly to understand that his political or religious creed is merely a matter of his own personal opinion and not the result of a revelation of any 'Objective', Immutable Truth, he might then hesitate to consign a fellow man to perdition simply for being unable to conform. It is a fact – a sad but well documented fact in the history of religion and politics – that many otherwise noble men have felt themselves called upon to spill the blood of other men for no other reason than that their victims were unwilling to acknowledge what were alleged to be Eternal Verities.

I ought to point out that none of the five points which I have noted in the analysis of Engels' comments on truth are peculiar to the philosophy of Marxism. Taken together, they amount to the same doctrine as the one which the famous American philosopher and logician C. S. Peirce was independently expounding in the early years of this century under the somewhat unusual title of 'Fallibilism'. That doctrine, together with an insistence on the intrinsic connection between knowledge and action which is also found in Marx (see his *Theses on Feuerbach*), was taken up and painstakingly developed by another American philosopher, John Dewey, under the general name 'Pragmatism' (another coinage of Peirce) or more often 'instrumentalism'. So it is bound to be perplexing and alarming to anybody not accustomed to dire Marxist polemics to learn that in the judgment of a noted British Marxist, Maurice Cornforth, in a book entitled, ironically, *In Defence of Philosophy*, the pragmatic theory of truth is 'a philosophy of capitalism . . . a philosophy of imperialism expressing the point of view of a class which has ceased to play any progressive role, for which there is no future and which inevitably therefore must base its practice on illusions and deception – a philosophy profoundly hostile to human progress and well-being'. Were such an enemy of mankind a citizen of a Marxist socialist state he would presumably, on being discovered, be given the opportunities of socialist correction in some dry and barren region where, amidst severities conducive to self-criticism, he might work out his wilfully delayed salvation on more dialectical lines, or perish.

It is well known that Marxist literature abounds in the sort of judgment, or lack of judgment, typified by this passage from Cornforth. It is equally well known that such declarations are not made purely in the promotion of theoretical enlightenment but for the practical, even forcible, regulation of other peoples' lives. History and the contemporary scene are both witnesses to the fact that, when attempts have been made to base social and political organisation on Marxism, results have tended to take the form of authoritarianism – monolithic single party supremacy, harshly enforced conformity to a single doctrine, and so forth.

We are here faced with a major paradox. How is it that a philosophy which advocates such an admirable doctrine as the humanistic conception of truth tends so often to lead in practice to the suppression of freedom of thought and expression? Is it by accident that this comes to be so? Or is it due to causes internal to the philosophy of Marx and Engels?

Faced with this problem, many good and reputable scholars sympathetic to the Marxist standpoint have taken the line of blaming the evils on the shortcomings of the individual politicians involved. The fault, they have said, lies not in the doctrine itself but in its practitioners. An explanation of this sort is likely, at best, to have only a partial validity, and is to be resorted to only in the proven absence of, or in addition to, more internal reasons.

As a relatively more internal explanation, one might point to the fact that adherence to what I have called the humanistic conception of truth is neither universal nor consistent among the Marxists. By the time we reach Lenin a kind of epistemological absolutism has already unmistakably set in. Engels himself, never perfectly consistent, already compromises his conception of truth with some concessions to absolute truth in *Anti-Dühring* (Foreign Languages Publishing House, Moscow, 1962). In chapter IX he writes soon after some highly unsympathetic remarks about absolute truth:

> But in spite of all these are there any truths which are so securely based that any doubt seems to us to be tantamount to insanity? That twice two makes four, that the three angles of a triangle are equal to two right angles, that Paris is in France, that a man who gets no food dies of hunger, and so forth? Are there then nevertheless *eternal* truths, final and ultimate truths? Certainly there are [p. 122].

Engels divides 'the whole realm of knowledge into three great departments', namely, the sciences dealing with inanimate nature

(p. 122), those dealing with the investigation of living organisms (p. 124) and those dealing with the historical group of sciences (p. 124). He grants that there are absolute truths in each of these divisions, but he is distinctly reluctant in this. With regard to the first department, listen to how he puts the matter: 'If it gives anyone any pleasure to use mighty words for simple things, it can be asserted that *certain* results attained by these sciences are eternal truths, final and ultimate truths; for which reason these sciences are known as the *exact* sciences' (p. 123). He is no more ungrudging with respect to the second in which, according to him, the seeker after absolute truths will have to be content with only 'platitudes'. He is positively derisive in connection with the existence of absolute truths in the last of his three great divisions: 'Anyone [therefore] who sets out to hunt down final and ultimate truths, genuine, absolutely immutable truths, will bring home but little, apart from platitudes and commonplaces of the sorriest kind – for example, that, generally speaking, men cannot live except by labour; that up to the present they for the most part have been divided into rulers and ruled; that Napoleon died on May 5, 1821 and so on' (p. 125). It is clear from this that if Engels were immediately asked whether historical materialism, for example, which presumably belongs to this third, historical, department, were an absolute, eternal, immutable, truth he would be bound by logic to say no. There is no doubt that he felt that the above concessions to absolute truth were trivial exceptions to his predominantly anti-absolutist conception of truth.

Actually Engels had no need to make these concessions. But, unfortunately, as is clear from the first passage quoted above from him conceding absolute truths, he confused the idea of a belief held with full certainty with the idea of an absolute truth. This confusion is apparent from his list of absolute truths. It is a collection of categorically heterogeneous propositions united in nothing but the firmness with which they are believed.

The confusion left the way open to a more unstinted absolutism. And, sure enough, Lenin took this way with alacrity. Here is how, referring to chapter IX of *Anti-Dühring*, he reconciles Engels' inconsistency: 'For Engels absolute truth is compounded from relative truths' (*Materialism and Empirio-Criticism*, Foreign Languages Publishing House, Moscow, p. 312). From this he proceeds to assert the following: 'Human thought then by its nature is capable of giving, and does give, absolute truth which is compounded of a sum total of relative truths' (p. 133). This is the fruit of Lenin's pursuit of his own advice that 'we must learn to put, and answer, the question of the relation between absolute and relative truth dialectically' (p. 131). Soon he informs us that 'In a word, every ideology is historically conditional but it is unconditionally true that to every scientific ideology (as distinct, for instance, from religious ideology), there corresponds an objective truth, absolute nature' (p. 134). The ideology of scientific socialism thus, presumably, corresponds to an objective truth, absolute in nature. Gone here are Engels' qualms about absolute truth, his playing down and even apparent disparaging of such truths ('platitudes and commonplaces of the sorriest kind'). One can be sure that when it comes to impressing upon the masses the absolute nature of the objective truth corresponding to scientific socialism all thought of its 'relativity' would be shelved. We may, accordingly, spare ourselves any logical worries about how adding up mere 'relative' truths could ever possibly produce an absolute truth or about what number of 'relative' truths one would need to put together in order to get that 'sum total' which dialectically yields an absolute truth – questions which threaten to push Lenin's epistemology into the most dire straits. One thing is clear: with Lenin, *truth* has recaptured its possibilities for authoritarian use.

This account, however, does not give a fundamental enough explanation of why Marxism has tended to lead to authoritarianism. The Marxist doctrine itself – or shall we say the Marxist assortment of doctrines? – has an authoritarian trait which can, I think, be traced to the conception of philosophy to be found in Marx and Engels.

As we have seen, Engels recognises the cognition of truth to be a legitimate business of philosophy and makes a number of excellent points about truth. As soon, however, as one tries to find out what he and Marx conceived philosophy to be like, one is faced with a deep obscurity. The problem revolves round what one may describe as Marx's conception of philosophy as ideology.

What, then, is an ideology? The term 'ideology' was first used by a group of philosophically inclined authors in France around the closing decade of the eighteenth century. These authors sought to elucidate ideas through anthropological study. Ideology was, for them, a science of ideas, a certain scientific approach to the interpretation of ideas. It so happened that their notion of the scheme of things differed markedly from that of Napoleon Bonaparte – a circumstance which evoked from Bonaparte, a contemptuous reference to them as the 'ideologists'. In Napoleon's intended meaning, an 'ideologist' was a visionary, a doctrinaire proponent of unrealistic conceptions. The jibe proved fateful. From then on and for a long time the term was to take on the pejorative significance with which Bonaparte had invested it. Marx's conception of ideology in the *German ideology*, a work which he wrote jointly with Engels, reflects the influence both of the original meaning of the term and the Napoleonic distortion of it. The two shades of meaning are, however, transmuted under Marx's systematic attention.

'Ideology', for Marx and Engels, meant a set of illusory beliefs constituting a reflex or reflection of material conditions in the minds of those who held them.[3] The relation expressed by the word 'reflex' is also frequently expressed by the word 'determination'. I shall try to substantiate this interpretation with quotations from the text of Marx and Engels. 'As individuals express their lives, so they are', declare the founders of Marxism. 'What they are [therefore] coincides with their production, both with what they produce and with how they produce. The nature of individuals thus depends on the material conditions determining their production' (*The German Ideology*, ed. R. Pascal, New York, 1947, p. 7). The individual, of course, 'expresses' his life, in part, by means of ideas. Hence the deterministic correlation suggested in the quotation must be held to apply to the relation between ideas and material conditions. Note that no exceptions are here allowed.

A little later in the same work, Marx and Engels are more explicit: 'The production of ideas, of conceptions, *of consciousness*' (my italics) or in other words, but still sticking to the words of Marx and Engels, 'conceiving, thinking and the intercourse of men'

---

[3] It is surely to be accounted something of a 'world historical' irony that the followers of Marx now yield ground to none in their insistence on the necessity and importance of ideology. Marx and Engels seldom used the term 'ideology' except in contempt. As late in life as 1893 (he died in 1896) Engels still spoke of ideology as 'false consciousness'.

are 'the direct efflux of their material behaviour'. 'The same,' they declare in the next sentence, 'applies to the mental production as expressed in the language of politics, laws, morality, religion, metaphysics of a people.' Still referring to these things, they remark in the same paragraph, that 'in all ideology, men and their circumstances appear upside down'. 'Ideological reflexes' are 'phantoms formed in the human brain' which 'are also, necessarily, sublimates of their material life-process' (*ibid.*, p. 14). When propounded by the thinkers of the ruling class, ideology is nothing, according to Marx and Engels, but 'the ideal expression of the dominant material relationship grasped as ideas . . . the illusion of the class about itself' (*ibid.*, pp. 39–40).

As for philosophy, it is, apparently, 'empty talk about consciousness' which should cease: 'Where speculation ends – in real life – there real positive science begins: the representation of the practical activity, of the practical process of development of men. Empty talk about consciousness ceases, and real knowledge has to take its place. When reality is depicted, philosophy as an independent branch of activity loses its medium of existence. At best its place can only be taken by a summing up of the most general results, abstractions which arise from the observation of the historical development of men' (*ibid.*, p. 15).

Philosophy, then, is an ideological reflex which is *ipso facto* a system of illusions. Where philosophy ends, there, according to Marx and Engels, real 'positive science' begins. The word 'science', thus pressed into service, proves to be a magic wand. Marx applies it to his own speculations – dialectical materialism and all – to transform them from the status of ideology, presumable under the given hypothesis, to that of empirical truth. The same is, of course, not conceded to 'bourgeois' philosophers, who are condemned to perpetual self-deception. There is obvious special pleading here; but for the moment, let us consider the epistemological consequences of the ideological conception of philosophy. To begin with, take any philosophical proposition, e.g. 'To be is to be perceived'. What does it mean to say that such a proposition reflects a certain set of material conditions? Normally, one should expect that if a proposition reflects a set of conditions, that would be considered good reason for saying that the proposition is true of those conditions. It is, moreover, exactly in this sense of the word 'reflect' that, in *Anti-Dühring*, Engels, and in *Materialism and Empirio-Criticism*, Lenin, insisted in their rather naïve theory of perception that our ideas (i.e. perceptual ideas) are reflections or copies or images of independently existing external things.

Presumably, what is wrong with ideology is not the alleged fact that it reflects material conditions but rather that it reflects them upside down. To revert to the relevant passages of the *German ideology* again, we find that Marx and Engels actually compare ideology to the phenomenon of inversion in a *camera obscura* and also on the retina. On this analogy a proposition belonging to the sphere of ideology must be supposed to invert the truth about the material circumstances of its author and his relationship to them. This implies, of course, that such a proposition must be false. Thus we have to say, on this showing, that a proposition like 'To be is to be perceived'[4] is false because (apart from any other possible reason) it is an inversion of the truth about the material circumstances of its author, Bishop Berkeley, and others of his class. Notice that, since the contradictory of Berkeley's thesis was maintained by people belonging to the Bishop's class, that too must be supposed to invert the truth about the same material conditions and must be declared to be false, contrary to, at least, the laws of classical logic. Notice, too, that the fact that the thesis in question does not seem to be about the material circumstances of its author at all does not apparently stop it from inverting the truth about them. It is not surprising that philosophy does not survive the easy devastation of such a critique.

The same devastation results from the ideological interpretation of philosophy when couched in terms of the notion of the *determination* of ideas by material conditions. The notion, itself, of determination is advanced with remarkable lack of ceremony. 'Life,' declare Marx and Engels, 'is not determined by consciousness but consciousness by life' (*ibid.*, p. 15). Note, incidentally, the curious use of the words 'life' and 'consciousness' in that sentence. The intended meaning of 'consciousness' here is obviously 'thinking, the production of ideas'. Thus, Marx earlier in the cited work uses the term 'consciousness' in straightforward apposition to the term 'conception'. He speaks of 'the production of ideas, of conceptions,

[4] On my own view as to the truth value of this proposition see chapter 8, pp. 113–14 and chapter 9 as a whole.

of consciousness' (*ibid.*, p. 13 passage already quoted). Yet, on the next page it is asserted: 'Consciousness can never be anything else than conscious existence and the existence of men is their actual life process' (*ibid.*, p. 14). If so, then, of course, consciousness is equal to life; and it is, accordingly, meaningless to talk of consciousness being determined by life. I am not simply hair-splitting in these animadversions. I am proceeding in this way out of a suspicion that such carelessness in the use of cardinal terms may be symptomatic of deep inadequacies of thought. Let us charitably suppose that all that the sentence in question means is that 'ideas are determined by the material conditions of life'. This is certainly something which Marx and Engels seem anxious to assert. The point now is that this particular doctrine of determination makes nonsense of the very concept of truth. It constitutes, moreover, a complete reversal of all the well delivered points about the nature of truth which Engels makes in the passages quoted earlier on from his essay on Feuerbach. If all ideas are determined; and to be determined is to be false; then it follows that truth is impossible.

This point is worth emphasising. The bite that the theory of ideology seems to have derives from just this implication: that if and when one has shown that a set of ideas are determined by a definite development of productive forces and of the relations corresponding to them, one has thereby shown them not to have any independent claims to truth. This, surely, is the point of calling the ideas 'phantoms' in the human brain, 'sublimates' of the material life-process. Were it to be suggested that the theory had no such implication, so that the alleged determination of the ideas by material conditions did not affect the question of their truth or falsity, it would be a deep mystery why the authors of *The German Ideology* could have imagined that they had made a case for the cessation of philosophy. Previously, metaphysicians had claimed to reveal the ultimate nature of reality. If the theory of ideology does not necessarily imply that their ideas were false[5] then by what logic does the theory assert an exclusive disjunction between philosophy and the depiction of reality? ('When reality is depicted, philosophy as an independent branch of activity loses its medium of exist-

---

[5] In the abstract there is the possibility that they may be not false, but meaningless. Marx and Engels' theory cannot be said to imply the meaninglessness of the ideas in question since meaningless propositions cannot invert anything.

ence.') Of course, if Marx and Engels are right about philosophy's being determined by material conditions, it would follow tautologically that it is not independent of them. However, if, in spite of this lack of independence, philosophical propositions might conceivably be true, then their demise can only be brought about by the kind of intellectual argumentation that is so strikingly absent from *The German Ideology*.

A defender of Marx might like to remind me that, as I myself have noted earlier, Marx distinguishes between scientific thinking and ideology. Truth, he might argue, is impossible only in the sphere of ideology not science. Marx's own philosophy being scientific, does not suffer from the inescapable disabilities of ideology. *The German Ideology* has already been quoted as saying that the place of philosophy is to be taken by a certain mode of generalising about the historical development of man, while in *Anti-Dühring*, having asserted that modern materialism has rendered all former philosophy superfluous, Engels proceeds: 'What still independently survives of all former philosophy is the science of thought and its laws – formal logic and dialectics' (p. 40).

I would ask such a defender of Marx to explain how Marx, an individual whose consciousness is, by hypothesis, determined by some mode of production could possibly attain to an undetermined truth. Or, are we to say that scientific thinking is not part of 'consciousness'? I concede that to suppose that scientific thinking is not part of consciousness would make it conceivable that the conceptions of Marx are true. However, in the absence of any pre-established rules for determining what does and what does not come under consciousness such a supposition is apt to be arbitrary. But let that pass.

Let us assume, for the purposes of argument, that scientific thinking is not part of consciousness and is not therefore ideological. We assume further, for the same purpose, that the theories of Marx are scientific. Now, to say that a proposition is scientific is not necessarily to say that it is true. It is merely to say that it belongs to a certain general class of propositions, i.e. the class of propositions arrived at through scientific method. In other words, saying that a proposition is scientific means simply that it is such as to be capable of being shown to be true or false, probable or improbable, by the processes of observation or experimentation or conceptual analysis or logical deduction or all of them jointly and that it is backed by some such processes of cognition. It follows that if a proposition is scientific, its negation also is potentially scientific. Furthermore, if a proposition is scientific, its strict contrary must be potentially scientific. By the strict contrary of a proposition I mean another proposition containing exactly the same concepts but in a different order such that this proposition and the original one cannot be true together but can be false together. What a proposition is about is determined by its constituent concepts. If two propositions contain the same concepts then they are about the same subject matter. They must, consequently, be both potentially scientific if one of them is.

Consider now materialism, a basic component of Marxism, and idealism, a doctrine of speculative metaphysics much berated by Marxists. Materialism asserts that matter is primary and mind, derivative. Idealism asserts, contrarily, that mind is primary and matter, derivative. Both, clearly, are *about* the same thing, namely, the relation between mind and matter, and must both be potentially scientific if one of them is. Thus if materialism is scientific, then idealism too is conceivably scientific and cannot be automatically called an ideology in the pejorative sense of Marx and Engels, on the supposition, that is, that what is scientific cannot be ideological.

Marx and Engels are, therefore, on the horns of a dilemma. If all philosophical thinking is ideological, then their own philosophical thinking is ideological and, by their hypothesis, false. If, on the other hand, their philosophical thinking is not ideological then the philosophical thinking of the bourgeoisie is not necessarily ideological.

Marx, as is well-known, had great respect for science. He consequently never declared science, even as developed by the bourgeoisie, to be ideological. Bourgeois thinkers apparently become inescapably ideological only when they venture into law, morality and metaphysics, etc. But to grant even so much is to grant that some aspects of 'consciousness' are independent, i.e. not *determined* in the relevant sense. (It is important to note that the determinism here in question is of a different category from the valid kind of determinism which we found to be involved in the humanistic conception of truth.)

As we have seen, Marx admits by implication that science represents an aspect of 'consciousness' which is ideologically undetermined. But if this much is admitted, then we need specific reasons for declaring other aspects of consciousness to be ideologically determined. Marx does not seem to have been aware even of the necessity of giving such reasons. He and Engels simply assumed for themselves the privilege of exempting their own philosophising from the ideological theory of ideas. Both of them continued to think and write in recognisably philosophical ways in spite of their theory. Such special pleading is neither philosophy nor science.

Although the ideological conception of philosophy is unacceptable, I believe that a certain amount of sense can be made of what Marx and Engels appear to have in mind. The result, however, would be without the polemical potential so welcome to Marxists.

In a sense which I have already explained in connection with our analysis of Engels' remarks on the theory of truth, it is quite correct to say that all knowledge involves determination by circumstances. It seems to me that the apparent plausibility of the conception of the social or economic determination of knowledge is derived, in part, from this fact. It is so easy to forget that any circumstance which can validly be spoken of as determinative of truth or falsity must be of a strictly epistemological character. The fact that the same notion, 'determination', is used must not be allowed to delude us, as it did Marx, into thinking that extraneous factors such as social and economic circumstances can determine truth or falsity. Nevertheless, there is another, quite different, sense in which we might speak of the social and economic determination of some aspects of human thought. Again, my suggestion is that the spurious plausibility of ideological determinism derives, in part, from the fact that there exists such a further valid and superficially similar kind of determinism.

Let us begin by making a set of distinctions. Thought may be about questions of truth or falsity, as in natural science; or about the logical implications of ideas and their relationships, as in formal logic and mathematics (and possibly metaphysics); or about what is good, permissible, beautiful, as in ethics, politics and aesthetics. Ignoring a number of refinements, we may divide the whole field of thought into two. We entitle our two domains 'evaluative' and 'factual' to refer respectively to the sphere of value, on the one hand, and that of truth and falsity on the other. Now, in the philosophy of value, that is, in moral philosophy and aesthetics, there is a doctrine which asserts that statements of value, i.e. about what is good, permissible, beautiful, are irreducible to statements which may be true or false. According to this view, evaluative judgments are *ultimately* concerned with desires, needs, feelings, attitudes. (This basic conception in the theory of value is denominated, in the subtle varieties of its elaboration, by an assortment of philosophical labels such as naturalism, subjectivism, empiricism, emotivism, positivism. We shall not, however, here involve ourselves in the finer points of philosophical terminology.)

A certain basic unanimity in human valuations is, of course, not ruled out by this theory, though it is peculiarly efficient in accounting for the well attested variety of morals. It may be that human beings have in common certain basic needs, desires and feelings. In that case, what men of different times and places think good, permissible, beautiful, might be expected to coincide, at some fundamental level. Still it is clear that even in one country needs, desires, feelings and attitudes tend to vary with differences in social and economic position. Hence, it is quite reasonable to suggest that the evaluative thinking of men tends to diverge, over a considerable area of thought, on class lines. A man's political outlook, for instance, is *determined* in a primary sense, by the *ends* which he seeks to realise. (Of course, the pursuit of ends necessitates attention to matters of fact in regard to means. But from this point of view, factual implications are logically secondary.)

Accordingly, one might, within certain limits, speak of the class (i.e. the social and economic) determination of such a thing as a political outlook. (I say, 'within limits', because one has to observe actual life only briefly to realise that rigid deterministic correlations in this kind of field simply won't do.) A similar, guarded correlation might be supposed in other spheres of evaluative judgment such as morality, aesthetics, and, within somewhat narrower limits, metaphysics.

I am, I may say, sympathetic to the type of philosophy of value which makes correlation possible in these fields. One merit of this kind of analysis is that it enables us to unmask the grandiose disguises involved in the tendency of many men, especially those in authority and privilege, to project their own desires, feelings and attitudes as immutable truths. Again, this kind of theory does not lead to any insoluble problems about truth and knowledge because it does not deal with truth or falsity at all. Further, even in its appropriate domain, it does not declare a judgment to be 'illusory' when it calls attention to its social and economic determination. It simply places the judgment in perspective. Of course, the theory of value referred to can, and often has been, challenged. Any attempt to expound objections and answer them, however, does not belong to the scope of this chapter. Suffice it to say, then, that the theory of value in question is, at least, a possible one.

If Marx had advanced some such theory of value, then much sense could have been made of some modified theory of ideology on the lines I have suggested. In his admirable passion to improve the lot of the poor, however, Marx tended naturally to be contemptuous of moralism. But he confused moral philosophy with moralism and assumed rather than argued a moral standpoint. In a merely practical revolutionary such an omission would have been excusable; but in a system builder like Marx – in spite of all the disclaimers, Marx was nothing if not a system builder – it was an extremely unfortunate omission. It was one which did not presage well for subsequent generations. In particular, it has led to a tendency for ambiguous amoralism in many of his most influential followers such as Lenin and Trotsky which has led to some of the most unattractive features of communist and pro-communist tactics. It is not without ironic significance that from the time of Kautsky and Bernstein down to the present day, Marxist apologists who are, or pretend to be, highly sensitive to the moral problems of political action have felt it necessary to supplement their Marxism with some ethical theory. Interestingly, they have, as a rule, gone back to Kant, irreverently dismissed by the founders of Marxism.

Marx offered precious little in the way of an explicit philosophical discussion of morality. Engels was more forthcoming; but his treatment of morality in *Anti-Dühring* does not go much beyond a perfunctory sociology of morals. Characteristically, he advances the thesis that 'morality has always been class morality' and that each class has its own morality. To the question, which naturally arises, as to which, if any, is the true one, his answer is that the true morality (true 'not in the sense of absolute finality') is 'that morality which contains the maximum elements promising permanence, which in the present, represents the overthrow of the present, represents the future, and that is proletarian morality' (p. 130). Thus ideological determinism somehow leaves 'proletarian moral-ity' unscathed, though to ask with what logical consistency is, presumably, an undialectical diversion. Since human history in the Marxist scheme of things is inevitably destined to culminate in the millennium of a classless society, progress in morality is conceived by Engels in terms of the advance towards a classless morality, which is the truly human morality: 'A really human morality which stands above class antagonisms and above any recollection of them becomes possible [only] at a stage of society which has not only overcome class antagonism but has even forgotten them in practical life' (p. 132).

This is essentially the sum of Engels' moral philosophy. It obviously gives no guidance on the conceptual problems that have perplexed moral philosophers. It is silent on the question of what are the *fundamental* principles of the ethics of revolutionary action. Granted that 'the present' must be overthrown in the interest of the proletariat, the fact still remains that problems of moral choice can, and do, arise with regard to the variety of potentially successful methods of struggle. Some ways of attaining the goals of the proletariat will be more morally acceptable than others. On what principles is a choice of this sort to be made, and for what general reasons? Faced with a question of this nature, it is quite unavailing to cite the interests of the proletariat since that is what generates the problem in the first place. Not in Marx, Engels, Lenin (who generally repeats Engels), or Trotsky (who wrestles violently with this problem in *Their Morals and Our Own*), do we find the required principle of moral discrimination.

There are further important ethical questions that are left untouched by the Marxist treatment of ethics. Marxist thinking about morality seems to be dominated by the external moral rela-tions of the proletariat, viewed *en masse*, with the other social classes. But the question of morality arises in the internal relations of the proletarians themselves. What is the basis of the morality that should govern inter-personal relations among members of the proletarian class? One is left in the dark in this matter. Nor can we glean from the pages of Marx and Engels what the basis of morality might be in the classless society itself. If human beings living in the classless society of the future will ever have occasion to make moral judgments, and if we may suppose them in that setting to retain their intellectual capacities, then philosophical questions will be raised about morality, questions which will concern the logical status and objectivity or otherwise of moral judgment, the definability of the moral predicates, the respective roles of motives, intentions and consequences in the evaluation of conduct, the best way of resolving the conflict of moral principles, and so on. These very questions are even now, in our class-ridden societies, pertinent to the intellectual understanding of morality and the practical guidance of life. Obviously the ideological interpretation of philosophy does not encourage sustained reflection on questions of this sort.[6]

We conclude that Marx fell deeply into error in his conception of ideology and its bearing upon philosophy. What he might judiciously have said is that philosophy – in general, human thinking – has its 'ideological' aspects. Even so, the notion of ideology would have had to be modified in such a way that to say of a given judgment that it belongs to the ideological aspect of philosophy would not be to imply that it is false.

It is, perhaps, appropriate, at this juncture, to give a historical lament. It is impossible not to feel it a matter for regret that Marx himself never found the leisure to expand fully on the purely philosophical aspects of his outlook as was always his intention – such was the vastness of the task of economic research which he set himself. If time had allowed him to devote extended attention to the development of the more abstract aspects of his conceptions, it is conceivable that more mature reflection would have led him to correct the philosophical aberrations of his younger days. (The *German Ideology* was written fairly early in the lives of Marx and Engels, being completed by 1846.) As it is, the careful student of Marxism is bound to be struck by the poverty of Marxist philosophy in spite of the volume of exegesis. History, unkind to the

---

[6] The most interesting attempt to derive a moral theory from the work of Marx known to me is that of William Ash in his book *Marxism and Moral Concepts* (Monthly Review Press, New York, 1964). It is obvious that Mr Ash is struggling desperately hard to remedy the inadequacies of Marxist ethics with a hindsight that has benefited from an acquaintance with twentieth-century moral philosophy. Inevitably he glosses over the more deleterious aspects of the ideological interpretation of philosophy.

self-proclaimed repositories of her dialectical mysteries, saddled
Engels with the role of Marxism's canonical theoretician in philosophy. Unfortunately, when left on his own, philosophical profun-
dity often eluded him, even though he was an extremely fluent
writer and a perceptive analyst of facts and events. Nor was the
doughty Lenin, who in his *Materialism and Empirio-Criticism*
essayed to reassert the philosophy of Marxism in the face of mount-
ing scepticism early in this century, blessed with a head for abstract
reflection in spite of his great intelligence and revolutionary ability.

So the philosophical errors of Marx and Engels have been perpetuated. The run-of-the-mill Marxists, even less enamoured of
philosophical accuracy than their masters, have made the ideological conception of philosophy a battle cry. Without the slightest
scruple, any philosophy propounded by the 'bourgeoisie' (a term
used almost indiscriminately to refer to non-Marxists, or better,
non-Marxist–Leninists) is liable to be declared to reflect bourgeois
class interests. It is then pronounced to be subjective, false, illusory, deceptive, destructive, pernicious, perverted, subversive,
reactionary . . . It is not necessary, mark you, that a doctrine thus
pilloried should be really incompatible with the relevant parts of
Marx's philosophy. This fact is illustrated by Cornforth's violent
reaction, which is typical, to John Dewey's pragmatic theory of
truth. On the other hand, the Marxist philosophy or any doctrine
officially decreed to be Marxist is said to reflect the noble interests
of the proletariat. Automatically, it is asserted to be objective, true,
progressive, uplifting, revolutionary, constructive . . .

So the followers of Marx and Engels are apt to declare philosophy to be intrinsically partisan in a political sense. Listen again to
Maurice Cornforth: 'philosophy has always expressed and could
not but express a class standpoint' (*In Defence of Philosophy*, p. 45).
This, of course, echoes Lenin who was given to saying things like
'materialism carries with it, so to speak, party spirit compelling one
in any evaluation of events to take up directly and openly the view
point of a definite social group'. With Lenin, indeed, non-
partisanship in philosophy is a term of abuse. (See, for example,
Materialism and Empirio-Criticism, pp. 350 ff.)

I contend that, in so far as Marxism as developed by Marx and
Engels easily leads to this class, and politically partisan, conception
of philosophy, it is injurious to philosophy. Party politics is notori-

ously not conducive to rigorous theoretical thinking. The probability is that a philosophy used as an instrument of party politics will become a set of hardened dogmas which people are more or less terrorised or brain-washed into accepting. Nothing is easier than for political ideologists – the notion of ideology is, of course, used now not in the original sense of Marx but in the modern, adapted sense – to reason, or rather fulminate, as follows: If a man does not accept dialectical materialism, does it not plainly show that, being hostile to the ideology of the party, he is an enemy of the people whom the party seeks to uplift? Does he not stand proven a die-hard counter-revolutionary, a spineless reactionary, an incorrigible subversive? How can we afford to leave such a dangerous person free to retard the salvation of the masses? Such is the logic by which the class conception of all philosophy tends to lead to persecution and the suppression of dissent. Inevitably philosophy suffers violation.

I hope I have given independent reasons for questioning the ideological, class conception of philosophy. A proposition is not false simply because belief in it leads to harsh consequences. If, however, good enough arguments can be independently given for supposing it false, then there is a justification for deploring it with a certain measure of moral indignation. I believe the class view of philosophy to be deplorable in this sense.

I wish now, in near-conclusion, very briefly – all too briefly, perhaps – by a direct confrontation with Marxism to show that it harbours further confusions. Speaking somewhat schematically, we may say that Marxism consists of three layers of thought: (1) Dialectical materialism; (2) Historical materialism; (3) Scientific socialism. Apparently in the minds of Marxists, dialectical materialism logically implies historical materialism and both imply scientific socialism. There are two basic fallacies in this kind of thinking, one relating to the step from dialectical to historical materialism, on which more below; the other, in relation to the transition from both to scientific socialism. This latter fallacy consists in the false supposition that a doctrine which claims to state the general nature of existence can *logically* imply a scheme of valuation, which is what scientific socialism is, in parts. As David Hume remarked in a celebrated passage, you cannot automatically *deduce* a statement of what ought to be the case from a statement of what is the case. In their claims of scientific superiority, Marxists are apt to forget that their choice of socialism is, at bottom, an evaluative matter.

Dialectical materialism is the theory that matter is primary (i.e. prior to mind) and that things are perpetually undergoing change according to certain, as it seems to me, mystical laws, for example, the dialectical law of the interpenetration of opposites. Historical materialism asserts that the ultimate determinative factor in human history is the mode of production, i.e. the ensemble of productive forces and the associated relations of production. To argue, as Marxists do, that the primacy of the material factor in history follows logically from the metaphysical primacy of matter is to be guilty of a fallacy based on nothing more complicated than a pun. 'Material' in dialectical materialism refers to matter in a neutral technical sense in which the material is simply that which has mass and position and is in motion. 'Material' in historical materialism refers to material things in an economic sense. (Historical materialism is, in fact, often called the economic interpretation of history.) A piece of matter or a certain disposition of matter is not relevantly material in the economic sense, unless some human being takes an evaluative attitude towards it. Conditions are not economic unless regarded from the point of view of human needs and estimations. In the technical, merely physical, sense of 'material', the term has no necessary reference to human valuation. If 'matter' in this sense is primary, why should we suppose it to follow that matter in the evaluative sense is also primary in the scheme of human valuations? As soon as one poses the question clearly, one realises that the claim is based on nothing other than the fact that the same word 'material' is used in both cases.

Given that matter, i.e. that which is physical, is metaphysically prior to mind, why may not the direction of man's life be controlled more by factors usually called 'spiritual' such as religion or the pursuit of theoretical truth than by factors of economic significance? A man has to eat to live. Accepted. He has to be clothed and find some shelter before he can think about scientific truth. Additionally, he may avidly pursue good food and drink, and women and fast cars, all of which aims are material (or even 'materialistic') in the evaluative sense. But is there anything, in the sheer fact, if so it be, that the world is composed of myriads of systems of electrical charges – is there anything in this which makes it logically necessary that people should be more actuated by material considerations than by 'spiritual' factors in life? The question only has to be put, I believe, to be answered in the negative.

I am not to be understood as saying either that dialectical materialism or historical materialism is false. The question of the truth or falsity of these doctrines is not the issue before us. The issue here is simply, 'does dialectical materialism imply historical materialism?' A negative answer is clearly forced upon us. The first doctrine is patently consistent with the negation of the second. A man may grant that matter comes first and mind only afterwards and yet consistently insist that, since the emergence of mind, mental, intellectual, spiritual, factors have dominated and are destined to dominate human history.

Again, it is false to say that historical materialism logically implies scientific socialism. 'Scientific Socialism' itself is not a clear concept. It is an amalgam of factual and evaluative elements blended together without regard to categorial stratification. It consists of two different strands. The first is an analysis of capitalism seeking to show that capitalism will inevitably, owing to certain internal 'contradictions', break down and give way, through an equally inescapable process of class warfare, to a socialist mode of production, i.e. production and organisation under the condition of social ownership of the means of production and distribution. The second is a judgment to the effect that socialism is the best mode of social and economic organisation. Clearly, one can accept the first and reject the second or vice versa, without contradiction. Suppose it to be scientifically proven, for example, that the world will be destroyed in a nuclear holocaust; why should one, merely on account of its inevitability, embrace the prospect as good? It would simply be evidence of weak thinking to suppose that if something is inevitable then it is good or, in comparison to other supposedly less inevitable things, the best. Further, it is evidently possible to believe that socialist organisation, such as it was pictured by Marx, is the best way of organising society, without being so sure that that mode of organisation will prevail. As for the automatic jump from historical materialism to scientific socialism, why, if material factors are the most determinative in history, must it be true, *simply in virtue of that supposed fact,* that capitalism will break down, or that socialism is good? Is it not logically consistent to say both that the material factor is the most important in human history and that capitalism will go from strength to strength? Further words are needless.

In the more narrowly technical sense, dialectical materialism is *the* philosophy of the Marxists. I have tried to argue that there is no logical connection between that philosophy and the belief in the goodness of socialist society. It is only by a series of crass fallacies that dialectical materialism is said to be a necessary part of the 'ideology' of the working class. I propose the following as the definition of 'ideology' most in conformity with the realities of contemporary political life. 'An ideology is a set of ossified dogmas used as a political weapon in the relentless pursuit of power or, when attained, the determined retention of it at all costs.'[7]

Ideology is the death of philosophy. To the extent to which Marxism, by its own internal incoherences, tends to be transformed into an ideology, to that extent Marxism is a science of the unscientific and a philosophy of the unphilosophic.

EPILOGUE

The foregoing discussion does not, of course, argue that socialism in general is wrong. Nor does it even make any attempt to evaluate many of the strands in the fertile thought of Marx and Engels. It simply calls attention to an aspect of Marx's conception of philosophy and attempts to provide the fundamental explanation of the tendency to authoritarianism hitherto noted in many Marxist regimes.

That explanation seems to me to be more fundamental than any account in terms of the fact that Marx used the phrase 'dictatorship of the proletariat' to characterise the social organisation which he envisaged as the immediate follow-up of the triumphant revolution for which he hoped. It is possible that Marx used the word 'dictatorship' in a Pickwickian sense. The fact that, faced with the task of translating the ideas of Marx into practice, Lenin and his friends found it necessary to insist on a literal interpretation of the phrase 'the dictatorship of the proletariat', may be – and my argument

---

[7] This, of course, is the degenerate sense of 'ideology' noted in the last chapter. (See pp. 52–4.)

implies that it is – suggestive of intrinsic authoritarian potentialities in the Marxist philosophy itself. It is interesting to note that Karl Kautsky, who was not confronted with the actualities of the problem of application, vigorously opposed Lenin's literal interpretation, arguing with the customary profusion of textual quotations that Marx did not really mean dictatorship when he used the phrase. (See Karl Kautsky, *The Dictatorship of the Proletariat*.) The resultant controversy between Kautsky and the Bolsheviks, a controversy which, on the side of the Bolsheviks, produced Marxist classics in acerbic polemics, may be studied in two intriguing texts by Lenin and Trotsky, namely, *The Proletarian Revolution and the Renegade Kautsky* (Lenin) and *Terrorism and Communism* (Trotsky).

It may well be that only some form of socialism can satisfy the quest for social justice. Two points, however, ought to be stressed. (1) Any concept of socialism not impregnated, in its internal constitution, by a good dose of libertarianism, is likely to lead to harsh consequences. From this point of view, there is every reason to expect that careful study of the libertarian styles of socialist thought as represented by Proudhon, Bakunin, Kropotkin and others will prove rewarding for peoples engaged, such as we in Africa are, in the search for social justice through new forms of organisation. But (2) any political or social creed, however libertarian in conception, is bound to negate freedom in practice if it is decreed a compulsory basis of statecraft.

6

In praise of utopianism

A man is called a utopian if his conception of the good society is so unlike society as it is at present as to be clearly impracticable in the contemporary context. It is this impracticable character of utopianism which is the ground of objection, or perhaps we ought rather to say derision, on the part of those who are pleased to call themselves practical men, realists. Yet, how can a social ideal be practicable? Imagine some such ideal to be fully realised in practice at some time and place. Then, we would inescapably be faced with the dilemma of either acknowledging that the ideal was not idealistic enough or pretending that man has become perfect, has ceased, in fact, to be a fallible mortal.

It is not only in the sphere of social organisation that this dilemma can arise. Consider the broad realm of the human quest for knowledge. The ideal for man is obviously that of, to borrow a phrase from Kant, 'systematic completeness of all knowledge' (*Critique of Pure Reason*, A655 B683, Kemp Smith's translation, p. 540, last paragraph). We wish to know everything, to grasp the inter-connection of things, to reduce the infinite variety of things to a systematic unity. Yet, surely, man would cease to be man if such an ideal were to be completely attained. What would human cognition be like? No longer the business of trial and error; no longer the discomfiture of hypotheses falling foul of facts, nor the pleasure of a well-conceived guess verified by the realities.

Faced with this sort of situation, call it a paradox if you like, Kant suggested that the proper use of such ideals – in Kant's own exposition he spoke of the 'ideas of pure reason' – is *regulative* rather than *constitutive*. (See the section on 'The Regulative Employment of the Ideas of Pure Reason', *ibid.*, pp. 532 ff.) The word 'regulative' here speaks for itself but to try to catch the Kantian meaning of the contrasted word 'constitutive' would involve us in too much textual interpretation. Suffice it to say that the *constitutive* idea corresponds to our idea of full realisation. Now, I want to suggest that a social ideal, or in one word, an ideology, can only be, and indeed ought to be, a regulative principle rather than a constitutive one. It directs our efforts towards a goal which in its fullness is actually an ideal limit, something we may approach indefinitely but never reach. In this sense any ideology is impracticable, utopian. Of course, some are more utopian than others, depending on the degree of sharpness of moral sensitivity to the inequalities of current society.

I will come back to the question of moral sensibilities. But before that let me point out the utopian character of the two competing ideologies of the modern world, namely, capitalism and Marxist socialism. Just because there are states which claim to practise one or the other of these two ideologies, people are apt to suppose that these social ideals have actually been realised and are *a fortiori* practicable. But look more carefully. You will find that in the so-called capitalist states the realities fall far short of the ideals. Capitalism in at least one form envisages a society in which employers and employees work in harmony, each for his appropriate rewards. It is a society in which there are economic classes but no class war: The haves and the have-nots and the intermediate classes all realise that they get what they get or do not get what they do not get through their own talents and exertions or lack of these, or through the circumstances of their birth. They are supposed to accept voluntarily that nobody is to be blamed for disparities in wealth and social standing. The Government is there to guarantee to all the minimum conditions for their full self-realisation and to protect the private property and personal safety of its citizens. It is to see to it that everybody gets a chance to do what he can for himself, his family, his friends and society at large. If through some unlucky circumstance a man should find himself incapable of acquiring the basic necessities of life, the government should come to his aid. The government itself is one that is freely chosen by the people in fair elections to translate into reality the wishes and aspirations of the people. It is needless to comment that the actual practice of capitalism nowhere approaches this description; and it is a bold man indeed who envisages the realisation to the full of this conception on this earth.

Marxist socialism as an ideology is even more radically utopian. Marx conceived of the good society as one in which there are no economic (and therefore social) classes and in which, consequently, there is no class antagonism. In the socialist, or, more strictly, communist, society dreamt of by Marx there is no political power, no government because government is necessary only when there is class antagonism. Things are administered, but not men. The wealth of society is engendered by co-operative effort and is distributed on the principle of 'From each according to his ability, to each according to his needs.' In this society, money does not exist. In the words of Marx, 'The producers may eventually receive paper cheques ... These cheques are not money. They do not circulate.' Moreover, there is no division of labour, which Marx regarded as a form of slavery. In the good society, 'nobody has one exclusive sphere of activity but each can become accomplished in any branch he wishes, society regulates the general production and thus makes it possible for me to do one thing today and another tomorrow, to hunt in the morning, fish in the afternoon, rear cattle in the evening, criticize after dinner, just as I have a mind, without ever becoming a hunter, fisherman, shepherd or critic.' (Marx and Engels, *The German Ideology*, International Publishers, New York p. 22.) Where in the world, I ask, is there any form of social organisation remotely resembling this ideal picture?

The disrepute which has overtaken utopianism is due in large part no doubt to the essential conservatism of the great mass of mankind. But it is also, to quite a considerable extent, due to the curious ambivalence of Marx and Engels. Since, as is clearly seen above, these two giants were themselves purveyors of a utopia, it is ironical that they should have formed the habit of distinguishing their own ideology, which they called 'scientific socialism', from other brands of socialism, which they called 'utopian' in contempt. Only a little reflection is needed, I believe, to see that the name 'Scientific Socialism' is a singularly inappropriate name for the ideology of Marx and his friend. There is nothing scientific about the ideal of a classless, non-political society. But also, of course, there is nothing unscientific about it. The scientific/unscientific contrast just does not arise in this connection. A social ideal is a moral projection; it is an embodiment of one's moral yearnings in the domain of social life.

What might conceivably be called scientific in the work of Marx and Engels are their analyses of capitalism both as a type of economy and as a historical phenomenon, analyses that aimed at showing that the collapse of capitalism is inevitable. Other parts of Marxism are utterly speculative. I refer to the species of metaphysical speculation known as 'dialectical materialism' and the only slightly less speculative philosophy of history known as the economic interpretation of history. All these strands in Marxism are logically distinct and might each be true or false depending on their own merits, independently of the others. What is more, they are, together or separately, independent of the merits or demerits of the notion of a classless, non-political, society.[1]

Now, on what criterion may we determine the merits or demerits of a social ideal? I believe that this is by and large a moral problem. The important question about an ideology is 'Is it a worthy ideal?' Compare the two ideals described earlier on, namely, capitalism and Marxist socialism. What is wrong with a society in which some individuals are employers and others employees, in which some are rich and some are not-so-rich, if the rich are rich through their hard work or ingenuity or good luck and the not-so-rich are so through their lack of some or all of these, provided that nobody is allowed to sink into abject poverty? Some men will have no difficulty in answering: 'precisely nothing', particularly, though not invariably, if they themselves have considerable assets. I know of no way of *proving* such an attitude wrong. Such an ideal falls harshly on my own moral sensibilities but I see no justification for pretending that this judgment is a deliverance of an 'objective' verity.

This matter of disparate moral sensibilities in respect of ideology is a difficult phenomenon to account for. People living in the same place with the same basic needs, the same training, even the same sort of social circumstances may come to develop different sensibilities about economic and other inequalities in society. And there seems to be no way of settling this kind of fundamental difference in attitude except perhaps through the kind of emotional impact that, perhaps, only poets, novelists and prophets are capable of. I am anxious however to emphasise that this does not

---

[1] See pp. 83–6.

imply that the choice of an ideology is an irrational one. The truth of the matter is, I think, that the rational/irrational antithesis does not arise; this is, in fact, a corollary of my earlier point that the scientific/unscientific contrast does not arise with respect to a social ideal.

There is a certain asymmetrical way of comparing the ideologies of capitalism and socialism which is apt to make the choice between them look rather less like a fundamental moral choice than it really is. Believers in capitalism tend to compare the actualities of existing socialist societies with the capitalist blueprint of an ideal society, while socialists, on their part, have rarely resisted the temptation to compare the actualities of existing capitalist societies with the socialist ideal. True, there is nothing wrong with comparing actualities with ideals; that, in fact, is in the best traditions of rational reflection. But, if it is a matter of comparing two *ideologies*, then one should compare the one ideal with the other ideal rather than the one ideal with the imperfect incarnation of the other. When the comparison of ideals is placed in this light it becomes easy to see that a preference for one over the other is a moral preference rather than anything else.[2]

Saying that such a preference is a moral matter does not, of course, exempt the proponent of an ideology from the necessity of backing his conceptions with practical thought. Regarding any ideology, two things, at least, are required. First there must be a rational assurance that significant progress in its direction is possible; and second, proposals must be forthcoming as to concrete steps that might be taken towards the transformation of the *status quo*. A utopian is not one on whom this point is lost. He differs from other advocates of social regeneration only in the degree to which he emphasises the necessity for the fullest consciousness and articulation of one's social ideals.

I wish to point out that the view that the choice of a social ideal, being a moral choice, is neither scientific nor unscientific, rational nor irrational, does not imply any minimising of the role of rational thinking in morals. Though choices that reach down to moral

---

[2] It is not suggested here that as a matter of psychological fact the way in which people come to adopt an ideology is always by comparisons of this sort. But such comparisons are often made at various stages of ideological reflection, and it is important to clarify their nature.

fundamentals are not matters for argument, this still leaves open a vast room for rational argument in the sphere of morals. The stuff of moral reasoning is made up of issues in which factual questions are intertwined with normative ones. A rational outlook in morals is manifested in the willingness and ability to disentangle norms from facts, to assess secondary norms in the light of more basic ones and generally to situate moral judgment about particular actions, practices, persons and institutions in the context of a consistent and coherent system of fundamental moral principles.[3] If human beings differed in an absolute, all-pervading and systematic way on fundamental moral principles, there would be no such thing as rational moral discussion among men. It is an empirical fact that such a scale and quality of disagreement does not exist and – one might say – cannot exist where there is a human *community*. Nevertheless, it does not follow that disagreements in fundamental moral preferences cannot exist over a limited number of issues. I maintain that, when carefully enough considered, ideological disagreements can sometimes be seen to boil down to disagreements of this nature. In view, however, of the vital importance in human society of rational discussion, care is needed not to locate such disagreements too prematurely in discourse across ideologies.

The current free use of the word 'ideology' helps to obscure the foregoing point.[4] Almost any suggestion about society is called an ideology. Then, it is either advocated or rejected with an emotional fervour that makes rational argument impossible. This tendency is very much in evidence in Africa today. But although the basic choice of an ideology is a moral one, there are any number of issues concerning means and even intermediate ends which are not ideological and which permit of a rational and, if you like, scientific treatment. For example, what sort of model of industrialisation should we adopt in Africa, the large scale urban-oriented type of industrialisation or the small scale rural-orientated sort? What kind of educational system is best suited to our present circumstances in Africa? What changes must be effected in our traditional ways of life in Africa in view of modern developments, and how? I wish to

---

[3] See also chapter 4, pp. 55–8, on human preferences and the subjectivity/objectivity distinction.

[4] See also chapter 4, pp. 52–4.

insist that even when a question relates to the best means of pursuing a particular ideology, such a question is not necessarily ideological. It will often be factual. In such a case moral passion is out of place. Indeed a man who does not share the given ideology might well be able to give a useful answer to a question of this sort, provided he is well informed about the question in hand and is willing to put his mind to it.

I find that Marxists are especially prone to confuse factual with ideological issues.[5] In point of fact the great majority of those who call themselves Marxists do not share the ideology of Marx. As anybody can see from the description I gave earlier on of Marx's conception of the good society, his ideology is not Marxism. And I say this not because of Marx's own quip that he was not a Marxist, which was obviously a facetious reaction to the failings of his interpreters in his own day; but, firstly, because the body of doctrine designated as 'Marxism' usually does not include the really ideological part of his thought, and, secondly, because Marx's ideal of *society without government* makes his ideology in essence the same as anarchism, which was not his brain child. Anarchism is much older than Marxism and has stronger and more splendid historical exponents.

I do not wish to enter here into a verbal discussion of the word 'ideology' though such verbal analysis can be important. Nothing in what I have been saying will be fundamentally affected if we substitute phrases such as 'social ideal', 'conception of the good society' for every occurrence of the word 'ideology' in this discussion. What seems to me important is to realise that what is usually called Marxism ignores or glosses over Marx's conception of what the good society should look like. Indeed, one cannot avoid the impression that many Marxists regard this part of the thought of

[5] The distinction between the factual and the ideological is, of course, correlative to the distinction between fact and value. Rational thinking in the evaluative sphere must cease if we cannot distinguish, at some levels of discourse, between the factual and the evaluative; for then, there would be nothing to evaluate in the first place. Any reservation about this distinction has merit only if it is an acknowledgement of the fact that issues, among them some having great social importance, which wear a factual look can sometimes be resolved into evaluative matters. Herein lies the chief strength of the theory of ideology propounded by Marx and Engels. (See particularly their *German Ideology*.) It should be noted, though, that 'ideology' in the usage of these two thinkers is not exactly synonymous with 'ideology' in contemporary usage. (See further chapter 5, pp. 70 ff.)

Marx as an embarrassment. Yet if one takes egalitarianism (which, of course, is an important component of the ideology of Marx) seriously, it is difficult to see how one can stop short of some form of anarchism. If economic inequality is felt to be morally unsatisfactory, why should political inequality (i.e. inequalities of power) be otherwise?

I have never ceased to be puzzled, amazed, and disheartened by the total insensitivity to the problem of political inequality on the part of many people who claim to be Marxists. On our own continent examples are not scarce of socialist politicians who have sought and obtained power on the platform of the wellbeing of the 'poor and oppressed' and have thereupon proceeded to set up dictatorships not *of* the proletariat – for that is a figurative contradiction, in any case – but *over* the proletariat. Since in Africa political power often means easy wealth, their egalitarian slogans are revealed to be doubly hollow. I do not think that this can be attributed exclusively to the personal degeneracy of those involved; the trouble must, at least in part, be traced to the limitations of their social and political outlook. I maintain that the most fundamental shortcoming in this connection is their lack of a serious utopianism.

If the talk of egalitarianism is not just a game of words, then any opportunity to change the structure of society must be used in a number of obvious directions. To be sure, there are difficult problems in the precise definition of egalitarianism; but if we take such specific factors of life as food, shelter, clothing, health, work, education, personal self-determination (i.e. freedom from coercion), recreation, and the like, it is possible to get in relation to these a reasonable, though admittedly rough, idea of egalitarianism and of the current impediments to it. The question is: What kind of social arrangement is most likely to ensure an equal distribution of these factors to all? Needless to say, it is impossible to be literal in the interpretation of 'equal', and here the famous utopian phrase of Marx in the *Critique of the Gotha Programme* comes in handy: 'from each according to his ability, to each according to his needs';[6] that is

---

[6] Of course, in respect of personal self-determination the *needs* of all normal adults are the same. Moreover, in all cases a man's needs are to be determined by him or with his explicit consent.

the ideal intension and intention of 'equal distribution'. If we now look at actual societies in the world, including our own, we are at once struck by the enormity of the obstacles facing this ideal. Let us disregard many and mention only three of the most fundamental.

There is, first of all, the structure of the wage system which in our societies, particularly, seems to be based on the principle of 'to him that hath, more shall be given'. To a few, the so-called mental workers, most is given; and to the many, the manual and semi-manual workers, only a little. The question of the moral justification of such an inequality seems never to be counted among important problems. Then there is the political system which, whether driven by one party or more, is nothing but a machine for tossing the individual about. But most fundamental of all, there is the conceptual trinity of Truth, Beauty and Goodness. These concepts are, of course, essential constituents of any outlook upon the world, man and society; but invested, as all too often they are, with authoritarian connotations, they provide the intellectual springs of aggression. I have commented elsewhere (pp. 54–5, 66–7, and 122–3) on the authoritarian uses of these concepts. Here I wish to point out that this phenomenom pervades all sides of the current ideological divisions of the world. There are dangers in this, for when you have ideologically divided power blocks in possession of mutually incompatible Truths (each conceived with an Olympian 'objectivity' that transcends mere human opinion) about what is Good for man and society, prospects of peace are bound to be precarious. Peace, by the way, is not identical with the absence of a nuclear conflagration. To leave the international plane and come to the intra-national plane, it appears that on the African continent there are everywhere groups privileged with direct access to *the* Truth, social and political; and woe betide those, who, not having eyes to see, do not at the very least stay silent.

It is a good measure of the reactionary character of the familiar socialist of Africa that he has spared hardly any thought for the radical restructuring of the wage system. His automatic procedure when in power is to extend public ownership of the means of production and distribution. In principle there may be no objection to this but the procedure takes the form, among other things, of the establishment of government corporations of production and distribution on the basis of the orthodox wage system. So-called socialists, vociferous in championing the cause of the poor, soon become part-time directors or full-time managers of government corporations with salaries and privileges to which any son of the bourgeoisie might aspire. Meanwhile, on the political side, a highly democratic one party system is established that will brook no subversive criticism. Incidentally, the opposite of subversive criticism is something described as 'constructive criticism', which, contrary to what a naïve student of political terminology might imagine, consists of an amply worded recognition of the noble and infallible achievements of the revolutionary leaders of the party. Naturally, in all this, the ideal of egalitarianism has to fend for itself.

On the philosophical front there is scarcely more ground for optimism. So long as the humanly indispensable concepts of truth, beauty and goodness retain the meanings artificially grafted onto them by common-sense as well as more recondite philosophy, authoritarian thought can mask itself in noble phraseology. So naturally the corrective office here belongs to the philosopher rather than anybody else. Moreover, recognition that the issue is germane in this context shows that answers to such abstract questions as 'What is Truth?' (in epistemology), 'What is Goodness?' (in moral philosophy) and 'What is Beauty?' (in aesthetics) are desirable, not just to gratify the curiosity of professional philosophers, but, more importantly, to make life more humane. The issue is whether or not truth, beauty and goodness are to be defined in terms of the basic needs and capabilities of human beings. It is not thought wildly paradoxical to propose an affirmative answer with respect to beauty and goodness, though such an answer is often dismissed as wrong-headed, on the grounds that these concepts refer to objective qualities whose existence and nature are independent of the conditions of human life. But to suggest that the meaning of truth itself depends upon some aspects of the basic needs and efforts of the human individual[7] is very generally regarded as straining the limits of philosophical sanity. Accordingly, one who believes, as I do, that the approximation to the Good Society on this earth is unlikely to come in advance of the

[7] On the theory of truth see chapters 8, 9, 10 (section III), 11 and 12.

general realisation of the human essence of such a concept as truth[8] (and, of course, also beauty and goodness) has no excuse to be over-optimistic.

A utopian is not necessarily an optimist; or let me put it this way: the optimism inherent in utopianism must be an extremely long-term optimism. Consciousness of the multifarious causes which currently operate to keep the prospect of true social regeneration locked in the dim recesses of the future must imbue the utopian with a sense of the tragic character of human life.

---

[8] Among philosophers Marx and Engels stand out as men who were thoroughly seized of the social importance of a humanistic conception of truth. In spite of its almost Delphic obscurity, Marx's second thesis in his 'Theses on Feuerbach' deserves to be quoted as a historic formulation of this conception: 'The question whether objective truth can be attributed to human thinking is not a question of theory but is a *practical* question. In practice man must prove the truth, that is the reality and power, the this-sideness of his thinking. The dispute over the reality or non-reality of thinking which is isolated from practice is a purely *scholastic* question.' Engels in his classic essay 'Feuerbach and the End of Classical German Philosophy' (see for example *Karl Marx and Frederick Engels Selected Works*, vol. II, Moscow, 1951) is very much less laconic on the problem of truth. This is not to say, though, that Engels was always consistent. See chapter 5, especially pp. 63–70.

7

Philosophy, mysticism and rationality

When Pontius Pilate put the question 'What is Truth' to Christ, he did not, according to the biblical report, stay for an answer. Evidently, he must have felt that it was none of his business to probe such speculative abstractions. Professionally, he may have been in the right. But he apparently conducted himself in a manner that betrayed a supercilious scepticism. I have neither the professional excuse nor philosophical rashness to trifle with so fundamental a question. Nevertheless, though by and large I am concerned with the problem of truth in this chapter, I will not proceed to discuss possible answers to the direct question 'What is Truth?'[1] Instead, I will address myself to a narrower problem. What that problem is will emerge presently. In the meantime I hope that my failure to come directly to grips with the more celebrated question will be seen to be strategic rather than Pilatian.

In a brochure issued by the Theosophical Society, I find an exposition entitled 'A Statement of Theosophical Principles' in which the author, W. Bendit, writes: 'Theosophy being wisdom is not knowledge – though based on knowledge – and can neither be taught nor learnt; it has to develop from within as intuition grows. Nevertheless, certain principles can be enunciated not as dogmas but points deriving from the universal experience of enlightened seers and mystics of all times and races.' These principles are that life is one and universal, manifesting itself as spirit and matter, that there are such beings as angels, that death is not the end but the beginning of a new cycle, and so on.

The reference to the universal experience of the enlightened seers is, of course, a reference to what is commonly known as

---

[1] The next four chapters are, however, practically all of them, devoted to exactly this question.

mysticism. What excites my interest here is the fact that mysticism is appealed to as a way of attaining truth – important truth about the world and life. What I wish to do here is to investigate the standing of mysticism as a possible source of truth of any kind whatever about reality. In doing this my only technique will be the technique of philosophical reflection.

What then, it might be asked, is philosophy? Short statements of the nature of complex things are apt to be mystifying, and I experience a certain sense of dilemma in attempting to say in a sentence what philosophy is.[2] But we must start somewhere, and provided the limitations of such starting points are borne in mind, no harm need be done. Philosophy, then, as I conceive it, is the free investigation of the first principles of human life – the most fundamental principles, that is, which underlie human life. What sort of principles are these? Examples are, fortunately, quite easy to give. Human beings are essentially active. They act not blindly but in order to achieve certain ends which they hold valuable. What, then, is the general nature of value?

Action, moreover, involves a certain conception of the adaptation of ends to means; it involves, that is, some claim to knowledge. But what are the basic standards of knowledge, i.e. the general criteria of the correctness of our claims to knowledge? Again, it is a manifest fact that human beings have a deep speculative tendency in their nature which drives them to ask cosmic questions like 'What is the origin of this world?' 'Who, if anybody, made it?' and 'Where do we ourselves go from here?' These are questions which are fundamental in the sense that we cannot derive them from other questions.

By what method then does philosophy investigate these problems? Again, subject to the reservations we have expressed earlier regarding such brief accounts, we may say that philosophy proceeds by analysis, generalisation and synthesis. This is hardly illuminating, and I can only hope that what I do with regard to the problem which I have set myself may, by way of illustration, improve matters somewhat. There is perhaps one point, however, that we can make fairly straightforwardly in this connection. It concerns the sorts of things that are involved in philosophical analysis or synthesis. It is important to realise from the outset that

[2] The question of what philosophy is is treated at length in chapter 9.

the elements that the philosopher deals with are *concepts*, and one (but, please note, only one) of his most pressing tasks is to elucidate them. Now, this is not at all the same as explaining the meaning of a word after the manner of a lexicographer or a language teacher. To elucidate a concept by analysis is to show the problematic concept to be equivalent to a certain organisation of a number of less problematic concepts. To explain verbal meaning is simply to introduce somebody to a new symbol related to a concept antecedently grasped.

Indeed the concept of *meaning* itself is one of the most basic for philosophical analysis, and since questions of Truth and Meaning are intimately connected, I should like to spend a little time on the concept of meaning.

That truth presupposes meaningfulness is perhaps too obvious a point to labour here. An expression must make sense, impart some meaning, in order to raise the question of truth or falsity. What is senseless cannot intelligibly, and hence intelligently, be spoken of as either true or false. But what do we mean by saying either that a given expression makes sense or does not make sense? By an expression we usually mean a word, and though not only words can make sense, it is, I think, needless here to introduce other complications. Now, words considered externally are artificial signs which in themselves are simply brute existences. The word 'coal' is either a sound, if uttered, or a series of marks, if written. In themselves, words are sheer physical existences exactly like chairs and tables and trees. They acquire the character of being able to impart a meaning only by being made in virtue of a process which is in principle conventional to stand for something beyond themselves. What do they stand for? The simple answer, which however perhaps merely names a whole cluster of problems, is that they stand for concepts or ideas.[3] Thus take the word 'chair': it is a meaningful word because it is part of a certain system of conven-

---

[3] To some contemporary philosophers any postulation of *concepts*, or *ideas*, is objectionable on the grounds that it introduces a class of entities which are ontologically rather mysterious. I share this distaste for abstract entities myself. (See my series of articles on 'Logic and Ontology' in *Second Order, An African Journal of Philosophy*, vol. II, nos. 1 and 2, January and July 1973, vol III, no. 2, July 1974 and vol. IV, no. 1, January 1975.) But I dispute that concepts, ideas, need be conceived as any kind of entities at all. I take the position that ideas are mental states, but with the proviso that mental states are *aspects* (not equivalents, as in the 'identity' theory of mind), of brain states. This is, however, not the place to argue the matter.

tionalised symbols in the context of which it signifies the sort of thing that people are apt to sit upon. There is no magical connection between the word and the sort of thing that it refers to. As a matter of fact, in my own language the word for the same sort of thing is *akonwua* not 'chair' and, of course, different words stand for the same sort of thing in other languages.

I have said that signs become meaningful by being conventionally made to stand for various sorts of things. I use the phrase 'sorts of things' advisedly. Signs cannot stand for things except through their significations. A sort of thing is not a thing but the idea of a thing. If we wish, we may reserve the phrase 'stands for' for the relation that a word has to that to which it refers in virtue of its signification. In that case, we might say that words *signify* ideas but *stand for* (or *refer to*) entities, situations, relations, etc., when these are available.

I have observed some linguists greet the notion that in every coherent discourse words signify ideas with amused impatience. They point out that a piece of communication such as 'Good day!' is, standardly, not intended to convey any idea but only to put acquaintances at ease or something like that. Fortunately, the matter can be resolved quite easily. When a linguist remarks that 'Good day!' does not express an idea, he means presumably that it is not (standardly) used to convey factual information. He can hardly wish to be understood to be saying that the form of speech in question has no significance; for, of course, what he himself says amounts to maintaining that it imparts a social significance. For us a *significance* is necessarily an idea. If for a linguist a significance is not an idea unless it satisfies some further conditions, a philosopher can take note of the disparity in *usage* with equanimity.

It is, of course, not being suggested that every word or set of words expresses an idea. On the contrary, philosophers not infrequently find that they are compelled to deny in quite a drastic fashion that certain formations of words signify any ideas. Given any word or group of words it is always a legitimate question whether it signifies anything. Often the fact that an expression is made up of familiar words is not in itself enough to ensure that it signifies any kind of thing. An example is the expression 'round square'. 'Round' is meaningful, 'square' is also meaningful, but 'round square' cannot define any *possible sort* of object. Why?

Because the phrase is self-contradictory, and a self-contradictory expression defines no possible object or situation or state of affairs. I think, further, that it is quite reasonable to say that an expression which refers to no possible state of affairs is a meaningless expression in the sense that it can communicate nothing. As remarked earlier on, words acquire meaning only by being associated with something beyond themselves. Therefore, if a word or a series of words signifies no possible thing or state of affairs, then it cannot be said to have meaning; and if it has no meaning, then it cannot be used to say anything true or even false. I may remark in parentheses that what I am saying is not that an expression is meaningless if it refers to no object; that would be false, for the word 'unicorn' has a meaning although there are no unicorns. What I am saying is that an expression is meaningless if it refers to no *possible* object or situation, etc.; and unicorns, of course, are possible objects.

As with 'round squares', so with contradictory expressions made up of sentences. Take, for example, the expression 'Mensah is tall and also not tall.' Discounting all verbal pranks, what this comes to is the conjoint assertion of two statements one of which is the negation of the other. Independently, of course, each statement makes clear sense, but do they make sense when put together? I suggest that they do not make communicative sense when put together because in combination they do not define any possible state of affairs. Note that it is not that we know what it would be like for a man to be both short and not short at the same time but fail to find the possibility actually realised. Rather, the expression as a *unity* registers nothing; it violates the conventions of communicative assertion. The expressions 'is' and 'is not', like all meaningful expressions, have meaning only through convention; they function, respectively, to construct and destroy, to speak somewhat picturesquely. Thus if you say 'A is B' and say again that 'A is not B', the second assertion cancels, destroys, the first. This is, of course, a familiar thing in the world: a man says something; he changes his mind; he then says 'A is not B' thus cancelling the former claim that 'A is B'. But suppose he says 'A is B and also A is not B'; then I suggest that the correct thing to say is not that he has communicated anything false, but rather, that the expression does not abide by the rules for constructing a thought-conveying assertion. Thus to say 'A is both B and not B' is *somewhat* on a par with an expression like 'Theosophy maximises the carburation of quadratics'. All the words involved are familiar; they form the shape of a sentence syntactically, but the expression is, nevertheless, meaningless because it does not abide by the semantical rules governing expressions like quadratics, carburation, etc. It is often not at all a simple matter to discover and expound the rules governing the use of concepts – indeed it is frequently a matter of philosophical rather than lexical analysis. Here, however, we have cited two cases where rules of construction are clearly violated. We say, then, that an expression which violates conventional rules of construction is meaningless.

I should emphasise that I do not mean to suggest that meaning is conventional. On the contrary, a meaning itself, the concept or idea which a word signifies, cannot in any way be conventional. What is conventional are the circumstances in which some given word imparts a certain particular idea; and what I am saying is that if an expression does not abide by relevant conventions, then there is no question of its imparting any idea at all. Now, I very much regret that we cannot here enter into the problem of the nature of ideas, because if we could, we would be able to confront the whole issue of mysticism, the topic we are approaching, at an altogether deeper level. However, these few remarks about meaning are probably sufficient to enable us to make one or two points about mystical experience and its claim to truth at a not-too-superficial level.

Mysticism, whatever one may think of its epistemology, has been a great force in the history of man. It seems probable that most religions have at their profoundest depths been based on mysticism in some shape or form. Certainly, Buddhism, Hinduism, Islam, Judaism and Christianity show varying degrees of dependence upon mysticism which should be sufficient to underline its importance. Although, incidentally, our own indigenous religions seem to dispense with mysticism altogether. This is a point very much worth investigating. It is one which, if established, may carry a wealth of significance. Our indigenous religions or, at least, some Akan religions known to me, seem to be quite empirically oriented. *Onyankopon* is indeed the All Mighty Creator, but he is apparently localised. Moreover, his less omnipotent agencies on earth, the fetishes, assume very physical guises. True, rather unusual feats are sometimes credited to these agencies, but these are specific claims regarding mundane causes and effects which are perceptually verifiable or falsifiable. It can, I think, safely be taken as one of the defining characteristics of mystical claims that they transcend sensible experience and are therefore not empirically verifiable or falsifiable. On this claim concerning our indigenous religions, I would be glad to be corrected or corroborated by researchers in this field. At all events, students of our religions may find it at least methodologically worthwhile to beware of automatically investing indigenous religious concepts with transcendental connotations received from alien religions.

There are broadly speaking (that is, ignoring possible borderline cases) two kinds of mystical experience which we may call, after the manner of some authors, introvertive and extrovertive.[4] Extrovertive mysticism involves the use of the (external) senses. The mystic attains to a condition of consciousness in which, according to well-known mystical reports, he sees all separate things as one. The mystic, Meister Eckhart, for example, says of this sort of experience: 'All that a man has here externally in multiplicity is intrinsically one. Here all blades of grass, wood, and stone, all things are one. This is the deepest depth.' The extrovertive mystic insists that though the blades of grass do not become wood or vice versa, and everything remains distinct qualitatively and numerically, nevertheless all things become one. This unity is also said to be conscious, and, in theistic mysticism, is declared to be God. Extrovertive mysticism, incidentally, comes to the mystic unsolicited. At times it comes in the most unexpected ways, e.g. the mystic Boehm is said to have had an extrovertive mystical experience just by gazing at the brilliant surface of polished glass. There is, at all events, no question of training a man to have an extrovertive mystical experience.

In this respect the introvertive kind of mystical experience is different. It can be attained, according to those who know, by strenuous preparation, such as the fantastic posture and breathing exercises that the Yogis practise. Sometimes, indeed, according to the mystics, an introvertive experience may come unsolicited. Still, the experience seems to result usually from careful prepara-

[4] See, for example, W. T. Stace, *Mysticism and Philosophy* (Macmillan, 1961), chapter 2, especially pp. 60–123.

tion. Introvertive mysticism makes no use of the external senses; the master arrives, through sustained concentration, at a state where all ideas both sensible and intellectual are emptied from the mind – indeed to empty the mind of all content is the aim of the wonderful exercises which the neophyte must assiduously cultivate. When the mind is thus void of all content, it becomes a unitary consciousness, a pure ego. It then feels its *identity*, or, according to some mystics, *union* with a universal self which is divine.

Ruysbroeck, a medieval Christian mystic, says that he is 'lifted above reason into a bare and imageless vision, wherein lives eternal indrawing summons of the Divine Unity'. He goes on to say that there follows 'union without distinction'. The experience is almost always said to be full of beatitude.

I will not multiply quotations from mystics. I shall raise straightaway a difficulty which, I think, calls for philosophical treatment. It is this: the language used by the mystics, whether extrovertive or introvertive, often seems paradoxical or self-contradictory. The unity which they are supposed to experience is without distinctions; yet at the same time, it is the source of all distinctions; the self is identical with the Divine Unity, yet separate; the experienced Reality is personal yet impersonal; it is static and yet dynamic. And so on. I hope the reader recognises these claims as thinly veiled examples of the self-contradictory forms of discourse that we looked at when discussing meaning.

Now, in conformity with the principle of meaning which we there set forth, I hope it can be seen that we have to make a choice here. Either what the mystic says is really self-contradictory, in which case, whatever the character of the experience which he undoubtedly must have had, his expressions are meaningless, or they are not really self-contradictory, in which case there ought to be other ways of expressing what he wants to say more intelligibly. I believe that one would search in vain amongst the mystics for the exploitation of the second alternative, i.e. the alternative of trying to reformulate or interpret the mystical expressions in such a way that they can be made to conform to the rules or conventions of meaningfulness. This is not just an arbitrary guess of mine; it is based on the well-documented tendency among mystics themselves to say that what they experience is *above* the ordinary rules and standards of meaning and discourse, and, therefore, of logic.

In his book *Mysticism and Philosophy*, W. T. Stace adopts the position that the sayings of the mystics are really self-contradictory but contends that the mystics' experience defines a sphere over which the laws of logic have no application. Not all knowledge lies in the sphere within which our senses are pertinent and over which logic holds sway. There are, according to this position, higher spheres wherein spiritual knowledge may be attained without any necessity to abide by logical laws.

It was to enable us to evaluate this type of approach to mysticism and, therefore, by and large, to the problem of mysticism as a source of truth that I prefaced this discussion with a few remarks on meaning. I now invite the reader to look somewhat more closely with me again at some of the mystical things that are said to be above logic.

Take for instance the expression 'God is identical with the Universe and yet not identical with the Universe'. How, taken literally, does it differ from 'Mensah is tall and yet he is not tall'? As far as I can see, they are of the same form and violate the laws of the construction of communicative assertions in the same sort of way. Therefore, according to our previous practice, we would seem to be entitled to declare the expression to be meaningless; and if it is meaningless, then it cannot possibly define any sphere above or below logic. Indeed, claims to the privilege of talking without abiding by some of the most basic rules of communication strike me as unfortunate from a moral point of view. Linguistic meanings are social. Social life is based on a certain community of shared ideas. To use an expression that already exists to communicate a thought, we must abide by a certain minimum of the socially recognised rules of the expression, otherwise we fail to keep linguistic faith with our fellow men. Again, to use the forms of language, e.g. affirmation, denial, etc., one must abide by at least the basic rules governing these forms. To remain within this language and yet claim to be above its rules is a whimsical claim to uniqueness which no experience can possibly justify. But it is not only morally exceptionable; it is futile because, as we have seen, by violating the conventions governing the meaningfulness of the expressions of an existing language one fails to make oneself intelligible to one's audience.

I concede that a case might be made for regarding contradic-

tions as having some sort of meaning; and there are many unmysti-
cally minded logicians who are prepared to press the case quite
firmly. For instance, W. V. Quine, an influential contemporary
philosopher and logician, a very empirically minded thinker,
argues vigorously that contradictions are meaningful (*From a Logical Point of View*, Harper Torchbooks, 1963, p. 5). The following
are two considerations that count in favour of this contention.
Firstly, it is quite obvious that the conjunction 'Kofi is tall and Kofi
is not tall' differs both syntactically and semantically from unmean-
ing word groupings such as 'if of it by and and up'. In the latter
combination of words no semblance of a sentence is offered, and
neither the whole nor any part thereof is capable of conveying even
the appearance of a complete thought. In the former, the reverse is
clearly the case: the two components are straightforwardly meaningful sentences. Accordingly, the conjunction cannot be as totally
impenetrable as the unguided jumble of words. Secondly, contradictory sentences are amenable to logical transformations. For
example, from 'Kofi is tall and Kofi is not tall', the sentence 'Kofi is
tall' is logically deducible on the principle (known as the law of
Simplification) that if any two propositions are asserted to be true
together then they are each assertible as true when taken separately.

It must be granted that the foregoing points – and there are
others that might be developed – do establish that contradictions
do have a formal, syntactical, kind of meaningfulness. However,
the type of meaningfulness here acknowledged for contradictory
sentences is patently not enough to enable such sentences *as wholes*
to *communicate* any message whatever; and it must be accepted that
there is a rather serious sense in which any expression which suffers
from such a disability may be said to be meaningless. The latter is
the species of meaningless that interests us in the present discussion.

It should be noted that Stace's position with regard to the status
of the kind of mystical claims that is under scrutiny is subject to a
further objection. He asserts both that those claims are genuinely
self-contradictory and that they are *above* logic. But to say that a
sentence is self-contradictory is, by definition, to say that it violates
the law of contradiction. If the mystical deliverances were *above*
logic, they could hardly violate its laws. An escape from this

difficulty might, perhaps, be sought by introducing a distinction between inconsistency and non-consistency. It might then be said that, although the mystical sentences are not consistent, they are not inconsistent either, being rather *non-consistent* in the sense that with regard to them it is inappropriate to raise the consistency/inconsistency issue at all. That, however, would be a particularly Pyrrhic manoeuvre, since it would amount to elevating mysticism above not only logic, but truth.

Whatever, then, the character of mystical experience may be, it cannot justify anybody in uttering contradictions. So long as people use language, it will be obligatory for them to observe rules of meaning and the laws of logic. Thus mystical experience cannot be an infallible source of truth about reality. It is, of course, conceivable that one may be led by some uncommon experience one has had to assert propositions which are true; but the criterion of truth cannot lie simply in the fact that one has had a particular kind of experience. If it were so, what would happen if two persons each had a wonderful experience and came up with two mutually contradictory propositions, as some mystics (e.g. theistic and non-theistic 'seers') occasionally do? If the mere fact of having had a certain experience were enough to establish the truth of a proposition inspired by the experience, then the two contradictory propositions would be true, which is impossible.

I am disposed to suspect that the position of the mystic is extremely difficult to articulate conceptually on account of the dissociation of his experience from the conditions of ordinary thought and action. Legalistic logicality for its own sake is, therefore, probably not a useful attitude to adopt towards the poetic outpourings of the mystic. There is, nevertheless, justification for deprecating the mystical tendency to exult in contradictory forms of discourse. Obscurantism breeds irrationality which, in turn, is a mainstay of arbitrariness in human society. Even though there is little danger in this direction from unmitigated mysticism, given, as it is, to the exclusive cultivation of internal peace, the world abounds in half mystics and credulous non-mystics probably even more inclined to esotericism. A rational man is (in the ideal) one who apportions his belief to the evidence and orders his conduct according to warranted belief. Any tendency to condone inconsistent discourse is obviously a set-back to rationality. A consistent belief is, of course, not necessarily a true or a justified belief; but an inconsistent belief is an absolute non-starter. It should never come as a surprise that people habitually unmindful of considerations of consistency should be found to be careless about the grounds for belief and impartiality in action. It must be taken, then, that the philosopher's insistence on consistency in thought and talk has deeper springs than mere intellectualism.

8

Truth as opinion

The problem of truth has been touched upon in various ways in the last four chapters. I wish in this chapter to confront directly the question 'What is Truth?' which was posed but not answered in the preceding chapter. The thesis which I am going to advance, as the reader will probably have inferred from the title of this chapter, is that there is nothing called Truth as distinct from opinion. As this sounds paradoxical, it will not be amiss to preface my argument with a little discourse on common sense and philosophical paradox. And I cannot think of a better way of introducing this subject than by recounting an anecdote which seems to me to be especially interesting in the present connection. I once gave John Dewey's book *How We Think* to an intelligent person quite innocent of technical philosophy to read, saying that in my opinion it contained excellent philosophising. After reading somewhat less than two thirds of the book, he returned it to me complaining that he was expecting to be furnished with profound thoughts but found the book to be filled, page after page, with nothing but commonplace remarks whose truth was so obvious that he could not understand why anybody could think it important to put them into print. After initial unsettlement, I was rather pleased by his comment as it seemed to be a concrete confirmation of a good point which Dewey himself was accustomed to make, namely, that a lot of the things he used to say were so obvious that he would not have insisted upon them so industriously were it not that many philosophers habitually denied them, if only by implication.

One would naturally and immediately want to ask: 'If the matters in question were so obvious then how do you account for the circumstance that many philosophers were disposed to dispute them?' In attempting to answer this question, I should like to call attention to the fact that what is obvious is apt to become extremely unobvious when subjected to protracted reflection. The problematic arises, and can only arise, from the unproblematic. A problem always relates to the significance of something taken as settled. In the philosophically interesting cases common facts are found to pose problems of significance the investigation of which leads us to form ideas of great abstractness, or to institute very general distinctions. There is, of course, no reason why the theoretical ideas and distinctions thus generated should be obvious. Nevertheless, it is required that philosophical ideas should not contradict, but rather illuminate, the facts of common experience. It happens, however, that when carefully examined some ideas proposed by philosophers will be found to conflict with obvious facts of everyday experience. This is possible because abstract ideas are apt to live a life of their own, spurning, as it were, 'the base degrees by which they did ascend'. It then becomes relevant to rehearse, as clearly as possible, the common facts in question and to indicate their relation to the more speculative ideas to which they give rise. This corrective function John Dewey fulfilled with unsurpassed competence.

The point of particular interest for our present purpose in all this is as follows: The theoretical abstractions which I have just alluded to are often to be encountered not only in philosophical treatises but also in everyday thought or common sense, and the principal difference between them lies in the greater elaboration and the technical sophistication of the former. For this reason, the denial of some philosophical theories may also imply the denial of certain common-sense conceptions. When that happens, we speak of a philosophical paradox. Since the kind of common-sense ideas we speak of here may be *in principle* as abstract and interpretative as their corresponding philosophical theories, there is no particular difficulty in the notion that even deeply ingrained common-sense beliefs may sometimes conflict with the facts of common experience. So it need not be a paradox to suggest that the motivation for denying common sense may be a desire to attain in thought greater harmony with common experience.

Let us now turn to an example: the phenomenon of visual illusion. It is a common fact of experience, surely, that we sometimes believe ourselves to perceive things as having certain properties which they do not, in fact, have. Scientifically, such occurrences are susceptible of fairly straightforward explanations in terms of the position and/or the state of the viewer, physiological or psychological. But the very fact that such explanations are available seems to compel us, even in our ordinary common-sense thinking, to institute an abstract and quite speculative distinction between *Reality*, that is, things as they are in themselves and *Appearance*, that is, things as they appear to us in our individual transitory, 'subjective' states. In confirmation of this, moreover, we are apt to reflect that things must exist and have their own natures when not being observed. In this way we seem led to the conception that the nature of things is independent of the cognitive relation between the knower and the known; independent, in other words, of the fact that anybody may come to perceive them.[1] And this, I take to be a conception very deeply embedded in common-sense thinking about the world in general.

There exist philosophical theories which adopt this common-sense conception, subtilising and developing it in varying degrees and directions. But against all such theories there is an objection which, to my mind, is conclusive. The objection is that it is a logical consequence of any such theory that it is impossible ever to know things as they are. For, any claim to know any given object as it really is in itself, will, on the view in question, merely be a report of how a certain thing appears to a certain observer or group of observers in some specific 'subjective' state. Indeed, any claim to know something *as it is in itself* would be a contradiction in as much as it would amount to a claim to know something *as it cannot be known*. But this consequence of the theory, which, remember, is originally a common-sense conception, flatly contradicts our premise that we sometimes perceive things as having certain properties which they do not, *in fact*, have. This premise, which is an indisputable datum of common experience, clearly implies that we can sometimes know things as they are. As the theory thus contradicts a common fact of experience, it must be false.

What then is the alternative? The only alternative, as it seems to me, is to restore the cognitive relation to reality. It was, at any rate, partly with this purpose that the British philosopher, Bishop

---

[1] Kant made this distinction one of the corner-stones of his *Critique of Pure Reason*. See pp. 133–7 of the next chapter for some further remarks on Kant on this subject.

Berkeley, in 1710 propounded his remarkable paradox that for physical things, to exist is the same as to be perceived. History has not been kind to him, as in arguing for his principle of *esse est percipi* Berkeley mixed it up with another quite separable thesis to the effect that to be a physical or, in his own word, 'sensible', object is to be a sensation,[2] and his critics have been unable to separate the two doctrines, and so have visited the opprobrium thought to attach to the latter upon the former. In consequence, attempts to refute Berkeley's contention that to be is to be perceived have always, to my knowledge, displayed *ignoratio elenchi*, the fallacy of arguing to the wrong point. After repeatedly offering the final refutation myself of the paradox in undergraduate and post-graduate exercises, I am now of the opinion not only that it is irrefutable, but also that it is in close harmony with common experience. I am even ready to defend it in a somewhat more general form: I should say that *for anything whatever,* to be is to be apprehended.[3] I shall, however, proceed here to argue only a special case of this principle, namely, that to be true is to be opined.

The steps by which I seek to recommend this contention about truth are exactly parallel to the steps we have just gone through. It is an incontestable fact of common experience that we sometimes know some propositions to be true and at other times make mistakes as to the truth. From this fact common sense is apt to infer that, since our opinions may fall short of the truth, we must draw an absolute distinction between truth and opinion. In philosophical development, this conception becomes an objectivist theory of truth. Truth is then said to be independent of, and *categorially* different from, opinion. Two things are said to be categorially different from each other if something which when said of one of them is either true or false becomes, when said of the other, neither true nor false but inappropriate or even meaningless. According to the objectivist theory, it makes sense to say that a man's opinions may change but it is meaningless nonsense to say that the truth itself may change. Once a proposition is true, it is true in itself and for ever. Truth, in other words, is timeless, eternal. Advocates of this view are not unaware of such apparent exceptions as that it may be true at time t_1 that it is raining but no longer true at time t_2 that it

---

[2] On the separateness of the two theses see pp. 132–3.

[3] This position is argued in the next chapter.

is raining as the rain may have stopped before then. Such cases are easily accounted for as follows: What is said to be true is not the strictly incomplete proposition 'it is raining', but the full proposition 'it is raining at time t_1 at place p_1'. If such a proposition is true, then, according to this conception, it obviously does not make sense to suggest that it might come to be false at a different point of time or space.

This theory about truth, however, goes aground on an objection which may by now be apparent. It is this: If truth is categorially different from opinion, then truth is, as a matter of logical principle, unknowable. Any given claim to truth is merely an opinion advanced from some specific point of view, and categorially distinct from truth. Hence knowledge of truth as distinct from opinion is a self-contradictory notion. But this consequence contradicts the fact of common experience from which we started, namely, that we sometimes know some propositions to be true. Therefore the objectivist theory must be incorrect.

To attempt to escape this conclusion by appealing to *correspondence* with *fact* as the criterion of truth would be of no avail, for that something is a fact must remain nothing more than an opinion.[4] Nor would any reference to perception help, for that any given perception is veridical is still an opinion. For the same reason no alleged faculty of direct apprehension such as intuition can serve. Now, it is an essential fact about opinion that an opinion is necessarily a thought advanced from some specific point of view. Hence, in the case of truth as in our previous case of 'Reality', we must recognise the cognitive element of point of view as intrinsic to the concept of truth. Truth, then, is necessarily joined to point of view, or better, truth is a view from some point; and there are as many truths as there are points of view.

Very likely certain obvious and, perhaps, not so obvious linguistic facts will prevent instant acceptance of this suggestion. The word 'opinion' is often used in such a way as to suggest uncertainty. One contrasts established fact with mere opinion. I do not, of course, mean 'opinion' in this sense. An established fact is simply an opinion felt to be secure from some individual point of view or set of points of view. What I mean by opinion is a firm rather than

[4] The correspondence theory of truth is beset by various other difficulties some of which are discussed in chapter 10, section III, especially pp. 154–8.

an uncertain thought. I mean what is called a considered opinion.
The word 'opinion' is also often used to refer to attitudes to
situations as opposed to factual accounts of them, but here I treat of
opinion as to facts. Another likely cause of objection is the
ambiguity of the term 'truth'. Quite frequently, the word 'truth' is
used to express not the cognitive concept of veridicality but the
moral idea of veracity. When political orators and public guardians
of morality praise truth, we may be sure that what inspires their
passionate eloquence under the heading of truth is not so dry a
topic as the cognitive concept of truth but rather the more sublime
subject of honesty or truthfulness. The Akans have separate
expressions for the two senses of the word 'truth'. '*Nokware*' is the
word which they use to express the moral sense of 'truth'. Literally,
'*Nokware*' means 'one voice', the idea being apparently that
truthfulness consists in saying to others only what one would say to
oneself. For the cognitive concept of truth the Akans use not one
word but a phrase which may be translated as 'what is the case' or
'what is so'. I venture to suggest on autobiographical grounds that
attention to their own vernaculars by Africans in their speculative
thinking may often yield useful dividends in philosophical clarity.
In the English language, nothing is easier than to confuse the two
concepts of truth which I have just distinguished, which often
makes it possible for the careless or disingenuous to import over-
tones of righteousness into the discussion of purely cognitive
matters. In this discussion, my primary concern is with the strictly
cognitive concept of truth.

Coming to a somewhat more logical level, we may anticipate an
objection to the view I am advocating which at first sight may seem
conclusive. The following argument is likely to be urged: Suppose
two people maintain two mutually contradictory propositions.
Then, if there are as many truths as there are points of view, both
propositions must be true. But of two mutually contradictory
propositions only one can be true. (For example, it cannot be both
true that $2 + 2 = 4$ and that $2 + 2$ does not equal 4.) Therefore, the
view that truth is opinion implies a contradiction. This objection
fails, however, because it does not hold fast enough to the element
of point of view in the concept of truth. A contradiction arises only
when two mutually inconsistent propositions are asserted from *one*

and the same point of view. If '2 + 2 = 4' is held true from one point of view and '2 + 2 does not equal 4' is held true from another point of view, there is no reason except lack of logical sophistication why a third point of view should hold both propositions true. In claiming to deduce such a contradiction from our conception of truth, our hypothetical objector simply does not bother to ask himself from what points of view the two contradictory propositions are supposed to be presented.

A variant of this objection is as follows: 'If there are as many truths as there are points of view, then the opinion of the fool will be as good as the opinion of the wise; which is absurd.' In inferring that the opinion of the fool will be as true as that of the wise, our wise man has forgotten to distinguish between his point of view and that of the fool and so has inadvertently displayed an affinity with him.

Another version of the objection is that if truth were nothing but opinion, anybody would be at liberty to believe whatever nonsense he pleases. The authors of the objection are presumably to be understood to hold themselves up as shining exceptions, which shows little logical acumen but rather more self-congratulation. Nonsense is nothing but one man's opinion forcefully declared by another to be defective in a particular way. Whatever theory of truth holds or may come to hold the field, some people will continue to consider nonsensical what others embrace as wisdom.

It may be helpful to note in this connection that 'belief' as I am using it is not a matter of will but of reason. One cannot reasonably say 'the evidence is in favour of proposition P but I choose to believe the opposite', or even 'I do not know any reason for or against P but I choose to believe it'. The psychologist and philosopher William James, once wrote a famous essay entitled 'The Will to Believe'. This somewhat over-suggestive title led many people to form the impression that James intended to suggest that believing was a matter of will and that one could believe anything which one found pleasing or advantageous. As a matter of fact, his main contention was only that when an issue of truth or falsity cannot be decided on intellectual grounds then, if acting *as if* the relevant proposition is true offers more advantages and fewer dangers, it is reasonable to act so. It is an unfortunate fact that when James himself came to apply his general principle to the specific matter of religious faith he failed to observe rigorously the distinction between actually believing a proposition and merely acting as if the proposition were true. But, at all events, the distinction is a clear one. Accordingly, any anxiety (genuine or feigned) that my theory could imply that people might believe anything that caught their fancy irrespective of their own appraisal of relevant evidence or arguments can be finally put to rest.

I can still imagine some objector insisting: 'Surely $2 + 2 = 4$; and that is the truth of the matter. If anybody believes anything to the contrary, he is wrong. He is simply misled by false opinion; and that is that. Nothing can change the obvious fact that there is such a thing as false opinion and that, therefore, truth cannot be identical with opinion.' This objection shows that the lesson about the logical importance of the concept of point of view as an element in the concept of truth value (i.e. truth or falsity) is still not learnt. It is not, of course, disputed that a proposition held to be true from one point of view may be held to be false from another. The phrase 'false opinion' only refers, with perhaps tendentious brevity, to the complex occurrence of assertion and counter-assertion. My contention is that it can mean nothing more. I too am reasonably confident in the belief that $2 + 2 = 4$ and that anybody who holds the contrary is mistaken. But I cannot help recognising that this is simply to affirm my belief and express my disagreement with any contrary belief. Neither the fact that I hold a given opinion nor that many reputable people share my opinion can transform it into something of a different category from opinion, and I must confess that the objectivist conception of truth often strikes me as an intellectualised sublimation of somewhat more primitive passions of the human soul.

Aside from any speculative psycho-analysis, however, reference to the phenomenon of assertion and counter-assertion brings us to the consideration of a rather important aspect of our subject. A counter-assertion is an assertion which contradicts another assertion to which it is a response. Let us take the liberty of using the term 'co-assertion' to mean an assertion which agrees with another assertion to which it is a response. Counter-assertion and co-assertion clearly involve comparison of assertions. Suppose we bring the two topics under the one comprehensive heading of 'comparative assertion'. Then, I contend that the concept of truth is relevant only to comparative contexts. Truth and falsity are concepts whose whole essence consists simply in indicating the agreement or disagreement of one point of view with another, antecedent or anticipated.

Although we are accustomed in common language to speak of the pursuit of truth in a manner which suggests that the aim of all rational investigation is the truth, a little reflection will show that this is a case where common speech is apt to be philosophically misleading. In the primary sense the aim of rational investigation is always to solve a problem or determine an issue one way or another. This, as we shall soon see, is not identical with seeking to determine the truth or falsity of a statement.

In reflecting upon this matter let us not be too impressed by what is standardly said. Rather, let us attend to what is standardly done and check what is said against what is done. As a preliminary to this exercise, we note that it does not make sense to speak of a question or problem as being either true or false. What is susceptible of truth or falsity is a judgment, statement, opinion, belief, assertion. Let us suppose that we are confronted with a problem occasioned, not by a statement advanced from some antecedent point of view, but by our own observation of phenomena, and that so far we have formed no judgment or opinion. At this stage there is nothing about which to predicate truth or falsity. To resolve the issue before us, we do not shut our eyes and 'assert' anything that comes into our heads. Such simplicity of approach is, I dare say, not dreamt of even in the most whimsical philosophy. We undertake an inquiry, investigation, or research. Let us take it that in this given case, we are able to bring our investigation to a successful close. This means that we are able to construct a judgment or form an opinion. Now I ask: can there be for us, at this concluding stage of our investigation, any question of truth or falsity?

I am aware that some may be disposed to answer: 'Yes, of course, there is a question of truth or falsity. After all, rational men seek not just any opinion, but the opinion that coincides with the truth.' That this answer will not do is easily shown by means of a concrete case. Take a rather serious example. Suppose a murder has been

committed and that we make an investigation and come to the firm
opinion that Mr *X* did it. I again ask the reader to consider whether
after arriving at this definite judgment it would be reasonable or,
indeed, even consistent, to go on to say: 'Very well, we are now
going to investigate whether it is true or false that Mr *X* did it.'
Surely such a speech presupposes that one has not yet arrived at a
firm conclusion. One does not first construct a firm judgment and
then ask whether the judgment is true or false.

There is a temptation, to which many logicians have succumbed,
to infer from the foregoing consideration that to assert firmly: 'Mr
X committed the murder' is equivalent to asserting that the statement that Mr *X* committed the murder is true.[5] But this temptation
ought to be resisted, for it obscures a subtle distinction which is
implicit in a number of remarks already made. To say of a statement '*P*' that it is true, presupposes that a statement is antecedently
available. But in our hypothetical case we are on our own, struggling to form a judgment without the benefit of prior counsel.
Therefore a conclusion of the form 'the statement that Mr *X*
committed the murder is true' cannot be appropriate. A statement
of this form is in the nature of what we have called a comparative
assertion. By contrast, a statement of the form 'Mr *X* committed
the murder' may be called a primary judgment. Not to resist the
temptation just referred to would mean confusing a primary judgment with a comparative one. If we call an inquiry which terminates in a *primary* judgment a primary inquiry and one which
terminates in a comparative judgment a *comparative* inquiry, then

[5] This remark applies to the theory of truth advanced by the English logician
Frank Ramsey in 1927 in a paper on 'Facts and Propositions' in *Aristotelian Society
Supplementary Volume VII*, July 1927, reprinted in Ramsey, *The Foundations of
Mathematics*, Routledge and Kegan Paul, 1931. He argued that 'it is evident that "It
is true that Caesar was murdered" *means no more* than that Caesar was murdered, and
"It is false that Caesar was murdered" *means* that Caesar was not murdered'
(*Foundations*, p. 142; my own italics). From considerations of this sort, he concluded that 'if we have analysed judgment, we have solved the problem of truth'
(*ibid.*, p. 143). The view of truth I am putting forward has a basic affinity with
Ramsey's in spite of the reservation expressed. Ramsey's view has come to be known
generally as the Redundancy Theory of Truth, for it followed from it that 'It is true
that' and 'It is false that' are redundant phrases which, in Ramsey's words, 'we
sometimes use for emphasis or for stylistic reasons, or to indicate the position
occupied by the statement in our argument' (*ibid.*, p. 142). The theory of the Polish
logician Alfred Tarski, which is known as the Semantic Conception of Truth, also
obscures the distinction mentioned in the text. On Tarski's theory of truth see
chapter 12, pp. 197–201.

the position at which we have arrived is that the concept of truth belongs not to the domain of primary but rather to that of comparative inquiry.[6]

Notice, however, that there is an intimate relation between the two types of investigation. The substantive problem of a comparative investigation is exactly identical with that of a corresponding primary investigation. To try to determine whether 'it is true that Mr X committed the murder' is, in substance, the same as trying to find out whether Mr X committed the murder. Nevertheless the two enterprises are not identical in their antecedents or in the logical structure of their results. The comparative inquiry is a response to the challenge of a pre-existing judgment, and its appropriate outcome is a judgment on a judgment. The primary investigation is, by contrast, a response to the challenge of a problematic situation and leads to a direct judgment on that. The relation between them, however, is obviously such that, whenever a primary judgment is made, a corresponding comparative judgment is automatic, *given an appropriate context*. It is this circumstance which seduces incautious reasoners into the error of supposing that every rational inquiry aims at truth. On the analysis given, it should, I fancy, be clear by now that truth belongs only to a comparative context wherein to be true is to coincide with a corroborative point of view.

The objectivist theory, which is also the prevalent conception of common sense, is, accordingly, to be rejected. But do we thereby reject objectivity and embrace subjectivism? Actually, the subjective/objective distinction apparently so beloved of intellectual controversialists is an exceedingly tricky one. It is rare indeed to find it employed with any rigour outside philosophy or even inside it. I regret that I cannot in the present discussion enter into an analysis of this matter. I can here only state my own opinion rather baldly. It seems to me that in the way of opinion, that is objective which is in

[6] I am thinking here of the concept of truth as it is used in ordinary discourse. In truth functional logic, however, the truth value *truth* belongs to the domain of primary, rather than to comparative, inquiry. In that logic, truth is that which, being added to a function (i.e. a content representable by a participal phrase), converts it into a declarative sentence. I have discussed the primary and the comparative concepts of truth in my 'Truth as a Logical Constant, with an Application to the Principle of Excluded Middle', *Philosophical Quarterly*, October 1975. The next paragraph in the text above may be taken as a clarification by implication of the relation between the two concepts of truth.

conformity with the principles of rational inquiry,[7] these in their turn, being susceptible of a naturalistic account.[8] Objectivity does not require that an abstract principle should be erected into an abstract object. Objectivity, in other words, ought not to be confused with objectivism.

So far, I have argued my thesis on what may *broadly* be called logical considerations. I now wish to make one or two moral remarks. First, however, a disclaimer: the morality of an opinion has not the slightest tendency to prove or disprove it. But, if logical grounds are independently adduced against a position, as I hope I have done in this case, then reference to moral consequences may serve to induce a legitimate sense of the practical urgency of the issue.

The concept of absolute truth appears to have a tendency to facilitate dogmatism and fanaticism which lead, in religion and politics, to authoritarianism and, more generally, to oppression. I do not say that this is a necessary consequence of that conception. Indeed, if human beings were always consistent, the doctrine of absolute truth should, as suggested earlier, lead to total scepticism rather than to dogmatism. Besides, it is not here suggested that all advocates of the idea in question are dogmatic or fanatical. It is a fact, nevertheless, that in matters of truth and falsity, drastic persecution is hardly conceivable without pretensions to absolute truth on the part of the persecutors. It is difficult to think that men could imprison and even kill their fellow men for doctrinal differences with a free conscience if they understood clearly that, in doing so, they were acting simply on their own fallible opinions. It is a totally different thing when people believe that they are in the service of absolute truth, particularly if they imagine that the destiny of a nation, or even, perhaps, of the whole of mankind, is in question. There is no end to the mischief and cruelty of which they are capable. Yet, translated into the terms of my theory, such assertions as 'The Truth will prevail'; and 'The Truth is on our side', amount to no more than 'Our opinions will prevail' or 'My opinions are on my side.'

On the practical plane, then, the identification of truth with

[7] See chapter 4, pp. 56–8 for more on the subjective/objective distinction.

[8] John Dewey, in his *Logic: The Theory of Inquiry*, attempted to give such a naturalistic account of the principles of rational inquiry.

opinion may be interpreted as a prescription for open-mindedness. This quality of mind consists not in affecting uncertainty but in recognising one's liability to error. Dogmatism, obversely, consists not just in expressing one's opinions with positive conviction but in the unwillingness or refusal to offer evidence for them or to consider objections with a view to revising them. Scientific practice, if not always the theory of it, has long been informed by an attitude of fallibilism. I dare say that the Humanities will never become completely humane until those disciplines are thoroughly imbued with a sense of the intrinsically human character of truth.

Let me conclude on a note of apparent anti-climax. That truth is nothing but opinion is itself nothing but an opinion; and should my argument prove fair game for a critic, I should rejoin with F. C. S. Schiller: 'Sufficient unto the day is the Truth thereof!'

9

To be is to be known

In the previous chapter I characterised the thesis 'To be true is to be opined' as a special case of the claim '*For anything whatever*, to be is to be apprehended', and indicated a preparedness to defend this more general claim. I now address myself to this task.

Many philosophers and probably all laymen are, or would be, scandalised by the suggestion that *to be is to be known*. The thesis may even appear to imply that there is nothing that is not already known. And surely any view which has such a consequence must be false, and absurdly so, but I wish to show that any discussion of the proposition must encounter issues which cannot be cavalierly disposed of.

Consider, to begin with, the phrase 'to be' or its synonym 'to exist'. Philosophically, it is a notorious infinitive. A comparison with other infinitives such as 'to dance', 'to sing', 'to dissolve' will easily bring out a subtle peculiarity of 'to be'. To dance, sing, or dissolve is an action undertaken or undergone by an object, be it a person, a bird or a piece of inanimate matter such as sugar. Speaking somewhat technically, we may say that the ability to dance, sing or dissolve can be an *attribute* of an object. Can we say the same of 'to be'? Is *being* or *existing* an action or a process undertaken or undergone by an *object*? One would without any hesitation answer in the negative. An object must exist before it can act or be acted upon. This remark is true enough but considerable care is required in order to extract its exact significance.

Suppose I point to an object, e.g. a table, and say, 'The table exists'. Do I communicate a message? Many people would be tempted to reply that the sentence is *tautological* in the ordinary, non-technical sense of the term in which a tautology is a sentence which does not impart any information but merely repeats something already presupposed. In the present case it might be urged that the mere demonstrative utterance of 'This table' already presupposes the existence of the table so that the assertion that it exists is redundant. This will not do, however; for this alleged presupposition is itself nothing other than the proposition that the table *pointed to* exists, which must, for the same reason, itself be tautological. But this in turn must mean that the existence of the table is already presupposed by the successful demonstrative utterance. By parity of reasoning this last alleged presupposition must itself involve a redundancy, and so on, *ad infinitum*. What this pass of events suggests is that there is something radically inappropriate about such a sentence as 'This table exists'.

Let us note an interesting corollary of this result. If a man, pointing to a table, were to say 'This table does not exist', we would naturally be tempted to protest that he is guilty of self-contradiction. But the temptation ought to be resisted because any attempt to specify the contradiction would force us back to the same unviable argument that the successful utterance of 'This table' presupposes that the table exists. Of course, if the alleged presupposition were valid, the sentence 'The table does not exist' would imply both 'This table exists' and 'This table does not exist', which would be a contradiction. The point, however, is that if there is something inappropriate about the affirmation 'This table exists', then one must expect the corresponding denial 'This table does not exist' to be similarly defective. It is important to note that when we condemn a sentence as inappropriate, we are not suggesting that it says anything false but rather that it fails to say anything at all.

We can reinforce our sense of the degeneracy of a sentence such as 'This table does not exist' by means of the following consideration. Imagine that a man pointing to a table were to ask: 'Does this table exist?' What sort of information would he be asking for? We might suppose him to be wondering whether he is dreaming or having a hallucination, or some allied form of perceptual illusion.[1]

[1] Macbeth and the dagger provide a dramatisation of this type of uncertainty:

> Is this a dagger which I see before me,
> The handle toward my hand?
> Come, let me clutch thee.
> I have thee not, and yet I see thee still.
> Art thou not, fatal vision, sensible

But suppose our man were to react indignantly: 'Of course not, I am absolutely clear in my mind that I see a table in front of me and I am sure that you also see it. I simply want to know whether this table which we all actually see, exists.' I suggest that it would be legitimate at this stage to suspect an imperfect grasp on his part of the semantics of 'exists'. It does not in general make sense to ask in the presence of a *given* object whether it exists or not. When we pose a question as to the existence of an object the happiest way of resolving the issue is to be brought face to face with the object.

We have just spoken of a question as to 'the existence of an object'. Obviously here is a phrase, which, though unexceptionable as a piece of common locution, calls for rather cautious interpretation philosophically. A question regarding the existence of an object would take some such form as: 'Does x exist?' For example, one might ask 'Does the Snowman exist?' When such a question is raised our investigations standardly take the form of trying to locate some object satisfying the description of the Snowman. It emerges, then, that in general 'Does x exist?' has the same meaning as 'Does "x" refer to an object?'[2] The symbol 'x' here, of course, indicates a position to be filled by a determinate term.

We are now in a position to see clearly why it is meaningless to point to an object and ask whether it exists. To assert that an object exists is to assert that a given term refers to an object. Existence, that is to say, is a relation between a term and an object, not an attribute of an object.[3] Questions of existence thus start with a term, or a description, not with an object. Consequently, to ask whether a presented object exists is to put the cart before the horse, semantically speaking!

Before returning to our troublesome infinitive 'to be' let us note parenthetically the implications of the foregoing clarification of the

---

To feeling as to sight? Or art thou but
A dagger of the mind, a false creation
Proceeding from the heat-oppressed brain?
(*Macbeth*, Act II, Scene I)

[2] I ignore here questions of logical and mathematical existence. I am concerned only with material existence.

[3] Frege held that existence is a property of a term. See Gottlob Frege, *The Foundations of Arithmetic,* English translation by J. L. Austin, Basil Blackwell, Oxford, second revised edition, p. 65^e. It is possible to interpret Frege's view in such a way that it agrees with that put forward here.

concept of existence for the ontological argument for the existence of God. St Anselm, and Descartes after him, had argued that existence is logically bound up with the correct conception of God. As against this contention, Kant pointed out that existence is not an attribute of objects and that, therefore, any entity (including God) can be exhaustively specified without any mention of existence.[4] I believe that in the explication of existence given above, we have a further substantiation of Kant's criticism. My argument is: An attribute of an object must be something which can in principle be affirmed of an object in its presence. Existence cannot in principle be affirmed of an object in its presence. Therefore existence is not an attribute of an object and cannot be logically bound up with the conception of any entity whatever. Or consider it from this angle: To assert 'God exists' is to assert that the term 'God' has a reference – i.e. refers to an object. One could not even begin to investigate the claim unless one could obtain an adequate conception of the significance of the term 'God' independently of the question of whether it, in fact, has a reference. It follows that, whatever the right conception of God may be, the issue of his existence is logically separate from it.

Enough of the digression; I come back now to our special verb 'to be'. It must now be clear that this infinitive does not denote an action or process undertaken or suffered by an object; further it does not signify any sort of attribute of an object whatever. On the contrary, what we have found is that it serves only as a means of claiming that a given term has a reference. 'To be' ('to exist'), then, means 'for a given term "x" to be asserted to refer to some object'.

It might be objected that this is not what the discussion so far has shown. What it has shown, it might be argued, is only that for a given term 'x' 'for x to be' means 'for "x" to have a reference'. The objection turns on a supposed difference between the meanings of the phrases 'for "x" to have a reference' and 'for "x" to be asserted to have a reference'. Any appearance of a difference is, however, illusory. Let us note to begin with that considering the meaning of the phrase 'for x to be' is the same as considering the meaning of the

---

[4] The relevant passages in St Anselm (*Proslogion* chs. II–IV), Descartes (Third *Meditation*) and Kant (*Critique of Pure Reason*, A592, D620 ff.) are conveniently collected together in *The Ontological Argument*, ed. Alvin Plantinga, Anchor Books, Doubleday & Co. Inc., New York, 1965.

sentence 'x exists'. (My usage here is thus innocent of any metaphysical distinction between being and existence.) We may then reformulate my claim as follows: 'For any given term "x", "x exists" means "it is asserted that 'x' has a reference".' The objection now is that the discussion so far only entitles me to assert that 'For any given term "x", "x exists" means "x has a reference".' But the sentence ' "x" has a reference' *asserts*, surely, that 'x' has a reference (and, of course, the same applies, *mutatis mutandis*, to 'x exists'). Hence the only difference between ' "x" has a reference' and 'it is asserted that "x" has a reference' is that the latter brings out explicitly the assertive significance of the former for the purpose of emphasis. Underlying my contention here is a rejection of the common distinction between propositions and assertions according to which a declarative sentence merely expresses a proposition and does not constitute an assertion until somebody actually uses it to make an assertion. In truth the reason for calling such sentences declarative is the very same reason why we should recognise them to be assertive. A sentence of this sort, by *its form*, declares something to be so (or not so). That is the essence of assertion.[5]

With the explanation of the first part of the maxim 'To be is to be known' established, the second part falls into place almost effortlessly. It is plain without argument that one cannot claim that a term 'x' refers to some entity while disclaiming all knowledge about the entity in question. What remains is to sort out certain ambiguities in the usage of the word 'know'. Take the knowledge of persons. One may *know* who Mr X is without really *knowing* him. I *know* him in the first sense if I have so much as seen him before and have enough recollection of him to be able to identify him in future. In the second sense, I need to have considerable insight into the character of the said Mr X before I can be said to know him. Obviously the first sense of *know* is sufficient as a correlate of the assertion of the existence of Mr X. But it is not even necessary to know so much. Surely I can know about Mr X without knowing him in either of the two foregoing senses. A man may be *known* all over the world and yet many of the people to whom he is 'known' may never have seen him or even seen a picture of him. Here 'to know X' means 'to know about X'. Now, evidently, for anybody to

---

[5] I have discussed the distinction between propositions and assertions at some length in 'Truth as a Logical Constant', *Philosophical Quarterly*, October 1975.

assert the existence of Mr X implies that he knows something at least about X. Again, this piece of knowledge may be as bare as you like. For example, I can assert the existence of the mother of Mohammed Ali. But all I know about her is that she is the mother of Mohammed Ali. However, this is not trivial. In some imaginable contexts knowledge that a certain contemporary object satisfies the description 'Mother of Mohammed Ali' can make all the difference between knowledgeableness and absolute ignorance. Thus to assert the existence of an object and to claim knowledge of it in a certain minimal sense is one and the same thing.

I suppose that notwithstanding the explanations already given, some readers may wish to enter an objection on the following lines: 'We agree that to *assert* the existence of an object is to claim some sort of knowledge of the object. But an object may exist without anybody asserting that it exists. In this case the existence of the object is absolutely independent of anybody's knowledge. Your discussion so far does not even begin to touch on this issue.' I should say at once that I regard the proposition that an object *may* exist without anybody asserting that it exists as being compatible with the thesis that to be is to be known. What needs to be combated, then, is the impression that the two positions are opposed.

I shall begin by trying to show that the statement 'an object may exist without anybody asserting that it exists' amounts to pointing out the distinction between statements of the form 'X may exist' and statements of the form 'X exists' both of which, of course, claim different degrees of knowledge. As soon as we ask ourselves what is the significance of the word 'may' in 'an object *may* exist without . . .', we cannot avoid noticing that it is an allusion to a mode of knowing rather than to an attribute of an object. If, as we have seen, the fact that an object exists is not an attribute of the object, then the fact that a certain object *may* exist cannot, *a fortiori*, be an attribute of the object. One would not, normally, use the phrase 'x may exist' when one is (epistemologically) in a position to assert 'x exists'. It is significant that one does not say 'Some object x exists without anybody knowing (not to talk of asserting) that it exists'. That would be inconsistent, for, of course, whoever asserted the statement would himself have asserted the existence of the object. The form 'x exists', then, corresponds to certain knowledge, while '*x* may exist' corresponds to, let us say, possible knowledge. The possibility may, admittedly, never be realised, but logically, that is nothing surprising. Accordingly, to the maxim 'To be is to be known', we may now add the rider: 'Possibly to be is possibly to be known.'

A critic may still comment: 'Full justice has not been done to the significance of the word "may" in a sentence like "an object may exist without anybody knowing that it exists". This "may" need not be interpreted as indicating insufficient knowledge. On the contrary, as used in the present context, it expresses in the most positive way possible the position that existence is logically independent of knowledge. This use of "may" is quite familiar. In the sentence "a man *may* be an African without being a Ghanaian", the word "may" has been employed to indicate the fact that being an African does not logically imply being a Ghanaian. In fact, in the matter of the relation between knowledge and existence, one can go a step further. It can be asserted quite confidently that there must be a great number of things which actually exist but are not known. This is simply because there are more things in the universe than we have knowledge of.'

On this let me make two remarks: (1) The analogy between a thing existing without being known and a man being an African without being a Ghanaian is defective. It is possible to give an example of a non-Ghanaian African. But it is not possible to imagine an example of an object which exists unknown. How could we possibly make the existence of *that* object an example unless we had some knowledge of it? (2) I accept the proposition that there are more things in the universe than we have knowledge of. The question is how to interpret it. One thing we can say at once is that it does not mean that some specific things *x, y, z*, exist unknown, which, as we have seen, would be a contradictory suggestion. Here, then, is something that looks very much like a paradox: There are things we do not know of but there are no specific things of which we do not know. I suggest the following resolution: An assertion of indeterminate existence can only be matched by an equally indeterminate knowledge of the objects postulated. The statement that there are more things in the universe than we have knowledge of is essentially an expression of our sense of the open-endedness of human knowledge. The significance of this thought is formally hypothetical. In sum it says: If we continue our investigations we will encounter new objects. The *categorical* force of this *hypothetical* proposition is to connect the existence of objects not as yet determinately known with the present state of knowledge.

We do not hesitate, for instance, to affirm that in various unprobed regions of the universe there must exist things of one sort or another. But the *existence* of these unprobed regions is an item of human knowledge. Admittedly we do not know the nature of the objects that populate the regions in question. But specifically this is the reason why we are not entitled to assert that a determinate x or a determinate y exists there. That kind of definiteness of existential assertion must await future exploration. Comparison with a more mundane example will probably help to clarify the point: I am now sitting before a table. When I survey it I am able to see only a part of the table. Yet I confidently believe that parts of it exist which I do not now see. Why? Because, to speak with enormous, though not unforgivable, simplification, I know from past experience that things such as tables do have a constitution which is such that at any particular moment that portion I see is continuous with much else that I do not see. And this is the basis of my conviction that if I were now to move round the table I would see parts that are now hidden from my sight. In other words, the *existence* of the unseen parts consists in a certain systematic connection with my present and past experience. The existence of the remote reaches of the universe too has exactly the same significance, though this is without prejudice to the greater complexity of the manner in which the connection is established between the experienced and the unexperienced in this case.

An objection closely allied to the one just discussed is that our analysis is inapplicable to statements of past existence. Suppose we come to find out that there existed a certain object x at an earlier time unbeknown to anybody whatever at that time. Then the statement 'x existed at time t' is true but it is not true that anybody knew, let alone asserted, that 'x' had a reference.

The reply is simple. It is not correct to suggest that on my view 'x existed' means 'It was asserted that "x" had a reference'. What it means is 'It is asserted that "x" had a reference'. It is true that x was not known at the material time, but *its existence* cannot be said to be independent of knowledge. Though independent of the knowledge of the people of the earlier time its historical existence is not independent of contemporary knowledge.

This is an opportune juncture to stress one thing: It is the *existence* of an object not the object itself that consists in being known. Readers who have followed our earlier arguments showing that it does not make sense to say of a *given* object either that it exists or that it does not exist will find no paradox in the distinction between an object and the existence of an object. If he has understood that when we talk of the existence of an object we are, in fact, considering a certain relation of a term (or if you like, a concept) to an object, then he will not be tempted to confuse a mere relation with the object that instantiates one of the terms of the relation.

The contention of the preceding paragraph is significant in that it distinguishes our position from the idealisms of Berkeley and Kant and also from all brands of phenomenalism, old and new. Berkeley held that for 'sensible' (i.e. physical) objects, to be is to be perceived. This is only a special case of the much more general thesis of the present paper. As we have argued it, the thesis is an epistemological rather than an ontological one, i.e. it is one having to do with our knowledge of objects rather than with the ultimate nature of objects. Actually, Berkeley, too, resorts at one stage to epistemological argument on this matter, albeit briefly. Treating of 'what is meant by the term *exists* when applied to sensible things', he says: 'That table I write on, I say exists, that is, I see and feel it; and if I were out of my study I should say it existed – meaning thereby that if I was in my study I might perceive it or that some other spirit actually does perceive it' (*Principles of Human Knowledge*, sec. 3). Taken by itself, the most natural interpretation of this passage would be to construe it as a remark about the relation between the *existence* of objects and our knowledge of them. The historical fact, however, is that Berkeley's remark on the meaning of the term 'exists' with respect to sensible objects (i.e. the objects of our sense perception) was made in the context of a philosophical theory of perception, largely taken over from his predecessor Locke, according to which human beings can perceive only their own *ideas*, by which he meant sensations. Given this peculiar premise, it, of course, follows that it is a contradiction in terms to speak of an unperceived sensible object. 'For, what are the aforementioned objects but the things we perceive by sense? and what do we perceive by sense besides our own ideas or sensations? and is it not plainly repugnant that any one of these, or any combinations of them, should exist unperceived?' (*ibid.*, sec. 4). It is thus easy to see why in the matter of the existence of sensible objects Berkeley failed to separate the epistemological thesis that to be is to be perceived from the ontological thesis that sensible objects are sensations. Obviously the latter implies the former. But the converse does not hold. If objects are sensations, then, sensations being nothing but a species of awareness or perception, it goes without saying that to say that an object exists is to say that it is perceived. However, from the position that the *existence* of objects consists in their being perceived – we are for the moment thinking exclusively of sensible objects – it does not follow that the objects are a species of sensation; for as already argued, to talk about the *existence* of objects is not the same as talking of their ultimate constitution.[6]

Kant also shared Berkeley's sensationalist theory of sensible perception, though he enveloped it in his own special kind of terminological sophistication. Having assumed that in sense perception we are only aware of our own modes of sensible awareness, in his own terminology the modifications of our *sensibility*, he too was led to give the view that the *existence* or *reality* of physical objects, which he called *appearances*, consisted in their being perceived in an ontologically 'subjective' orientation. Thus we read:

> Save through its relation to a consciousness that is at least possible, appearance could never be for us an object, and so would be nothing for us; and since it has in itself no objective reality, but *exists* only *in being known*, it would be nothing at all [Kant: *Critique of Pure Reason*, A120. Kemp Smith's Translation, Macmillan, London, 1929, pp. 143–4].

or

> The appearances, in so far as they are objects of consciousness simply in virtue of being representations, are not in any way

[6] The last two paragraphs substantiate a claim I made in chapter 8 that Berkeley's thesis that for sensible objects to be is to be perceived is separable from the doctrine that sensible objects are nothing but sensations.

distinct from their apprehension [*ibid.*, B235, A190, p. 219 para. 3].

or

> [For] since a mere modification of our sensibility can never be met outside us, the objects, as appearances, constitute an object which is merely in us [*ibid.*, A129, p. 149, last para.].

Kant tried to distinguish between his idealism which he decorated with the term 'transcendental' and Berkeley's which he described – some may say stigmatised – as 'empirical'. Referring to Berkeley, he remarked: 'He maintained that space, with all the things of which it is the inseparable condition, is something which is in itself impossible; and he therefore regards the things in space as merely imaginary entities' (*ibid.*, p. 244. This occurs in a section entitled 'Refutation of Idealism'). Berkeley maintained no such position, and this passage must be counted among the most remarkable cases of one great philosopher's misreading of another. Berkeley, in fact, distinguished between the real and the imaginary or illusory in the realm of sensible things in his own way. According to him, the real is different from the imaginary or illusory only in being law-like and orderly in a certain basic sense. Both the real and the unreal are forms of awareness, differing only in the superior overall coherence of the former.[7] This, again, is the same in principle as Kant's own account of the distinction between the real and the unreal or the objective and the subjective.[8] As far, then, as sensible objects are concerned, Kant's idealism and Berkeley's are basically the same.

The real difference between Kant and Berkeley consists in two facts: (1) Kant, but not Berkeley, had a highly complicated account of the processes of the mind, which he called *syntheses*, by means of which the mere modifications of our perceptual faculties result in the perception of 'objects';[9] (2) Kant introduced the

---

[7] See George Berkeley, *Treatise Concerning the Principles of Human Knowledge*, sections 29, 30, 33, in, e.g. *The Works of George Berkeley*, ed. A. C. Fraser, vol. 1, pp. 170–3.

[8] See, for example, the 'Second Analogy', op. cit., B233ff, pp. 218ff.

[9] It is a disputed point of Kantian exegesis whether the various 'syntheses' which Kant talks about are processes or merely logical stages in the analysis of perception. I think that they are akin to processes but this is not the place to argue the point.

concept of *the thing in itself*, the *noumenon*, to which human beings have no access whatever. We can take it that Berkeley would have dismissed this notion as a gross illogicality. Indeed, Berkeley saw the postulation of entities independent of perception as the root cause of scepticism. In any case, Kant is, I think, inconsistent in introducing the notion of *the thing in itself* as absolutely independent of our cognition, for he himself may be taken to have shown in the *Critique* (in the metaphysical and transcendental deductions) that the general concept of *a thing* reflects our fundamental capacities for knowing.

These points of difference, however, are irrelevant to the following difficulty which faces any theory which resolves material objects into forms of apprehension. How can such a theory accommodate the fact that at any given time there are countless objects not perceived by its propounder? Berkeley tries this answer: If I am not actually perceiving an object then either it is a possible object of my perception – i.e. a possible sensation of mine, or it is actually being perceived by another perceiver. (See the quotation from Berkeley above on the existence of the table in the study.) The 'either . . . or' implies that one alternative is supposed to suffice. But consider the first alternative: On this showing the sensible world consists of actual and possible sensations. J. S. Mill adopted this position and epitomised his phenomenalism in the oft-quoted definition of matter as 'the permanent possibility of sensation' (*British Empirical Philosophers*, ed. A. J. Ayer and R. Winch, Routledge & Kegan Paul, London, 1952, p. 550). The trouble with this theory is that the possibility of a sensation is simply not a kind of sensation and cannot meaningfully be added to an actual sensation to constitute a whole. It is as if a man of modest means were calmly to declare himself a multi-millionaire on the ground that his wealth consisted of his slight actual assets plus unlimited possible assets. Presumably Berkeley realised the untenability of this metaphysical arithmetic, for in the end he rested everything on the second alternative: What is not actually perceived by me is actually perceived by another spirit which is a constant perceiver of everything – God. Thus, fundamentally, the material world consists of God's awareness and, derivatively, of the sensations of mortals induced in them by God.

Unfortunately Berkeley does not favour the reader with details of how God (who presumably has no sensations himself) induces sensations in our bodies which are, meanwhile, nothing but types of God's own apprehension. Kant does not drag God into his difficulties; but neither does he advance beyond Berkeley's first thoughts. He embraces Berkeley's first, phenomenalist, alternative. Thus he says:

> That there may be inhabitants in the moon, although no one has perceived them, must certainly be admitted. This, however, only means that in the possible advance of experience we may encounter them. For everything is real which stands in connection with a perception in accordance with the laws of empirical advance [op. cit. A493, pp. 440–1].

One cannot forbear asking at once: What is the 'them' which we may possibly encounter? Suppose we try to translate this quotation into a phenomenalistically stark language, then we should obtain something on some such lines as follows:

> That there may be certain possible sensations (or 'intuitions') of the sort that are called 'inhabitants' as part of those sensations which are called the moon must certainly be admitted. This, however, only means that when sensations increase, some of them may come to satisfy the description 'inhabitants on the moon'. For every sensation is genuine which stands in connection with a present sensation in accordance with the laws of the increase of sensations.

Of course, this translation is incomplete, for if one were to encounter inhabitants on the moon they would be seen by means of the eyes, possibly touched by means of the hands, and so on. Since such organs, indeed, all the bodily parts of a person, are themselves supposed to be sensations, actual or hypothetical, the present writer must confess himself completely overwhelmed by the task of having to translate the clause 'although *no one* has perceived them'. In general, it does not emerge how one is to translate the notion of 'my sensation' or 'his sensation'. The reader can raise more difficulties, e.g. how do sensations increase?

Phenomenalism is often traced to Mill, but, as must be plain, it exists full-blooded in the *Critique of Pure Reason*. Modern phenomenalism attempts to introduce a refinement by claiming that the theory is not a thesis about the ultimate constitution of matter but rather one about language to the effect that all talk about material objects can be translated without remainder into talk about sensations. One must be excused for looking upon this as an exercise in evasion. For, suppose material objects are not sensations, then even if all speech about material objects could be translated into a sensationalist language, that fact by itself would be of no philosophical interest. On the other hand, if material objects are, in fact, sensations, then it would be philosophically pusillanimous not to say so. However, as of the present day no phenomenalist has succeeded in carrying through the projected translation,[10] which should not surprise any reader who tries to complete the translation of the Kantian quotation of the previous page into a phenomenalistic language.

Suppose, now, that we return to this quotation and view it in complete isolation from the problematic doctrine that material objects are mere forms of sensible apprehension. Then the passage acquires a new lucidity. That its import, which I have called the epistemological thesis, is valid I have already argued. I conjecture that the confidence which Berkeley and Kant displayed in their varieties of metaphysical 'subjectivism' is a spillover from their legitimate sense of the correctness of the epistemological thesis which they failed to keep apart from the ontological one. Henceforward any critic of the thesis that to be is to be known will have to do better than attacking the claim that to be is to be a mode of awareness.[11]

Finally let us briefly dispose of a tempting objection to the thesis of this paper. It may be asked: 'Is it not conceivable that all cognitive beings could perish? And would not the world of material objects still exist?' The answer is simple. This question is raised, and can only be raised, while we are all still around, and it is raised

[10] Ayer who appeared, in *Foundations of Empirical Knowledge* (London, Macmillan, 1940), to be bent on such an enterprise gave up in *The Problem of Knowledge* (Pelican, 1956). Hospers in a critical discussion of phenomenalism tries to go as far as is humanly possible in phenomenalistic translation, thereby bringing out the difficulties with the utmost clarity. (See John Hospers, *Introduction to Philosophical Analysis*, Routledge & Kegan Paul, second edition, 1967, pp. 530–47.)

[11] G. E. Moore in his famous essay 'The Refutation of Idealism' (included in his *Philosophical Studies*, London, Routledge & Kegan Paul, 1922, paperback, 1960, originally published in *Mind*, 1903) argues against the doctrine that objects are forms of awareness while claiming to refute the thesis that to be is to be known.

from our *point of view*. That the world of material objects *would* still exist in the event of the universal calamity is what we envisage we would observe if we were able to. To repeat a point earlier made, to hypothetical existence we can only correlate hypothetical cognition. If we forswear all hypothetical resurrection, then the question of existence just does not arise in a desolate world such as the one imagined.

10

What is philosophy?

Earlier, in chapter 7, I attempted a little rashly to say what philosophy is in three paragraphs or so. I now wish to enlarge on and make good those brief remarks. Philosophy is, indeed, a well-established subject, but its issues are so riddled with controversy that there is hardly a single question to which there can be said to be an established answer. Not even on the question of what philosophy is is there agreement, and any definition is apt to be personal.

The uninitiated may not immediately appreciate the connection there is between disagreements about particular questions in philosophy and differences with respect to the nature of the subject itself. But a little study will reveal to him that a philosopher's attitude to particular questions very often reflects his general conception of the nature of philosophy. Yet, paradoxically, in the actual maturation of philosophical thought as a process of personal development the attainment of a definite and articulate notion of the nature of philosophy comes last or nearly so. What actually starts off the would-be philosopher is a particular puzzle or cluster of puzzles. In a celebrated case – that of G. E. Moore, one of the most influential figures in British philosophy in the first half of this century – a whole life of earnest philosophical investigation was touched off by puzzlement at the sayings of other philosophers. For instance, he would ask: What could a philosopher possibly mean by saying that the external world is unreal or that reality is spiritual? Schopenhauer, an often outspoken German philosopher of the preceding century, had some unkind words for this inducement to philosophical activity. According to him, only false philosophers are made by way of reaction to the doctrines of other philosophers. Whether Schopenhauer's animadversions are just or

not, it is certainly more usual for philosophic stimulation to come
as a result of the encounter with life, society and the environment.

In comparison with other sorts of questions that are capable of
engaging inquiring minds, philosophical questions have a special
kind of generality. It is, for example, an interesting and important
question whether state participation in an economy is good. This
question has its own, quite high, degree of generality. But in
consideration of the passion (and frequently even violence) with
which conflicting answers are canvassed, one might be moved to
ask: 'What, to be sure, is meant by saying that something is good?'
We are then faced with a philosophical question. Since such questions are very abstract some may be disposed to doubt their practical importance. But it is surely remarkable that all the major
historical figures who have advocated fundamental changes in
the *practical* arrangements for conducting social life have felt the
need to find answers to a series of inter-related questions of this
sort. So that it should not sound fanciful to suggest that the
asking of questions of such rare generality is the beginning of
wisdom. We will go further into the character of such questions,
amplifying and illustrating, but the reference to wisdom calls for
elaboration.

Philosophy used to be said to be the love of wisdom, and this is
true to its etymology. The idea is not as immodest as it might seem,
for any but the most idle love must seek actively to possess its
object, and the endeavour has, of course, to be on the basis of an
acknowledgement that the object is not already possessed to start
with. An open-minded humility, therefore, is the first requisite for
the study of philosophy.

But what is wisdom? We may start with the remark often made
that wisdom is not identical with knowledge. Heraclitus, one of the
early Greek philosophers, is credited with the comment that the
learning of many things does not suffice of itself to make a man
wise, else certain of his predecessors would have been wise. It is
intriguing to note that one of these berated predecessors, mentioned by name, is Pythagoras, immortalised as the inventor of
Pythagoras' Theorem. Heraclitus denies wisdom to Pythagoras
even though he expressly concedes that the latter practised scientific inquiry beyond all other men. In our own traditional homes if
book learning should incline a man to be too pretentious, he would

be promptly reminded of the distinction between knowledge and wisdom.

Not only will the acquisition of knowledge not automatically make a man particularly wise; it will not even make him an intellectual, for the true intellectual is not just one whose mind has become a store house of facts. The intellectual is one who, through education, has developed the cast of mind that is capable of processing facts and extracting their significance *for human life*, and whose participation in the affairs of society is thoroughly imbued with the desire to bring his intellect to bear upon human problems, so as to liberalise and humanise and, in a word, enrich life.

However, when it is said that wisdom is not the same thing as knowledge, it ought to be remembered that a man cannot become wise on an unfurnished mind either. Consider what sort of man the wise man is conceived to be in a traditional society.[1] He must be a man deeply learned in the traditions and usages of his society, a man of ripe judgment matured in careful reflection and enlarged by keen observation. He must be steeped not only in the values and ideals of his society but also in the general principles underlying them. If one wants to understand a traditional society, there are, of course, a few ways of going about it, but one of the most rewarding ways must be to go to their sages for they can inform not only about norms but also about the reasons behind them. Again, when there is a personal misunderstanding between a man and his neighbour, it is to the wise man that they would voluntarily appeal. Why? Because they can expect impartial judgment from a man who knows the relevant customs, appreciates the importance of general rules and is capable of a disciplined survey of facts. The application of general rules to the solution of inter-personal problems can never be carried out mechanically; and this is why knowledge of rules without insight into their supporting reasons is not good enough. Nevertheless, it should be obvious that knowledge is indispensable to wisdom. Adapting a Platonic phrase, one might even say that wisdom is nothing but humanly oriented knowledge *with an account*. Correspondingly, the wise man is one who is skilled in turning this kind of knowledge to serve the purposes of human relations.

[1] By *traditional society* I mean a society in which the march of industrialisation has not appreciably eclipsed the authority of pre-industrial tradition in the spheres of belief and general outlook.

This suggests a way of characterising the relation between wisdom and intellectuality. The intellectual has knowledge and appreciates its relevance to the broader needs of society, but he does not necessarily have the skill of ordering personal relations harmoniously. Conversely, the wise man is a master of personal relations, but not for that reason a savant of any particular branch of knowledge. Both, however, have this in common that their particular excellences consist in a certain way of going beyond mere knowledge of facts. How does the philosopher fit in this scheme of relations? It is exactly here, in the transcending of brute fact, that the philosopher comes in. Take, for example, the wise man of the tribe. We have said that he is able to go behind the customs of his people to expound the reasons for them. The philosopher, for his part, seeks to understand and evaluate the principles underlying the reasons for the arrangements of men. Both the philosopher and the wise man are concerned with fact and practice, but the philosopher in his more theoretical moments operates at a more rarefied level. Naturally, his cogitations will be more abstract. However, there is nothing that sharply demarcates the philosopher from any other interpreter of life – a fact which accounts for the broadness of applicability of the word 'philosophy'. It is idiomatic to describe the reason behind any action as the *philosophy* behind it, and any fairly comprehensive collection of practical maxims, far down the scale of abstraction, is legitimately entitled a *philosophy*.

Although a philosopher is not necessarily a wise man, enough has already been said to disclose a real similarity in the concerns of the philosopher and the wise man. Wisdom in the common imagination is too often narrowly identified with the ability to succeed in day-to-day family, social and business life, and the philosopher is frequently teased with alleged incompetence in the down-to-earth affairs of this world. This attitude to philosophy is a very old one. The following anecdote, apocryphal or not, illustrates its longevity, but also its falsity. The ancient Greek sage, Thales, often considered the father of Western philosophy, is reported to have been reproached with the supposed uselessness of philosophy. Wishing to confound the scoffers, he took a little time from philosophic meditation to make a quick fortune in skilful speculation in olive presses. He anticipated in advance of all others a bumper olive harvest in a forthcoming winter and hired all available olive presses at very low rates. When the time came and olive presses were in great demand he was able to hire them out again, charging at will. 'Thus,' comments Aristotle, 'he showed the world that philosophers can easily be rich, if they like, but their ambition is of another sort' (Aristotle, *Politics*, 1259²).

Any impression engendered by these remarks that philosophers are a breed apart must be combated at once. Not everybody need become a *professional* philosopher, but, to a certain degree, everybody is a philosopher. In truth, no one has a choice whether to have some philosophy or none at all. In this connection we may recall the words of Jesus Christ: 'Man,' he said, 'shall not live by bread alone, but by the word of God.'

But if man shall not live without the word of God, even less shall he live without a philosophy; for how, otherwise, shall he attain the very conception of God? How shall he attain a conception of value – of what to live for? How, in short, shall he attain a general and integrated outlook upon the world in which he lives? Clearly, the choice is not between having and not having a philosophy but rather between having one that is consciously fashioned or an inherited and largely unexamined one.

In our traditional societies philosophy tends to be of the inherited type. In such societies philosophy is, in the main, an accumulation of the thoughts of the folk mind. The philosopher, that is to say the sage of the tribe, is fairly rigidly tied to tradition. There are bound, of course, to be a number of adventurous minds remarkable in their ability to think *critically* about the foundations of the folk mentality and make original contributions to the fund of public philosophy.² But the lack of writings robs many traditional societies of the richness in depth, rigour and variety which a continual dialectic of individual efforts preserved in script can yield. This is not to belittle traditional philosophy. In any society, 'developed' or 'developing', there is a subtle interaction between the intellectual productions of even the boldest minds and their background of immanent public thought. Bertrand Russell was surely right when in the preface to his *History of Western Philosophy* (Allen and Unwin, London, new edition, 1961) he deprecated the practice of depicting philosophers as if their thinking occurred in a vacuum. He tried, rightly, in that book 'to exhibit each

---

² See the remark in chapter 3, p. 37.

philosopher, as far as truth permits, as an outcome of his *milieu*, a man in whom were crystallised and concentrated thoughts and feelings which in a vague and diffused form, were common to the community of which he was a part'.

It is a fact, nevertheless, that as the impact of science becomes more and more felt in various areas of life, the need becomes felt among elements of the educated population of a traditional society for a new philosophy, a philosophy new not in basic intent but in the manner of its pursuit. Philosophy becomes more self-conscious because more individualised, more urgent because now more of a personal responsibility, more ramifying because now based on a more sophisticated background of knowledge, and more universalist because now sensitive not only to the ideas of one's own society but also to ideas and systems from other cultures.[3]

As science advances and achieves ever more spectacular results, it is natural that men should be increasingly inquisitive about the nature of human knowledge. Science itself is, strictly, not so much a body of hardened knowledge as an organised and co-operative effort to carry on inquiry by a certain method – the method of hypothesis, experiment and observation. Scientific method has in practice attained a high degree of complexity but, in bare essentials, it is characterisable as follows. The mind is challenged by a problem and casts about for a solution. Soon an idea emerges as a possible solution. However plausible it may be, it is not immediately asserted as true. It is merely entertained as a *hypothesis*, a tentative proposal, to be put to the test. But before that, its significance has to be explored, that is, its logical implications have to be unravelled in conjunction with other known facts. This is the stage of elaboration of the hypothesis, which often requires techniques of deduction available only in quite advanced mathematics. The result, however, is always of the logical form of an implication: 'If the hypothesis is true then such and such other things should be the case.' The stage is then set for empirical confirmation or disconfirmation. In the more elementary phases of the taxonomical sciences straightforward observation often suffices, but in methodologically complicated sciences such as physics very technical experiments may often be called for. If results turn out not to be in agreement with the implications of the hypothesis, it is said to be falsified. It

[3] For more discussion of these matters see chapter 2.

is, accordingly, either abandoned or modified. In the latter case there is a repeat of the process. On the other hand, if results prove to conform with the elaborated hypothesis, it is said to be confirmed. But even so, it is not claimed to be verified as an absolute truth. Usually, it is only said to be confirmed with a certain degree of probability. It is implicit in scientific practice that no hypothesis can ever be accounted so well-established as to be exempt from the possibility of revision. Of course, the best attested hypotheses hold the field. Regarded as laws, they constitute the main corpus of scientific knowledge at any point in time. (See, for example, Carl G. Hempel, *Philosophy of Natural Science*, Prentice-Hall, Inc., Englewood Cliffs, NJ, 1966, at least the first three chapters.)

To repeat, this account of scientific method is highly simplified; but there is a certain advantage in this. The simplicity enables us to extend the epithet 'scientific' to all rational inquiry whether in daily life or in the remoter reaches of academic research. Indeed, inasmuch as the virtues of the scientific approach to problems are of great relevance to many of the problems of life, it would be a mistake to tie the general conception of scientific method too closely to the characteristics of the more specialised forms of scientific investigation.

Notice in the above description of scientific method the occurrence of the following notions among others: truth, significance, logical implication, deduction, verification, confirmation, assertion, law, fact, observation, knowledge, and probability. Complacent common sense might take these concepts for granted, but a few preliminary questions would quickly reveal perplexities.

II. LOGIC

Let us take logical implication and deduction. The systematic investigation of these and allied concepts belong to logic, the most successful branch of philosophy, a branch so successful in modern times that, mindful that philosophy has been a veritable battle-field of endless controversies – the phrase is an adaptation of Kant's[4]

---

[4] It should be pointed out, however, that the phrase alluded to was used by Kant only in preliminary soul-searchings to the vast enterprise of the *Critique of Pure Reason*. Actually, the ambition of the *Critique* was to put Metaphysics on the 'sure

description of metaphysics – some have sought to set it up as an independent discipline. In fact, however, the methods of logic are extremely well adapted to illustrating the characteristics of philosophical investigation – its heightened generality, its quest for systematic unity and coherence, its inevitable technicalities but, notwithstanding this, its practical motivation.

In all domains of human thought and communication where issues of truth and falsity are germane, problems of validity arise sooner or later. The truth of a statement relating to the external world depends not – never! – on the special state of the author of the statement, but on its grounds. To give the grounds of a statement involves giving an argument having that statement as its conclusion. An argument is a group of statements one of which, the conclusion, is claimed to follow logically from the rest, known as the premises. In standard form the premises come first and the conclusion last. The grounding is satisfactory if and only if the premises are acceptable and the argument is valid. This last remark implies that an exercise in grounding a statement might fail to be satisfactory even though it incorporated true premises and a true conclusion. The point is easily illustrated: 'All Ghanaians are Africans;[5] all Ashantis are Africans; therefore all Ashantis are Ghanaians' satisfies the description. Accordingly, in seeking for a justification, a judicious man asks to be furnished not just with any series of true propositions but only with true propositions linked with the conclusion by valid reasoning. Obviously, then, validity is a matter of the utmost practical moment.

Students of various disciplines concern themselves with the evaluation of particular types of argument; the general nature of validity and its principles are matters that are left to the logician. However, there is no suggestion that only logicians understand the meaning of validity. On the contrary, anyone who can react disapprovingly to an argument like 'All men are mortal, all dogs are mortal, therefore all dogs are men', must be credited with some

---

path of science'. Whether he succeeded or not is a question that the reader is invited to investigate himself – a course of action upon which he should, however, not embark without due preparation. The most widely used translation of the *Critique* is by Norman Kemp Smith, first published in 1929 by Macmillan and Co., London.

[5] One means here natural Ghanaians, of course. The point here is that all the premises are true and the conclusion is true but the conclusion does not follow.

conception of validity, a consideration which gives a certain pointedness to Locke's quip that God did not make man barely a biped and leave it to Aristotle (the father of the Western tradition in logic) to make him rational.

Nevertheless, it is one thing to have an intuitive understanding of a concept and quite another thing to have the ability to give a rigorous exposition of it. It is unfortunately clear that God has left it to Aristotle and others to undertake the latter task for the generality of mankind as far as the concept of validity is concerned. Suppose we ask any average man, intelligent but untouched by logic as an academic discipline, why he believes that the first example given above is invalid; he might point out that if the argument of that example were valid, then we might just as well accept the second example too as valid. Here he would be resorting by instinct, as it were, to a very legitimate form of argument, known technically as refutation by logical analogy. But if he were to be pressed to discuss the principle underlying this procedure, he would very probably come to a stand-still.

The basis of refutation by logical analogy is to be found in the fact that validity is formal. In other words, if an argument is valid, then any other argument which has the same form must be valid also. It is a simple matter to exhibit the identity of form in the two illustrative arguments given above. Consider the following argument form, which is simply an arrangement of letters such that 'M', 'P', 'S', are *term* variables (i.e. letters standing indifferently for the subjects or predicates of judgments) and 'a' stands for a logical connective, in this case 'All ... are ...', which joins the predicates to the subjects:

$$S \text{ a } M$$
$$P \text{ a } M$$
$$\therefore P \text{ a } S$$

Now, if we substitute 'Ghanaians' for 'S', 'Africans' for 'M', and 'Ashantis' for 'P', we obtain the first example. Attending to the same form, put 'Men' for 'S', 'mortal' for 'M', and 'dogs' for 'P'; the result is the second example. The point, then, is that since the second example is patently, even scandalously, invalid, the first must also be invalid, even if it wears a somewhat tempting appearance.

But we still have not explained why the second example is invalid. Let us reproduce the argument here in more schematic arrangement for ease of reference:

> All men are mortal
> All dogs are mortal
> ∴ All dogs are men

From a layman's point of view the unacceptable thing about this argument is presumably that it starts from true premises and ends with a false conclusion. However, from a strictly logical point of view, this is not a general enough characterisation of the defectiveness of the argument. It does not, for instance, automatically enable us to fault the other example which starts with true premises and ends with a true conclusion. We should say rather that the trouble with the argument in question is that it has a *form* which *makes it possible* for one to start from true premises and end with a false conclusion. It is for this reason that the conclusion may be said not to follow logically from the premises. To say that a proposition follows logically from a set of others is to claim that if the latter is true, it would be logically impossible for the former to be false. This fact gives rise to a variety of equivalent definitions of validity as applied to arguments. An argument is said to be valid if and only if its premises logically imply its conclusion. We may also say that an argument is valid if and only if, if its premises are true, then its conclusion must, *as a matter of logical necessity*, be true also. Alternatively: a valid argument is one which is such that the assertion of its premises jointly with the negation of its conclusion yields a logical contradiction, i.e. a statement of, or reducible to the form '*P* and not *P*', where '*P*' is a variable for any proposition whatever. Or yet the matter may be put this way: An argument is valid if and only if the conditional statement which corresponds to it is a logical truth. By a conditional statement is meant a statement of the form 'If ... then ...' which seeks to exclude the situation in which the first component, the antecedent, is true and the second, the consequent, is false. The conditional corresponding to an argument is the result of converting its premises conjunctively into the antecedent, and its conclusion into the consequent, of a conditional statement. Thus the conditional version of the argument under scrutiny is: 'If all men are mortal and all dogs are mortal then all dogs are men.'

If we could develop a dependable method for deciding in any given case whether the conditional corresponding to an argument is logically true or not, we would thereby secure a procedure for assessing arguments which would be very much superior to the procedure of refuting an argument by logical analogy. For one thing, refutation by logical analogy is of use only when one is opposing a spurious argument. For another, the method suffers from the circumstance that its effectiveness depends upon there being agreement between the parties concerned that the analogical argument proposed as a counter case indeed has true premises and a false conclusion. Though in the present example featuring statements about men and dogs, truth-value (i.e. the truth or falsity of the statements) is easy to determine, little imagination is needed to conceive of cases in which the attempt to settle such questions might prove less convincing.

The examples studied so far belong to the field of the traditional logic of terms, also called 'syllogistic logic'. In comparison with modern systems of logic it is of a rather simple type. We can convert the syllogistic examples into arguments falling within modern propositional logic by transforming the import of the terms into propositions in a certain way. Thus the first example might become something like this – note, though, that exact correspondence is not claimed:

> If Kofi is a Ghanaian then he is an African
> If Kofi is an Ashanti then he is an African
> ∴ If Kofi is an Ashanti then he is a Ghanaian

The logical form of this argument may be depicted as follows: Let 'p' replace 'Kofi is a Ghanaian', 'q' replace 'he is an African',[6] and 'r' replace 'Kofi is an Ashanti'. Also let the symbol '$\rightarrow$' represent the logical connective 'If ... then ...' We then have:

$$p \rightarrow q$$
$$r \rightarrow q$$
$$r \rightarrow p$$

[6] Strictly the sentence is 'Kofi is an African'.

The corresponding conditional obviously is:

$$[(p \to q) \ \& \ (r \to q)] \to [r \to p]$$

The symbol '&' means 'and'. The brackets are simply punctuation marks. Incidentally, the name 'propositional logic' for the logic that treats of such formulas derives simply from the fact that the variables stand for, or range over, propositions. The beauty of this logic is that a mechanical procedure is available in it for deciding in the case of any arbitrary formula whether it is logically true or not within a finite number of steps. This, of course, secures for us a dependable method of checking the validity or invalidity of any argument whatever in the field of this logic.

Actually various such procedures, called, technically, *decision procedures*, are known in the field of propositional logic. But perhaps the most familiar of them is the method of truth tables. This method begins with precise definitions of the basic statement forms, namely, 'not-p', 'p and q', 'if p then q', 'p if and only if q' by means of tabulations of their truth values under all the possible ways of assigning the truth values *truth* and *falsity* (represented by T and F) to their variables. Using these tabular definitions, one can always compute, step by step, proceeding from the simpler to the more complex parts, the truth values of any formula, however complex, under all the possible truth value assignments to its variables. If the formula takes T in every case, it is a logical truth; if it takes at least one T and one F, it is logically contingent, and if it takes only Fs, it is a self-contradictory formula. One great advantage of the method is that it makes it almost pictorially clear that logical truths or tautologies, as they are called in this particular domain of logic, owe their truth to their form, that is, the manner in which variables and logical connectives are arranged, rather than to their content, that is, the actual sentences that might happen to occupy the places of the variables.

Given, then, the availability of the method of truth tables, the problem of the validity or invalidity of any given argument that falls within the domain of propositional logic can be solved by the following recipe: Obtain the conditional formula which corresponds to the given argument and construct a truth table for it. If it turns out to be a tautology, the argument is valid; otherwise it is invalid.

Theoretically, the method of truth tables may be applied to check any argument as to validity irrespective of its complexity. But in practice it is tedious to test arguments involving more than four variables in this way. An alternative method, namely, the method of deduction, may accordingly be resorted to. A limitation of this method, though, is this: If an argument belonging to propositional logic is valid, we can show its validity by the method of deduction, but, if it is invalid, we cannot establish the fact by this method of deduction, may accordingly be resorted to. A limitation of this method, though, is this: If an argument belonging to interest.

The idea underlying the method of deduction is that if we could specify a manageable set of logical truths or rules, acceptable as such by some sure method of computation or reflection, and if we could, further, show that every other logical truth expressible in the language of propositional logic is deducible from these, then we would be able to demonstrate the validity of any valid argument. For, if an argument is valid, its corresponding conditional is a logical truth and can therefore be deduced. Several such sets (i.e. systems of propositional logic) have, in fact, been offered in the literature of modern logic. We shall, however, not present an example here, as any moderately useful discussion is apt to become symbolic and technical.[8] Suffice it to say that the successful construction of such systems provides one of the most perfect examples of the attainment of systematic unity in the field of human knowledge.

Let us now recall that our motive for undertaking this brief account of some aspects of logic was the desire to elucidate the concepts of logical implication and deduction. Has the attempt at elucidation been successful? As in all philosophical enterprises no dogmatic answer can be given. In fact, on a little further reflection,

---

[7] Indeed, outside truth tables and other mechanical procedures in propositional logic, decision procedures are hard to come by in logic generally.

[8] An elementary exposition of logic will be found in I. M. Copi, *Introduction to Logic*, New York, Macmillan. A somewhat more advanced presentation of logic is given in *Symbolic Logic* (New York, Macmillan) by the same author. A very great number of other competent introductions to logic exist. I have given an example of a logical system together with a brief development in my 'On the Formal Character of Logic Part I', in *Ghana Social Science Journal*, vol. 3, no. 1, May 1976.

difficulties emerge. So far, we have conceived the relation between logical implication and deduction in the following manner: A deduction is valid if and only if its premises logically imply the conclusion. And we have appeared to hold that if a conditional (interpreted after the image of a truth table) is logically true then this means that the antecedent logically implies the consequent. Consider now the following conditional: $p \rightarrow (q \rightarrow p)$. It needs only a trivial mental effort to verify by a truth table that this formula is a logical truth. We seem, then, entitled to say that:

$$p$$
$$\therefore q \rightarrow p$$

is a valid argument form. But now suppose we substitute 'Two plus two equals four' for 'p', and 'Mao Tse-tung is a Ghanaian' for 'q'. We are then committed to defending the validity of the following deduction:

> Two plus two equals four;
> therefore, if Mao Tse-tung is a Ghanaian,
> then two plus two equals four

I can imagine the general reader protesting in scandalised impatience. 'Surely this can't be a valid deduction. What has a false claim about the nationality of Mao got to do with the sum of two plus two?' Actually, the sympathies of a good number of professional philosophers are on the side of the general reader in this matter.[9] Yet arguments can be marshalled in favour of the disputed deduction which, whether ultimately correct or not, nobody has a right to dismiss hastily. Moreover, it should not be assumed that the truth about such abstract matters as the exact nature of validity need be unsurprising.

---

[9] A non-technical discussion by a very distinguished philosopher of alleged disparities between the use of 'If ... then ...' involved in the conception of validity in question and ordinary language uses are given in Strawson, *Introduction to Logical Theory*, Methuen, London, 1952, pp. 78–93. For an early but hardly supplanted defence of this kind of interpretation of 'If ... then ...' see W. E. Johnson, *Logic*, Part 1, Dover Edition, 1964, pp. 38–46 (first published 1921). For a slightly more technical discussion see my 'Material Implication and "IF ... THEN ..."', *International Logic Review*, December 1972.

III. THE THEORY OF TRUTH

The last remark ought to be borne in mind in considering philosophical elucidations generally. It must be remembered that uncriticised common sense is unlikely to represent the deepest insights in such subtle matters. In 1960, a panel of Oxford philosophers in a discussion on *truth* broadcast on the BBC disagreed sharply among themselves on the suggestion that what makes a statement such as 'The town hall is Gothic' true, if true, is the *fact* that the town hall is Gothic. An exasperated layman, commenting later on the performance of the philosophers – a curious manifestation of the British democratic spirit, by the way – deplored the fact that anybody could dispute so obvious a point. A philosopher is one who has outgrown this kind of innocence.

The question of the nature of truth is, in fact, a particularly tricky but fundamental topic in epistemology (or the theory of knowledge), the branch of philosophy which considers such notions as perception, truth, belief, opinion, observation, memory, knowledge, illusion, verification. To be sure, the philosopher panellists were not directly disputing the verbal or nominal definition of truth as 'agreement with reality, that which is ... according to the facts of the case' (*Chambers's Twentieth Century Dictionary*). Kant long ago expressed himself as follows on the question 'What is truth?':

> The nominal definition of truth, that is, the agreement of knowledge with its object, is assumed as granted; the question asked is as to what is the general and sure criterion of the truth of any and every knowledge [*Critique of Pure Reason*, Trans. N. Kemp Smith, p. 97].

Kant's own answer to this question would appear at first sight to be a rather inauspicious introduction to a discussion of the philosophical theory of truth. He said:

> [Now] a general criterion of truth must be such as would be valid in each and every instance of knowledge, however their objects may vary. It is obvious, however, that such a criterion (being general) cannot take account of the varying content of knowledge (relation to its specific object). But since truth concerns just this very content, it is quite impossible, indeed, absurd, to ask for a general test of the truth of such content. A sufficient and at the

same time general criterion of truth cannot possibly be given . . .
such a criterion would by its very nature be self-contradictory
[*ibid.*, pp. 97–8].

This passage is, however, extremely useful in showing clearly what
a philosophical theory of truth is not and cannot be. In offering a
theory of truth a philosopher is not seeking to teach fresh language
learners how to use the word 'true' in the English language (or the
corresponding word in any given language). Nor could he possibly
be proposing a 'sufficient and at the same time general criterion of
truth'. On the absurdity of such a programme Kant has most likely
said the last word. Revisiting the nominal, dictionary, definition of
truth, we may sum it up as: 'Truth is correspondence with fact.'
This is a convenient starting point for clarifying the philosophical
concern with the concept of truth. We may say that what the
philosopher does is to take this definition of truth and try to
elucidate the nature of assertion, fact and correspondence.

Probably the most widely held theory of truth among
philosophers is what is known as the *correspondence* theory. A naïve
approach to this theory might lead one to suppose that it is simply a
reaffirmation of the ordinary verbal definition. In fact, the correspondence theory of truth seeks to set up a realm of facts as an
ontological order distinct from the realm of statements and entities
such as trees and houses. According to this theory, there are facts
which mirror the import of those statements that are true. A
statement may be about a tree, but the fact which makes it true
would not itself be a tree. Let the statement be: 'The tree is tall.'
Then the fact which makes it true, if it is true, is the *state of affairs*
that the tree is tall. The state of affairs in this case is not the tall tree
but an apparently complex entity which contains elements corresponding to the tree, the tallness and the 'is' which subsists between
the two. The statement is true if it agrees with this complex entity
point for point.

The fundamental cleavage in the theory of truth is between those
who interpret fact in this ontological manner and those who give it a
logical interpretation. To give something *ontological*[10] status is to

---

[10] There is a somewhat old fashioned, though not for that reason pointless,
classification of philosophical subjects according to which metaphysics has two
divisions, namely ontology, which deals with the types of existence, and epistemology, which deals with the conditions of knowledge.

bestow on it a nature and type of existence. Those who oppose the ontological interpretation of the distinction between a statement and a fact maintain that a fact is simply a statement which stands in a certain relation to certain other statements. This is why their standpoint with regard to the nature of facts may be said to be of a logical type, using the word 'logical' in a broad sense. There is here a saving in the number of types of entity admitted into one's world view. The correspondence theorists admit into their world such things as trees and statements about them and facts *over and above* both; their opponents admit that there are facts but not *over and above* the other categories of being. Not, of course, that ontological economy is necessarily a virtue.

An almost picturesque illustration of our point about the purport of the correspondence theory is provided by a version of the theory which Bertrand Russell propounded at an early stage in his philosophical odyssey. In *Philosophical Essays* (Allen and Unwin, London, first published 1910, revised edition 1966), Russell said: 'We feel that when we judge truly some entity "corresponding" in some way to our judgment is to be found outside our judgment, while when we judge falsely there is no such corresponding entity' (p. 152). And then elaborating, he went on:

> When we judge that Charles I died on the scaffold, we have before us, [not one object, but] several objects, namely, Charles I and dying and the scaffold. Similarly when we judge that Charles I died in his bed, we have before us the objects Charles I, dying, and his bed ... Thus in this view judgment is a relation of the mind to several other terms: when these other terms have *inter se* a 'corresponding' relation, the judgment is true; when not, it is false [p. 153].

(It should be noted that the terms of the relation here are objects, not words.)

Russell later came to abandon the theory of judgment advanced in the passage just quoted but he held fast to the basic thought that truth consists in a certain relation between statements and facts as extra-linguistic entities. Thus in *My Philosophical Development*, pp. 188–9 (Allen and Unwin, London, 1959) he still quoted with undisguised satisfaction the definition of truth which he stated in

Human Knowledge: Its Scope and Limits, p. 170 (Allen and Unwin, 1948) as:

> Every belief which is not merely an impulse to action is in the nature of a picture, combined with a yes-feeling or a no-feeling; in the case of a yes-feeling it is 'true' if there is a fact having to the picture the kind of similarity that a prototype has to an image; in the case of a no-feeling it is 'true' if there is no such fact. A belief which is not true is called false.

Not many philosophers who support the correspondence view of truth find such metaphysical literalness to their taste. Accordingly, the ontological status of facts comes out in many statements of the theory only indirectly. A celebrated case is J. L. Austin's definition:

> A statement is said to be true when the historic state of affairs to which it is correlated by the demonstrative conventions (the one to which it 'refers') is of a type with which the sentence used in making it is correlated by the descriptive conventions ['Truth', in *Proceedings of the Aristotelian Society, Supplementary Volume XXIV* (1950)].

Consider now a statement such as 'Some men are infallible'. Though it is not clear what Austin could possibly mean by the descriptive and demonstrative conventions relating to this kind of statement, one thing is clear: We are invited to imagine as the reference of such statements a realm of 'states of affairs' distinct from men and their statements. To repeat: when certain philosophers reject the correspondence theory it is not the idea of *fact* that they oppose but its metaphysical transcendence which is explicit in Russell's formulation and implicit in the verbal sophistication of Austin.

There are, in fact, several difficulties in the correspondence theory. First of all, there is the problem of how a statement *as a whole* can be said to refer at all. A statement always contains a finite verb which gives it its assertive character. How can this *assertive* factor have a correlate 'outside' the statement? Let us return to our example: 'The tree is tall.' It is agreed on all hands that if this statement is true, a certain particular use of the term 'the tall tree' will have a reference. But here it is not the statement as a whole that refers but what we might call its *ideational* content, namely, the idea: 'tall tree'. Further, the referent is not a fact but a tall tree. Indeed, the whole message of the assertion, 'the tree is tall', is that the ideational content has a reference. Obviously making the referential claim is the function of the assertive element. To say that the claim that a certain conceptual complex has a reference itself has a reference is, surely, to compromise plausibility. If one should now comment: 'But when the tree is, in fact, tall, isn't there a fact that the tree is tall?' The answer is: 'Exactly so. The fact in question is *that* the tree is tall, i.e. *that* the ideational content has a reference.' If the one who asserts that *the claim that the tree is tall* is a fact is talking responsibly, then the presumption is that he has made the necessary inspection. All that we have here, then, is the coincidence of the propositional results of two confrontations with the environment. On this showing, a fact is nothing but a confirmed claim. Any feeling that in rejecting the transcendent conception of facts one is cutting off the anchorage in *reality* can thus be dispelled at once: The claim which is said to be confirmed in the given case is confirmed only by an observation of a tree – a part of the furniture of the real world.

There is a further difficulty in the notion of the reference of a statement, an assertion or a belief. It seems to be suggested in the correspondence theory that in raising the question of truth one starts with a belief antecedently formed and then wonders whether this belief 'refers' or 'corresponds' to a fact. But this is quite clearly putting the cart before the horse, methodologically speaking. A rational man does not first form a belief and then ask for the evidence in support of it. On the contrary, in facing a problem one starts with an idea, a tentative proposal, as is the practice in all scientifically accredited inquiry (on which see the account of scientific method given earlier). Truth-claims enter into the picture only at the close of inquiry; they indicate the attainment of warranted judgment. It is therefore absurd, *given an identical point of view*,[11] to ask 'When is a belief true?' And to answer 'When it

---

[11] One can, of course, wonder whether a belief held from another point of view is true, but this is *ipso facto* to convert the belief into a problem. Also a man may consider whether an old belief of his is true, but here again this means suspending that belief, at least, hypothetically. The concept of point of view introduced here is crucial in the analysis of truth. A weakness of Dewey's theory of truth is a failure to treat of the importance of point of view. See chapter 8 on the connection between the

corresponds to fact' is to give an absurd answer to an absurd question. The proper question is: 'When is an "idea" true?', and the answer implicit in these reflections is 'When it becomes the ideational content of a warranted judgment'. In basic essentials this view is in accord with John Dewey's 'instrumentalist' or 'pragmatist' conception of truth as 'warranted assertibility'.

There is yet another difficulty in the correspondence theory of truth. Suppose that, against all good sense, a man were to embrace a proposition and only afterwards try to see whether it 'corresponds' to fact. How is he to set about it? Should he try to find reasons to justify or evidence to support the proposition? But in this way he can only arrive at a warranted assertion, if he is successful. And yet what we are looking for is a fact over and above a warranted judgment which is to confer truth on the assertion. Clearly, as far as ordinary inquiry is concerned, there is nothing further to do after reaching a fully grounded belief. To compare a warranted assertion with a fact is thus a totally mysterious activity.

In discussions of the philosophical theory of truth two alternatives to the correspondence theory are usually given, namely, the *pragmatist* and *coherence* theories of truth. The first is frequently described as the theory which defines truth as *useful* belief. There is a certain justification for this characterisation in *Pragmatism* (Meridian Books, New York, 1955, originally published in 1907), the work in which William James first popularised the pragmatic theory of truth. James' was a restless intellect in whom basic philosophical insight was combined with a literary flair for exhilarating prose. But his passionate and enthusiastic exposition of the pragmatic theory was not always sufficiently rigorous. Consequently he was capable of certain lapses which might even be described as unpragmatic. The most serious error of this sort was his failure to distinguish between belief and idea. This important distinction was made by Dewey, who gave a more philosophically

---

notions of truth and point of view. There is in the paragraph above a close interplay between what might be called the primary concept of truth and the comparative one. When we consider the question of the truth of a belief advanced from a different point of view we are employing the comparative concept of truth. This is the concept of truth normally operative in ordinary discourse. The truth of an 'idea' is a rather technical concept. It corresponds to the truth value *truth* of truth functional logic. However, it is the base of the comparative concept of truth. See chapter 8, pp. 120–1.

rigorous formulation of the pragmatic theory in various of his numerous works. James was apt to define truth indifferently as the *idea* or *belief* that has satisfactory consequences. And this way of speaking laid him open to the charge that pragmatism is a licence for believing whatever one finds pleasing. Dewey pointed out in his review of James' *Pragmatism* (included in *Essays in Experimental Logic*, Dover, originally published by University of Chicago Press, 1916) that the consequences of a belief were of no purely epistemological interest. According to Dewey what is relevant and crucial to the problem of defining truth is the role of 'ideas' in the construction of warranted judgment. An *idea*, that is, a hypothetical proposal, is true if it leads to the satisfactory solution of a problem. Of course, having said this the next problem is: What is the nature of satisfactory problem solving? To this question Dewey devoted one of his most substantial works, *Logic: The Theory of Inquiry*[12] (Holt, Rinehart and Winston, 1938); indeed, some would say that he devoted his whole life-work to this problem.

I come now to the coherence theory of truth. A pithy formulation of this theory is given in the maxim: Truth is coherence. Truth, according to this view, lies not in any relation between a statement and an independent realm of being but in its harmonious fit with the received *system* of knowledge. This fit, or coherence, is not easy to define. It is not mere logical consistency. If it were, the theory would be unthinkably absurd, for any whimsical proposition will be consistent with some potentially infinite set of propositions. Consistency is presupposed, of course, but something more is involved.

What this something else is will be appreciated if we develop the

[12] The reader new to Dewey is, however, not advised to tackle the *Logic* at once. The style of this work is loaded with his special terminology. More lively accounts of his general approach to the problem of truth may be found in ch. vi of his *Reconstruction in Philosophy* (Bacon Press, 1957, original edition, 1920) and in 'The Development of American Pragmatism' included in his *Philosophy and Civilization*, 1931 (Capricorn Books edition, 1963). An earlier, more vigorous, even entertaining, discussion of truth is to be found in his 'A Short Catechism Concerning Truth' written in 1909 and included in his *The Influence of Darwin on Philosophy and Other Essays in Contemporary Thought* (1910; Indiana University Press, 1965). While on bibliography, it may be mentioned that the origin of pragmatism is attributed by William James to C. S. Peirce whose 'How to Make our Ideas Clear' is frequently cited in this connection. This paper is included in, for example, *Values in A Universe of Chance*, ed. by P. P. Wiener, Double Anchor Books, 1958. In the matter of the definition of truth, however, Peirce's pragmatism did not remain very stable.

exposition in relation to an example. Suppose a staid acquaintance should break in suddenly (at Legon) with the following announcement: 'Have you heard? London is burning. The whole city is on fire. I heard it on the BBC news at 5.00 p.m.' I dare say that one's curiosity would be immediately aroused. Presumably if one trusts the acquaintance, one would more or less take the message as true. Hearing a later BBC broadcast oneself would certainly confirm it decisively. Now, as regards purely logical consistency, both the supposition that London is burning and its negation would 'cohere' with one's actual state of knowledge. Yet, surely, it just would not fit into the scheme of things, as far as one can conceive it, for the BBC to announce such a calamity unless it were so. The BBC has a solid reputation for not relaying simple and straightforward lies, and it is hard to imagine what could possibly motivate such a lie. Of course, an unusually fastidious person could remain sceptical. 'Could not Maoists be using BBC wavelengths to strike panic into the capitalist world?' And so they could, but suppose hastily evacuated relatives from London were to give vivid eye-witness accounts of the disaster. Then it would be carrying incredulity beyond *reason* not to accept the story as true.

In this account we have what one might call three degrees of coherence. First, our knowledge of the acquaintance predisposes us to take his word seriously, i.e. to credit his report that the BBC has actually carried such news. Not to take the report seriously would jar with our whole appraisal of him. Secondly, we have the BBC announcement itself to consider. It would conflict with our outlook extensively to treat the BBC lightly in this matter. Our friend may, for once, be playing a joke on me, but what about the BBC itself? When we come to the third stage, with corroborating eye-witness accounts, one might almost say it is impossible not to believe the story. To entertain any doubts at this stage would imply abandoning the received procedure for investigating matters of this sort; it would be being *unreasonable* to the third degree.

This last reflection suggests that coherence is nothing but reasonableness. How do we judge the reasonableness of a suggestion? The answer is that a suggestion is reasonable to the degree to which it can be supported by rational investigation. Thus to say of a claim that it *coheres* with our system of knowledge is to say that it is warrantably assertible. What the new proposition has in common with our antecedent 'knowledge' is substantiation by the method of rational investigation. Indeed, it is this method which gives *system* to the bits of information and deductions which we call our *knowledge*. Moreover, it is only in virtue of this consideration that we can explain how a new development may lead to large-scale revision of previously accepted conceptions. Various bits of putative knowledge may fall, but the method itself stands. For this reason, the coherence theory is strictly to be understood as saying, not that truth is what coheres with our knowledge – which would be circular in any case, since knowledge involves truth – but rather that which coheres with our *system* of beliefs.

In the light of this discussion it is easy to see what Otto Neurath, one of the principal modern proponents of the coherence theory, is driving at when he says:

It is always science as a system of statements which is at issue. *Statements are compared with statements*, not with 'experiences', 'the world' or anything else ... Each new statement is compared with the totality of existing statements previously co-ordinated. To say that a statement is correct, therefore, means that it can be incorporated in this totality. What cannot be incorporated is rejected as incorrect. The alternative to rejection of the new statement is, in general, one accepted only with great reluctance: the whole previous system of statements can be modified up to the point where it becomes possible to incorporate the new statement ['Sociology and Physicalism', included in A. J. Ayer (ed.), *Logical Positivism*, The Free Press, Glencoe, 1959, p. 291].

Hitherto it has been generally supposed that there is a fundamental difference between the coherence theory of truth and the pragmatic one. This discussion shows that they are, at bottom, one, at least as far as the Deweyan version of pragmatism is concerned.[13]

[13] This account of the coherence theory applies more immediately to the scientifically oriented version of it. An exposition of this type of coherence theory will be found in Carl G. Hempel, 'On the Logical Positivists' Theory of Truth' in *Analysis*, vol. II, no. 4 (1935). The metaphysical version of the coherence theory is elaborately expounded in *The Nature of Truth* by H. H. Joachim (The Clarendon Press, 1906), *Essays on Truth and Reality* by F. H. Bradley (The Clarendon Press, 1914), and more recently in *The Nature of Thought*, vol. II (The Macmillan Co., 1940). To my mind the metaphysical theory of coherence is a layer of doctrine superimposed on coherence as a cognitive concept. This comes out clearest in ch. VII of Bradley's essays on *Truth and Reality* entitled 'On Truth and Coherence' which, but for a few remarks on an apparently wide-ranging metaphysical existent called the Absolute

IV. PHILOSOPHICAL METHODS

On a review of the foregoing discussion of the concept of truth, it will be seen that we have been trying to establish a conceptual relationship between truth, on the one hand, and such other concepts as fact, statement, belief, reason, reality, knowledge, inquiry, on the other. We have been trying to construct an equation between truth and a certain arrangement of these other concepts in such a way as to throw light on that important aspect of the interaction of human beings with their own kind and with their environment called *cognition*. To fashion out an equation of this sort is what is called philosophical analysis; for this equating of one concept with a certain configuration of a number of others may be described somewhat figuratively as a breaking down of the original concept into its component parts. Accordingly, many philosophers have said that the method of philosophy is the method of logical or, more appropriately, conceptual, analysis.

In view of the impression which apparently has a hold on some laymen that analytical philosophising is a sort of glorified verbal hair-splitting, it is important to repeat emphatically that conceptual analysis is not concerned with expounding the verbal meaning of words. Even at the height, two decades ago or so, of the conversational tendency in the style of British philosophy that was known as linguistic philosophy, it was never the intention of philosophical analysis to give instruction in the ordinary use of words. On the contrary, more than average linguistic competence was usually needed for the understanding of this kind of philosophy. The motivation was generally to make ordinary usage a basis for clarifying the relations of certain fundamental concepts. There are, of course, various ways of relying on ordinary usage in philosophy, but there is no way of not relying on it at all.

It is worth remarking also that analysis is not the only method open to philosophy, although many modern philosophers appear to take the contrary for granted. Analysis takes its material (i.e. the concepts to be analysed) as antecedently ready made. This is inevitable in the nature of things. But there is no reason why the philosopher should remain professionally incurious about the origin of concepts. Historically the problem of origination has led

---

and a certain disparity in terminology, is indistinguishable in content from Neurath's exposition.

to two highly dissimilar modes of philosophising – to what is known as the *transcendental* method of Kant, and the *genetic* method of John Dewey. A transcendental inquiry is a search into the structure and capacities of the human mind itself for the basis of certain very fundamental concepts such as space, time, object, cause, and the modes of knowledge immediately associated with them. Consider, for example, a geometrical proposition such as 'Two straight lines cannot enclose a figure'. Kant pointed out that the truth of such a proposition is not derivable from experience, that is, observation through the senses. Pairs of straight lines, both actual and possible, are infinitely numerous, and no one can survey them all. Were our knowledge of such a truth based on observation, we would only be entitled to claim a comparative, rather than an absolute, certainty. Yet, insisted Kant, mathematical propositions are certain and without qualification. Therefore, he concluded, there must be a way of knowing which is independent of experience, and this he called the *a priori* mode of knowing.

There is a type of *a priori* knowledge which does not, at any rate as far as Kant is concerned, precipitate any epistemological crisis. For example, we know that all sisters are female. Any attempt to verify this proposition empirically would, presumably, involve rather delicate observations; but the effort would be totally pointless because any supposed sister who turned out not to be female would be said not to be a sister. The reason is plain: a sister may be defined as a female sibling. Hence a sister who was not female would be a female sibling who was not female – a manifest contradiction. Kant entitled a proposition of this sort, whose negation leads to a contradiction, 'analytic'. A proposition which is not analytic he called 'synthetic'.[14] Now, it is immediately obvious that all analytic propositions are knowable *a priori*. The question is whether all *a priori* propositions are analytic. An affirmative answer is plausible and highly tempting, and many philosophers have proposed it;[15] but Kant stoutly maintained a negative answer. It

[14] Kant's discussion of the analytic/synthetic and *a priori/a posteriori* distinctions is in the introduction to the *Critique of Pure Reason*. This portion of the work is comparatively easy reading. (Incidentally, the opposite of *a priori* is *a posteriori*, i.e. that which is based on sense experience, so that *empirical* and *a posteriori* are synonymous.)

[15] The affirmative answer is, in fact, the cornerstone of the brand of philosophy known as logical positivism.

was this negative answer that set him on the path of transcendental inquiries.

To say that not all *a priori* truths are analytic implies that there are synthetic *a priori* truths. How can we explain the possibility of this species of knowledge? Returning to our example, how is it possible for us to know with absolute certainty that two straight lines cannot enclose a figure, when this knowledge is (according to Kant) not the result of observation or of conceptual analysis? Kant's answer is that it is impossible to explain the possibility of this kind of knowledge except on the supposition that it arises from the basic structure and functioning of the human mind itself. The first half of the *Critique of Pure Reason* is devoted to explaining in great detail the manner in which the fundamental organisation of the human mind makes synthetic *a priori* knowledge possible in mathematics and natural science. This might sound like armchair psychology, but the matter is somewhat more complicated than that. Psychology studies the facts of observable mental life or, if you like, behaviour. Transcendental epistemology, on the other hand, studies what is *presupposed* of the human mind by the possibility of the synthetic *a priori* mode of knowing. In other words, psychology operates on the empirical level while a transcendental investigation seeks to delve beneath experience.

Exactly this attempt to delve beneath experience is the ground of objection on the part of empirically orientated philosophers to all transcendental inquiries. The empirical approach to the problem of the origin of concepts is to attend to basic aspects of life with a view to seeing how our most fundamental concepts reflect environmentally-determined needs. Take, for example, the concept 'good reason'. Is it plausible to suppose that the genesis of this concept is completely unrelated to the exigencies of action? Human beings must act one way or another to live at all. In action we must depend on all sorts of hypotheses about means and consequences. The good hypothesis is obviously the one that will carry us safely to our destination. However, if we try to relate the concept 'good reason' – and, therefore, also truth – too immediately to the multifarious purposes of action, we fall into a gross form of wishful pragmatism. It is different if we try to relate our cognitive standards to the basic conditions of life. Such genetic inquiries are, perhaps, also 'transcendental' in their own way, in that they seek to go beyond, more specifically below, the level of full-blown human experience. But, in as much as every level of life appealed to is open to empirical examination, the non-empirical connotations traditionally associated with the word 'transcendental' are bound to cause serious misunderstandings in the context of genetic epistemology.

Comparatively speaking, the genetic method in philosophy is as yet undeveloped. There are, however, important hints in the philosophy of David Hume. This eighteenth-century British philosopher is famous for bringing out with the greatest clarity and force certain fundamental difficulties relating to the basis of inductive reasoning, though this is by no means his only claim to fame. Text-books of logic usually distinguish between two forms of reasoning, namely, the deductive and the inductive. We have already discussed the nature of deductive argument (see section on logic), and can therefore be brief. A deductive argument, it will be recalled, is one which is such that the joint assertion of the premises together with the negation of its conclusion leads to contradiction, which is a reflection of the fact that in a deductive argument the premises logically imply – or, to use a frequent synonym, entail – the conclusion. By contrast, an inductive argument is generally said to be one in which the premises give varying degrees of rational support to the conclusion without logically entailing it. For example, we can assert with a very high degree of rational confidence that all men are mortal. The argument that would be given in support of this proposition is essentially that in the past, to our knowledge, all human beings have died. Now, a determined sceptic might admit the evidence of past experience and yet deny the conclusion. Such a person could be said to be very unreasonable, blind to the evidence, but one thing we cannot say is that he would be contradicting himself. A literally immortal human being would be a rather remarkable sort of creature but, at all events, not a contradiction. We can imagine a figure like Methuselah, living on and on, with his cells perpetually renewed; and if the thought of such a human being is so clearly conceivable, then it must be consistent. As Hume puts it, 'whatever is intelligible, and can be distinctly conceived, implies no contradiction' (*Enquiries Concerning Human Understanding* and *Enquiries Concerning the Principles of Morals*, edited by L. A. Selby-Bigge, second edition 1902, Oxford at the Clarendon Press, p. 35).[16] So, then, the acceptance of the evidence for the proposition that all men are mortal together with the rejection of that proposition involves no contradiction. And yet if any inductive conclusion is strongly supported by the evidence, this is.

Proponents of the formal distinction between deduction and induction never tire of pointing out that induction is our main instrument for the acquisition of factual knowledge. If so, induction is an affair of the most overwhelming human importance. The question now is: what is the justification of this mode of reasoning? It does not seem to follow from the mere fact that something has been so in the past that it will be so in the future. This remark implies more than that inductive arguments are not deductively valid – an observation that would be utterly trivial, given the distinction between deduction and induction just explained. The point is that not every conclusion based on the assumption that the future will resemble the past, an assumption known as the principle of the uniformity of nature, is valid. In *Problems of Philosophy*[17] (Oxford Paperbacks, University Series, 1967), Russell commented on the fate of a presumably inductively orientated chicken as follows: 'The man who has fed the chicken every day throughout its life at last wrings its neck instead, showing that more refined views as to the uniformity of nature would have been useful to the chicken' (p. 35). But even for man the achievement of a 'more refined' formulation of the principle of the uniformity of nature which would enable us to discriminate between the good and the bad in the way of inductive reasoning proves to be highly problematic. What Hume did was to offer an impeccable proof that no such principle as the principle of the uniformity of nature is of any use whatsoever in the matter of justifying induction. More drastically, he showed that no inferential justification of induction is possible.

Before coming to Hume's argument it may be useful to touch briefly on the question whether induction is really a form of reasoning distinct from deduction. The orthodox view which will be

[16] The *Enquiry Concerning Human Understanding* is available in a separate edition published by the Liberal Arts Press, New York.

[17] This work, by the way, is a classic. In the space of ninety-four pages, Russell contrives to provide an instructive introduction to philosophy unsurpassed in its lucidity and elegance.

found in most text-books of logic is that induction is, in fact, a distinct form of reasoning. As we have seen, induction in this sense takes the form of inferring from the fact that observed cases have had a certain property that unobserved cases will also have the property in question. One text-book[18] exhibits the claimed contrast between the deductive and inductive forms by the following illustration.

(a) *Deductive:*   Every mammal has a heart
                All horses are mammals
     .˙. Every horse has a heart.

(b) *Inductive:*   Every horse that has ever been observed has a heart
     .˙. Every horse has a heart.

There is, however, a significant group of logicians who find this schematisation of inductive reasoning unsatisfactory. It does seem that in all cases of inductive reasoning such as the one given in the above illustration some general factual proposition can be formulated, such as in this case, 'it would not have been the case that every horse that has been observed had a heart unless every horse, by nature, has a heart', which could function as an additional premise and thus give the argument the form of a deduction. On this view, an inductive argument is, as far as form is concerned, a cryptic deduction. At best, the distinction between deduction and induction would pertain only to the character of the propositions involved. It might be said that the starting-point (and, consequently, the conclusion) of an inductive argument is always factual while the initial propositions of a deductive argument may be analytic.

This view[19] which is sometimes called the deductivist view of

[18] The illustration is taken from page 14 of *Logic* by Wesley C. Salmon (Prentice-Hall, Inc., 1963). It should be mentioned that Salmon's discussion here of the distinction between deduction and induction is deliberately simplified for elementary readers. A more advanced discussion is given in his *The Foundations of Scientific Inference* (University of Pittsburgh Press, 1966).

[19] Elementary presentations of the 'deductivist' view may be found in Morris R. Cohen and Ernest Nagel, *Introduction to Logic and Scientific Method*, ch. xiv, sec. 1 (Routledge & Kegan Paul, London, 1934) or more recently, David Mitchell, *An Introduction to Logic*, ch. 9 (Hutchinson University Library, London, 1962). The latter is particularly interesting. For more advanced treatments of a similar persuasion see Karl Popper, 'Philosophy of Science: A Personal Report' in *British Philosophy in the Mid-century*, ed. C. A. Mace (Allen and Unwin, London, first edition

induction is probably right to a very large extent, but it makes no difference to the problem of induction, for one still has to give an account of how the general factual assumptions which emerge as suppressed premises are to be justified. As Strawson justly remarks in his *Introduction to Logical Theory*[20] (p. 235), 'by regarding those general statements as suppressed premises of the arguments . . . we do not get rid of the general problem of explaining how we can reasonably draw conclusions from premises that do not entail them. We merely shift its emphasis to the narrower question: How do we establish general propositions such as these?' It is difficult to see how any attempt to provide an inferential justification for such general propositions can avoid an appeal to some form of the principle of the uniformity of nature. By an inferential justification of a proposition I mean an acceptable argument that has that proposition as its conclusion.

Hume's argument against the possibility of any such justification of induction is devastatingly simple. In a somewhat modernised paraphrase the argument is this: Either such a justification starts from conceptual propositions (i.e. propositions stating relations between ideas) or it starts from some general factual proposition. In the first case, only a conceptual conclusion could conceivably be reached which, of course, is not what is wanted; in the second there is a circularity, for we were supposed to be finding the justification of all general factual assertions. (See *Enquiries*, Section IV, Part II, especially p. 35.) It is no exaggeration to say that since Hume propounded this argument, every philosopher from Kant[21] onwards who has tried to reflect seriously on the nature of factual

---

1957; the second edition does not contain Popper's paper); Morris R. Cohen, *Reason and Nature*, ch. III (Collier-Macmillan Ltd, London, 1964, first edition 1931).

[20] Strawson's chapter on induction is one of the most celebrated modern treatments of the problem of induction. In it he tried to show that the general problem of induction is the result of an inappropriate question. According to him, it is the inductive procedure itself that defines the concept of good reason. Hence it is misconceived to ask if we have a good reason for trusting in that procedure.

[21] Kant said in his *Prolegomena to any Future Metaphysics* that it was Hume's argument which awoke him from his 'dogmatic slumbers'. The *Prolegomena* is, incidentally, a fairly easy introduction to the *Critique of Pure Reason*, written in the light of the reactions of reviewers to the *Critique*. An accessible edition with an introduction by Lewis White Beck is published by The Liberal Arts Press, New York, 1951.

inference has had, one way or another, to settle accounts with Hume.

Yet, paradoxically, not enough attention has been paid to Hume's own solution to the problem which he so brilliantly disclosed as the base of factual inference. Hume stated the fundamental step underlying all factual inference by means of the following two propositions:

> *I have found that such an object has always been attended with such an effect and I forsee, other objects, which are, in appearance, similar, will be attended with similar effects* [Op. cit., p. 34, Hume's own italics].

The point he established is that there can be no rational justification for this step. But, in his solution (Section v, Part I) he pointed out that 'if the mind be not engaged by argument to take this step, it must be induced by some other principle of equal weight and authority' (p. 41). He continued: 'This principle is Custom or Habit. For wherever the repetition of any particular act or operation produces a propensity, without being impelled by any reasoning or process of the understanding, we always say that this propensity is the effect of *custom*' (p. 43). Further, 'custom, then, is the great guide of human life. It is that principle alone which renders our experience useful to us, and makes us expect, for the future, a similar train of events with those which have appeared in the past' (p. 44).

This principle of Hume's has been widely misunderstood. In the ordinary acceptation of the words, to be controlled by *habit* or *custom* alone in argument is to argue *irrationally, blindly*. Indeed reason is legitimately contrasted with custom or habit in this sense. Accordingly, Hume has been credited with the view that factual reasoning is simply a matter of habit. Thus A. E. Taylor, for example, commented: 'Belief in the truth of a scientific statement thus comes to be with [Hume] always a blind faith.'[22] This is a very

[22] A. E. Taylor, *Does God Exist?*, p. 42, n. 7 (Fontana Books, 1961, first published by Macmillan & Co. Ltd, London, 1945). Taylor is here defending religion against the criticisms of Hume, and the point is that if for Hume belief in scientific truth is nothing but blind faith, then his criticisms of religious faith as irrational is arbitrary. There are two 'mischievous' sections in the *Enquiries* (Section x: 'Of Miracles'; and Section xi: 'Of a Particular Providence and of a Future State') but Hume's fullest examination of the belief in God is contained in his *Dialogues Concerning Natural Religion*, considered by some philosophers to be the finest piece

radical misunderstanding of Hume indeed. In talking about 'custom' and 'habit', Hume is, in fact, alluding to a level of life far below the level of conscious thought and cognition. He is not speaking immediately of habits of thought or belief concerning specific matters. On the contrary, he is referring to a natural, or better, biological, principle which underlies the whole activity of inductive inference. Thus his principle does not bear on the problem of how specific factual propositions are to be validated;[23] it relates rather to the very possibility of validation. The genetic motivation of Hume's principle is made virtually explicit in a rarely discussed section of the *Enquiries* entitled 'Of the Reason of Animals'[24] where he points out that the principle of custom lies behind the basic capacity to learn from experience seen 'in all the higher, as well as the lower classes of sensitive beings' (pp. 106–7). The easy victory which critics of Hume, such as A. E. Taylor, have won over him on his doctrine of *custom* is clearly attributable to the mislocation of it in a domain for which it was never intended. Whatever the ultimate merits or demerits of Hume's doctrine of *custom* may be, it is certainly admirably suited to illustrating the genetic style of philosophising.

Another important modern philosopher whose thought had a decidedly genetic dimension was John Dewey. He saw the fundamental features of our conceptual framework as a cumulation of developments arising out of the needs of life in its 'transactions' with the environment. Thus in his *Logic* he vigorously defended

---

of philosophical writing in Western philosophy. This and other writings are selected and introduced by Richard Wollheim in *Hume on Religion* (The Fontana Library, London, 1963).

[23] As to the problem of the better conduct of factual investigations, Hume himself offered a series of very pertinent rules in his *A Treatise of Human Nature*, a work of genius started at about the age of 21 when the author was still at university, and finished before he was 25. The *Enquiries* are a more even and briefer statement of the principles first expounded in the *Treatise*. The rules mentioned are given in Book I, Part III, Section XV of the *Treatise*, under the title 'Rules by which to judge of causes and effects'. Hume believed that all factual inferences turn upon beliefs regarding cause and effect. (See e.g. *Enquiries*, Section IV, Part I, especially p. 26.) The section on 'Rules by which to judge of causes and effects' is a much neglected part of Hume's work; my attention was first called to its importance in the scheme of Humean things by Ryle.

[24] One philosopher who has long been seized of the importance of Hume's section 'Of the Reason of Animals' is Prof. A. G. N. Flew, whose *Hume's Philosophy of Belief* (Routledge and Kegan Paul, 1961) puts him in the top rank among contemporary interpreters of Hume.

what he called a 'naturalistic' theory of logic. He tried to illuminate the nature of inquiry – its structure and canons – by first investigating how 'intellectual operations are foreshadowed in behaviour of the biological kind, and the latter prepares the way for the former' without glossing over the 'extraordinary differences that mark off the activities and achievements of human beings from those of other biological forms' (p. 43).[25]

V. CONCLUDING REMARKS

The mention of the term 'naturalistic' brings us to an important type of philosophical outlook which may be regarded as the genus of which the genetic approach is a species. 'Naturalism' in philosophy is a broad rubric covering every manner of philosophising in which explanations and elucidations are developed exclusively in terms of factors relating to man and external nature. (Thus, obviously, genetic epistemology is naturalistic, though not every naturalistic theory is genetic.) The most direct antithesis to naturalism is supernaturalism, but there are a variety of shades of anti-naturalistic tendencies in all the branches of philosophy.

The contrast between naturalism and supernaturalism comes to the sharpest focus in moral philosophy or ethics. This branch of philosophy investigates the fundamental concepts and principles underlying our judgments of good and evil, right and wrong, the obligatory and the optional.[26] It is a familiar contention of popular theology that morality needs a backing in religion. This doctrine links up in moral philosophy with a rather more fundamental doctrine to the effect that the concept of goodness itself is only definable in terms of the will of God. Opposed to this is the basic naturalistic thesis that the concepts and principles of morality derive their whole meaning from the nature and needs of man as a social being. The issue thus raised is of the profoundest theoretical, as well as practical, bearing. It manifests itself on the practical plane in the opposition between those who advocate religious instruction as a necessary foundation for moral education and those

[25] See chs. II and III of *Logic: The Theory of Inquiry*. These early chapters are comparatively straightforward in style.

[26] An allied branch, aesthetics, deals with the concepts and principles underlying our judgment of the beautiful and the ugly. Both ethics and aesthetics are concerned in varying ways with the notion of value.

who insist on a secular approach to moral education, regarding religious studies as simply one among academic pursuits. This is only one example of the practical implications of ethical theory, but its importance is so obvious as to impress every reader with the practical significance of ethical investigations. On the theoretical side the affiliations of the naturalism/supernaturalism issue are legion in religious and metaphysical disputes about the essence and destiny of man and the ultimate nature of the world.

Ethics, moreover, may quite naturally be considered as a preliminary to political or, more broadly, social, philosophy, which is concerned with the fundamental problems of the social institutionalisation of the concept of the good.[27] Social philosophy is, indeed, the crown of all philosophy. But for this very reason it should not be approached in haste. The religious, moral and social areas of philosophy are the areas in philosophy which impinge most directly on feelings, emotions and aspirations; they are consequently the areas in which prejudices are most likely to impede the course of objective reflection. From a pedagogic standpoint, therefore, it is preferable to prepare the way to these studies through the mind-disciplining exercises offered by the comparatively unemotional subjects of logic and epistemology. And this accounts for the pride of place given these branches of philosophy in the present essay. There is a further reason. It is in these areas that the tools for the effective treatment of the problems of moral and social philosophy are sharpened.

And now a couple of closing remarks. First, philosophy seeks to be comprehensive and endeavours to transcend the ordinary levels of insight in both accuracy and depth. As a result it is complex and often technical in a tantalising way, because it deals in uncommon ways with ideas which are the common stock of our ordinary thought and experience. For many purposes of practical life and discourse quite fundamental concepts can serve adequately although only impressionistically apprehended. But it should be no surprise if these same concepts when rigorously analysed do not wear their simple and familiar appearance. I hope that the discus-

---

[27] A beginner of reasonable intellectual persistence can read at once G. E. Moore's *Ethics* (Oxford, 1966, first published, Home University Library, 1912). J. D. Mabbot's *The State and the Citizen* (Grey Arrow Books, 1958) offers an absolutely painless introduction to political philosophy.

sions of logic and the theory of truth that have been given will go some way not only to illustrate these features of philosophy but also to show their basic practical motivation.

This matter of practical motivation is one which ought never to be lost sight of. The beginner who is unapprised of the practical motive and therefore, ultimately, the practical relevance of philosophy may, however well intentioned initially, find, in the face of the theoretical complexities, that his sympathies incline towards the opinion of Marlowe's Dr Faustus that philosophy is difficult and obscure to no particular purpose; while the initiate, having mastered the technicalities, might possibly become so enamoured of his intellectual virtuosity as to take delight in spinning even more of them merely for their own sake.

Secondly and finally, it should be stressed, above all, that philosophy should be approached in a spirit of openness and freedom or not at all. In philosophy one should early form the habit of asking for the reasons for other people's assertions and making sure that one has reasons for one's own. In the widespread cultivation of this habit lies the hope for the improvement of human relations.

11

In defence of opinion

The thesis that truth is nothing but opinion has been much criticised. My statement of the thesis, nearly ten years ago in a paper entitled 'Truth as Opinion',[1] has received such close and careful attention from Dr Oruka[2] that I must now return to its defence.

Let me, first of all, in the briefest possible compass, attempt a sort of natural phenomenology of opinion. In a quite basic sense the holding of opinions is not an option; it is a human necessity. Indeed, I am tempted to call it an animal necessity. We must act to live at all; and we must think to act at all. Even the most rudimentary action-oriented thinking must involve or, at any rate, presuppose, taking some things to be related in one way rather than another. This taking of things to be such or not-such must, within recognisable limits, conform to reality, or we would fail to execute our simplest intention. But this still leaves great opportunities for error and confusion in large fields of thought and action. Hence the problem of truth.

Now, to take something to be so or not so with certainty is to hold an opinion on the matter in question. In this sense 'opinion' can interchange with 'belief', 'contention', 'position', 'view', 'judgment', 'assertion', etc., subject, of course, to idiomatic constraints. Doubtless, there are other senses in which 'opinion' and most of its cognates have another status, a weaker one. A matter of opinion – 'opinion' here being used in the weaker sense – is a matter with regard to which criteria are unclear or even possibly non-existent or the evidence is scanty and there is, consequently, doubt and uncertainty. For instance, is this year's Beauty Queen the most beautiful woman in the country? Well, this, as we say, is a matter of opinion.

[1] Chapter 8 above.
[2] H. Odera Oruka, 'Truth and Belief', *Universitas*, vol. 5, no. 1, November 1975.

In this sense, the proposition that two plus two equals four is not a matter of opinion. However, in the stronger sense of 'opinion', it is still an opinion; it is a taking something to be so. It is still an outcome of a mental effort, the result of the mind's activity of systematisation and validation. It is undoubtedly among the most robust of statements, but anyone impatient of the suggestion that such a proposition can be called an opinion *in any sense at all* ought to be reminded or informed, as the case may require, that, after all, it is part of an over-all system which in its deeper reaches bristles with paradoxes, uncertainties and even undecidables.

In philosophy it is often instructive to bring together what common sense has thrown apart. This is not surprising because common-sense thinking is motivated by limited tasks of understanding whereas philosophy – and this applies in varying degrees and styles to all systematic disciplines – is a search for systematic coherence. In the matter of the philosophical problem of truth the deepest problem, it seems to me, is whether the world contains cognitive beings and their thoughts and perceptions and the objects of their thoughts, plus something over and above all these which confers truth on their thoughts.[3] From the point of view of a question of this sort the difference between a factual proposition of ordinary life or of natural science and a formal proposition of logic or mathematics is of no special significance. If an opinion can ever be conceived of as a thought advanced with full assurance from some point of view, then there is nothing amiss philosophically in classing scientific and mathematical propositions alongside others as opinions. Besides, if one holds, as I do, that truth does not consist in any relation between our statements and anything outside the general context of statements, then this classification has the advantage of emphasising the human character of truth. This does not mean that we do not in our statements refer to objects and situations. On the contrary, the function of a factual statement, for instance, is to claim that a certain ideational content applies to an object or situation. Thus the 'general context of statements' is firmly in the realms of man and nature.[4]

It is a fact worthy of the greatest emphasis that we cannot choose

[3] In chapter 10 I have discussed this matter among others relating to the concept of truth in section III on 'The theory of truth', see especially pp. 154–6.

[4] On this see again chapter 10, pp. 156–8.

to hold or not hold an opinion at will. The formation of opinion is governed by rules – rules of evidence and of formal logic. A person can choose what problems or fields of inquiry he may turn his mind to, but once faced with a specific problem, he cannot decide just anyhow what conclusion to adopt. This fact is of paramount importance for my view of truth. Truth, according to that view, is nothing but opinion; but opinion is normally the outcome of rational inquiry. It was to emphasise this aspect of the matter that Dewey defined truth as *warranted* assertibility.[5] In chapter 8 I was at pains to emphasise the relevance of reason to opinion. If I may quote from that chapter, I said: '... "belief" ... – which incidentally I here use interchangeably with "opinion" – is not a matter of will but of reason. One cannot reasonably say "the evidence is in favour of proposition P but I choose to believe the opposite", or even "I do not know any reason for or against P but I choose to believe it"' (p. .117). Now, the general relations between premises and conclusions of both the deductive and inductive types are complex matters that require mental discipline to grasp. And the ways in which these are instantiated in specific subject matters are, even more evidently, matters often requiring keen observation and careful judgment. If we are rational persons we will not – we cannot – form our opinions anyhow. Confronted with a problem about any phenomenon, 'we do not shut our eyes and "assert" anything that comes into our heads. Such simplicity of approach is ... not dreamt of even in the most whimsical philosophy. We undertake an inquiry, investigation, or research' (p. 119). Inquiry, in the standard sense, is a process involving the use of the combined resources of observation, logic and imagination. We are not born into the world ready-made masters of the art of inquiry, of the art, that is to say, of arriving at opinions. Hence the necessity for education – education in logic, formal and informal (academically or through daily experience) and in such subject matter as our circumstances may require or permit. It is the insistence on the need for belief to be in accordance with the canons of rational investigation which distinguishes my view from relativism. Truth is not relative to point of view. It *is*, in one sense, a point of view. But it is a point of view born out of rational inquiry, and the canons of rational inquiry

[5] See chapter 10, pp. 158–9 for some discussion of Dewey's theory of truth and of the pragmatic theory in general.

have a universal human application. (See, further, pp. 216–23 below.)

Unfortunately, although a rational animal, beyond the most basic levels of thought man is nevertheless only sporadically rational. In various spheres of thought and action, men will throw rationality to the winds and revel in wishful thinking, believing things as they please. All men of good sense agree in deploring such conduct. Moreover, irrationality is not consciously avowable. A man pushing a doctrinaire line does not in the standard case say 'I know that the policy I am pursuing is not reasonable but I don't care.' What usually happens is that his sensitivity to observation and reasoning is dulled by emotion; his perception is distorted and consequently he honestly regards his line as the best. This demands an intellectual modesty from all theorists of truth. Our own minds are, in principle, as subject to this as the minds of others. So, just as we offer our firm and honest opinions as truths, so may others offer theirs as truths, however stupid we may think them to be. This is almost banal; but I insist that it has a consequence of theoretical importance, which is that in describing others as doctrinaire, dogmatic, unreasonable, wrong-headed, etc., we are not standing on any rock of Eternal Truth but on the unsteady platform of our own opinions; we are purely and simply expressing in various shapes and forms our disagreement with them. It is to be hoped that the divergence will be based on careful observation and rational reflection; but that does not make it one whit different from opinion. If truth is something beyond opinion, then, on this showing, it has no relevance to the disagreements of men.

The disagreements of men can in suitable conditions be resolved by rational discussion. Sadly, suitable conditions are not always available. Be that as it may, to press our opinions as truths transcending 'mere' opinion and to stigmatise opposing opinions of others as 'mere' opinion is often to display nothing more than self-glorification. Dr Oruka in his 'Truth and Belief' does not make this mistake. He does not advance a transcendent concept of truth. Accordingly, in responding to his criticisms of my 'Truth as Opinion', I am conscious of a certain affinity in our epistemological standpoints. Nevertheless, there are important points where we differ. Also, his criticisms express with great logical sophistication objections that have often been made to me in discussion by friends not all of whom have been professional philosophers, a fact which makes Dr Oruka's criticisms all the more important.

One point which is, I believe, rather basic relates to the very conception of opinion. Dr Oruka comments that my view, that truth is nothing but opinion, implies that 'there can be nothing true outside the whims and beliefs of the individual, no matter how wicked and stupid' (op. cit., p. 182). It follows naturally enough that 'if [my] thesis is consistently maintained and applied, then any principle of learning or education must be regarded as being purely arbitrary' (p. 182). But since to describe an opinion as the whim and belief of a wicked and stupid individual is to dissociate one's own point of view from it, why should a thesis which says that truth is nothing but the affirmation of a point of view be supposed to imply that all opinions, even the whims of stupid people, are true? True from what point of view? I will return to the question of point of view at more length in another connection, but for the present let me remark that I discern in these quotations a devaluation of opinion *as such* which in the light of the human importance of opinion, as already explained, seems less than justifiable. It is hard to imagine that a judicious man used to apportioning belief to the evidence, would, on accepting the thesis that truth is nothing but opinion, thereupon say to himself: 'Now that I know that truth is nothing but opinion I will no longer bother to base my opinions on evidence and careful reflection.' No, the problem of irresponsible belief belongs not particularly to epistemology but to psychology. And, decidedly, the student in Dr Oruka's comic opening dialogue (intended as a reflection on my view of truth) is a psychological case. The dialogue goes as follows:

Student : I believe that 2 + 2 is not equal to 4. And I am perfectly confident that no professor is able to impart any knowledge or truth to anybody.

Professor: You are completely mistaken and absurd.

Student : But that is just your opinion which I am sure can never be true or communicate any knowledge to anybody.

Observer: What is truth? What are the standards for determining what is true and what is false?

Student : Whatever they are, no professor can enumerate them to you. [*Ibid.*, p. 177.]

Truth, I have maintained, is nothing but opinion; but this student obviously thinks that opinion is nothing but caprice. There should be no difficulty in separating the student's views from mine.

Incidentally, the observer's request for 'the standards for determining what is true and what is false' is not quite clear. If he is asking for the meaning of truth, then he is welcome to the abundant literature on this problem in philosophy. On the other hand, if he is looking for 'standards' that shall determine the truth or falsity of every particular knowledge claim, then, *mirabile dictu*, the student has hit on the right answer in remarking that no professor can enumerate them. Since every such 'standard' would have to take the peculiarities of the relevant problem into consideration, no such enumeration is possible.[6]

Before leaving the question of responsible and irresponsible belief it is appropriate to make one or two remarks about contradictory beliefs. 'If Wiredu's thesis is valid or correct,' says Dr Oruka, 'then it is impossible for anyone to maintain simultaneously contradictory propositions' (op. cit., p. 181). His argument is that since it is, in fact, perfectly possible for a person to hold a conjunctive belief that is contradictory, my thesis must be wrong. Presumably, he thinks that my view implies the impossibility of contradictory beliefs because he understands it to imply that every opinion is true. My view, however, has no such implication, as I have already suggested and as will become clearer below. Once this is understood, the problem of contradictory beliefs is seen not to be a special problem for my view of truth. Nevertheless, since the problem is an interesting one on its own account, I would like to venture a few remarks on it here. My own inclination is to regard an explicitly contradictory belief as a form of mental illness. We all, possibly, harbour some undetected contradictions in our thinking. But our respect for the principle of non-contradiction implies that as soon as we become aware of such contradictions we should, and would, try to do something to resolve them. This is straightforward

[6] Kant long ago gave an elegant proof of this impossibility. See *Critique of Pure Reason*, translated by N. Kemp Smith, pp. 97–8. The passage is quoted and commented upon in chapter 10, pp. 153–4.

enough. But, then, there are people who seem actually to exult in contradictions. Tertullian is a famous case in point:

> What is unworthy of God will do for me . . . the Son of God was born; because it is shameful I am not ashamed; and the Son of God died; *just because it is absurd, it is to be believed*; and he was buried and rose again; it is certain because it is impossible.[7]

Shorn of its sophistication such a piece of discourse must be a symptom of some abnormality of mind.

Mystics seem particularly enamoured of contradictions: Every thing is one, identical, yet separate, different. Personally, I suspect some genuine and deep problems of communication in the verbal articulation of mystical experience. It seems to me unlikely that the well-documented inclination of mystics to self-contradictory forms of discourse is evidence merely of a taste for verbal sport. In saying this, I am, of course, suggesting that, conceivably, the contradictions are only apparent. There are, however, some philosophers who believe that the mystic's contradictions are genuine and yet communicative, by virtue of some spiritual realm beyond the reach of logic.[8] This fundamentally obscure suggestion may be taken to pay a sort of back-handed respect to the principle of non-contradiction, for it seems to carry the realisation that anything violating it must seek accommodation outside this world.

Hegelians and Marxists are another group apparently undaunted by contradictions. However, it is at least arguable that the species of 'contradictions' that fires their enthusiasm, a species christened 'dialectical', is distinct and separate from the type of contradictions against which formal logicians guard.[9] 'Dialectical contradiction', it seems, refers to that struggle of opposites which, according to Hegelianism and Marxism, is the principle of all development. If

[7] Quoted by Bernard Williams in his 'Tertullian's Paradox' in *New Essays in Philosophical Theology*, edited by Anthony Flew and Alisdair MacIntyre, London, SCM Press, 1955, p. 190 (italics not in original).

[8] One philosopher taking this view is W. T. Stace in his *Mysticism and Philosophy*. I have given some attention to Stace's view and the general question of mysticism and contradictions in chapter 7.

[9] See, for example, the elegant interpretations to this effect in 'Marxist Dialectics and the Principle of Contradiction' by the famous Marxist sociologist and philosopher, Adam Schaff, in the *Journal of Philosophy*, 1960. This article is included in I. M. Copi and J. A. Gould, *Readings on Logic*, London, Collier-Macmillan, second edition 1972.

so, the dialectical philosophers are in principle, if not necessarily always in speech, innocent of formally contradictory beliefs. The trouble, however, is that, at least with Engels, there is the occasional flirtation with actual formal contradictions in addition to trafficking in 'dialectical' contradictions. Thus Engels can say: 'Motion itself is a contradiction, even simple mechanical change of position can only come about through a body being at one and the same moment of time both in one place and in another place, being in one and the same place and also not in it' (*Anti-Dühring*, Foreign Languages Publishing House, Moscow, 1962, p. 166). Notice that the negation involved in this example of a contradiction, a full-blooded formal contradiction, is a formal negation, the type of negation which consists simply in affixing a negation to a thought. Yet later in the same book Engels says 'Negation in dialectics does not mean simply saying no, or declaring that something does not exist, or destroying it in any way one likes' (p. 194), and he goes on to characterise the 'negation of the negation' which consists in 'alternately writing and cancelling *a*, or in alternately declaring that a rose is a rose and that it is not a rose' as a 'childish pastime' from which 'nothing eventuates but the silliness of the person who adopts such a tedious procedure' (p. 195). But there seems to be precious little to choose between saying that a rose is a rose and also not a rose, on the one hand, and saying that a thing is in a certain place and also not in that place at one and the same time, on the other. It is noticeable that he is pushed into actual formal contradictions when trying valiantly to show that Dialectics offers a logic that is a genuine and superior alternative to classical logic. I am afraid I can hardly distinguish between Engels' mentality in these passages and that of Tertullian. Not all Marxists have resisted the temptation to follow Engels in this matter, but the more logically alert have tended to join the classical logicians in doing their best to steer clear of formal contradictions.

It will be seen that I am chary of the idea of there being people who, unperturbed, carry in their heads explicitly contradictory beliefs in full consciousness of their contradictoriness. This is not because of any felt theoretical impossibility but simply because of the peculiarity of such a frame of mind.

Incidentally, Dr Oruka seems to suggest, following D. M. Armstrong (*Belief, Truth and Knowledge*, Cambridge, 1973 ch. 8), that

David Hume is an example of a person who fully consciously believed a contradictory conjunction of propositions. In substantiation of this he refers to the following remark of Hume's in the Appendix to his *A Treatise of Human Nature* (ed. Selby-Bigge, p. 636): 'there are two principles which I cannot render consistent nor is it in my power to renounce either of them'. It is, however, a mistake to think that Hume regarded the two principles as irreducibly contradictory. Nor was he satisfied with the two principles as they stood; otherwise that passage would not have been an agonised confession of perplexity. By this very confession the Appendix stands as a historic example of intellectual honesty. Listen to what Hume says in the same paragraph with regard to the problematic pair of principles:

> For my part I must plead the privilege of a sceptic, and confess that this difficulty is too hard for my understanding. I pretend not, however, to pronounce it absolutely insuperable. Others, perhaps, or myself, upon more mature reflexions, may discover some hypothesis that will reconcile those contradictions.

When we turn to other parts of Dr Oruka's criticism of my 'Truth as Opinion' our task is made easier by his admirable flair for logical schematisation. This way of treating the issues does not only make for clarity in what is said but also helps to highlight crucial implications and presuppositions on both sides. We meet the first such exploitation of logic in Dr Oruka's representation of that part of my discussion in which I claimed that the objectivist conception of truth is contrary to a fact of common experience, namely, that 'we sometimes know some propositions to be true . . .' He writes:

> The argument can be shortened and sketched as follows:
> 1. If truth is categorially different from opinion, then we cannot know truth.
> 2. But we can know truth.
> 3. Truth is not categorially different from opinion (follows by *modus tollens* from 1 & 2).

He continues:

> Although the above argument is valid one cannot correctly infer from it the conclusion that truth is identical with opinion. That

truth is not categorially different from opinion may mean that there is a connection or relation between truth and opinion, but it does not imply that truth and opinion are identical as Wiredu has inferred [op. cit., p. 178].

Dr Oruka is right in this comment, but the above representation of my argument is not quite complete, for it does not take account of the following sentence which Dr Oruka himself quotes: 'Any given claim to truth is merely an opinion advanced from some specific point of view, and categorially distinct from it. Hence knowledge of truth *as distinct from opinion* is a contradictory notion' (op. cit., p. 14; italics not in the original). Note that the conclusion follows even if we omit the word 'categorially' or even the whole phrase 'and categorically distinct from it' from the premise. This argument obviously warrants the following supplementary schema:

1. If truth is distinct from opinion, then we cannot know truth.
2. We can know truth.
3. Therefore truth is not distinct from opinion.

which is, of course, a valid argument. No one is compelled to accept the conclusion of a valid argument unless he accepts the premises. Dr Oruka seems to regard at least one of the premises, which is common to both schemata, as in some way illegitimate. The premise in question is the second one, namely, 'We can know truth'. I had claimed that 'it is an incontestable fact of common experience that we sometimes know some propositions to be true'. In direct reference to this, Dr Oruka remarks: 'But this fact of common experience (henceforward simple *fce*) I believe has been over-interpreted by Wiredu to mean (imply), more than it actually does. What the *fce* proves is not "that we sometimes know" but only that we sometimes are certain, assert or opine that we know' (op. cit., p. 178). Since the *fce* itself is nothing more nor less than the claim that we sometimes know some propositions to be true, I am quite mystified by the charge of 'over-interpretation'. It is open to Dr Oruka to deny the claim that we sometimes know some propositions to be true. But that would mean embracing scepticism; and I doubt whether he is intent on that.

There is another matter which I would like to dispose of. Dr

Oruka observes not long after the charge of over-interpretation: 'Wiredu's mistake lies in using the plausible principle that knowledge entails belief ... to infer and assert the very implausible idea that for anything or proposition to be true is to be opined' (p. 179). In actual fact neither in 'Truth as Opinion' nor at any time have I reasoned in this way. On the contrary, I take a particular interpretation of the proposition that knowledge entails (and is entailed by) belief to be a consequence, rather than a premise, of my view. Dr Oruka regards the first part of this equivalence, namely, the claim that knowledge entails belief, as plausible. However, it is not as unqualifiedly plausible as it is apt to seem. In the weaker sense of 'belief', it is quite plainly incorrect to say that knowledge entails belief. Belief in this sense is a state of mind involving some degree of doubt, uncertainty or tentativeness. It is in this sense that it is natural to say things like 'I believe that *p* but I am not sure'; 'I believe that *p* but I don't really know if it is so'. Thus to say that knowledge entails belief in this sense is to suggest that knowledge implies doubt, which is absurd. Accordingly, we must recognise that it is only in the strong sense of 'belief' that it is correct to say that knowledge entails belief. But, then, in this strong sense, it certainly is the case that belief entails knowledge, *given an identical point of view*. Consider a man who says in the strong sense: 'I believe that *p*.' What reason could he have to be cautious of a knowledge claim? The only reason for such caution would be the existence in his mind of some doubt or tentativeness. But any such lack of assurance would render belief *in the strong sense* illegitimate. Therefore, in the *first person sense*, belief (in the strong sense) entails knowledge. I need hardly repeat that in maintaining a certain kind of equation between truth and belief (or opinion), I have always explicitly taken belief in the strong sense and have always based the equation on an identity of point of view.

The orthodox account of the relation between knowledge and belief is vitiated by neglect of the role of point of view. This weakness is manifested in the common objection to any suggestion of an equivalence between knowledge and belief. The objection is that since a belief, no matter what the strength with which it is held, can be false but the same cannot be said of knowledge, it follows that knowledge and belief cannot be equivalent in *any* sense. The answer is simply that this ignores the first person context. In this kind of perspective there just is nothing like a *false* belief, for it is nonsensical to say 'I believe that p but p is false'. Talk of false belief is sensible, then, only when a disparity in point of view is envisaged. Thus one can only say 'X believes that p but p is false' where the falsity claim obviously originates from a point of view other than X's.

Nevertheless, one notices in this connection a certain difference between the concepts of knowledge and belief. To say that 'X knows that p'[10] implies that the assertor of the statement is himself prepared to say 'I know that p'. On the other hand, if a man says 'X believes that p' he is not thereby committed to saying 'I believe that p'. We must, however, beware of exaggerating the significance of this difference. It relates merely to the manner of communicating commitment. It does not disclose any new cognitive dimension which any actual case of knowledge in itself has and any corresponding case of belief in itself lacks. If there were such a dimension to knowledge, it would be reflected in the first person context also, but it is not. In epistemology we ought to learn to recognise the primary, and hence fundamental, significance of the first person context.

The question of point of view becomes absolutely crucial when we come to the concept of truth, which is the heart of the matter. On my view truth is primarily a first person concept. Now, of course, disagreement is a simple fact of the human situation. And we might from a neutral meta-theoretical point of view record this, as far as it touches the concept of truth, by saying that there can be opposing truths, each expressing a different point of view. A difficulty in the interpretation of this remark arises from the very first person character of truth which we are trying to bring out. Any reference to a truth seems to commit the speaker to the proposition involved, so that to talk of opposing truths seems to imply a contradiction. Certainly, in any situation in which we seek to determine an issue of truth or falsity this must be so: I cannot – at any rate, not with logical good sense – affirm two contradictory propositions both as true. However, in discussing the meaning of truth we are not seeking to determine specific issues of truth or

---

[10] In such symbolism the small letter 'p' has been used throughout to stand for any sentence that one may care to consider.

falsity; we are talking at a meta-theoretical level. We are, if you like, not making truth claims but only talking about them. If in this kind of context we refer to conflicting truths specifically in order to elucidate the constitutive role of point of view in the concept of truth, then we are not entitled to identify the meta-theoretic point of view with each of the opposing points of view. Syntactically, it might be thought that a suitable compromise could be achieved by saying not that there can be conflicting truths but rather only that there can be conflicting 'truths', the quotational encumbrance serving to distinguish the levels of point of view. But this would be a trifle too orthodox. Such a form of statement would, in fact, smother the significance of point of view in the analysis of truth.

Consider the logical relation between the concepts of husband and wife. Given existing semantic conventions a wife is necessarily the wife of a husband. In a monogamous society each wife will have one husband and each husband, one wife. Suppose a man, himself a husband, were to remark in such a society: 'There are as many wives as there are husbands', nobody would, presumably, be tempted to protest that he was thereby claiming all the wives for himself. Now, the relation between truth and point of view in my account is logically analogous: Every truth is necessarily a truth from some point of view. Yet when one says 'There are as many truths as there are different points of view' in the course of pointing out the essential relation of truth to point of view, one is promptly saddled with a commitment to the truth of every point of view. But in that case there would not be as many points of view as there are truths but only one point of view amidst myriad truths! When, therefore, Dr Oruka comments: 'An unconsidered belief or opinion is still an opinion and must, on Wiredu's opinion, be considered as true as any other; otherwise there would not be "as many truths as there are opinions"' (op. cit., p. 182), it is obvious that he has not given due weight to the explanations which I gave in 'Truth as Opinion' about the logical relation between truth and point of view.

There is another point closely related to this one regarding which I am sure Dr Oruka and others – for I have often heard this objection – will now be able to revise their criticisms. 'We are,' he says, 'used to contrasting truth with falsehood. And it is never disputed that truth and falsehood are opposites. Wiredu's thesis implies that truth and belief are identical or that the following formula is sound: p is true = p is believed.' It is fortunate that Dr Oruka's penchant for logical schematisation comes into play in this connection too, for it thus becomes possible to pinpoint clearly and exactly what is wrong here. And it is this. My formula is not just 'p is true = p is believed' but 'p is true = p is believed, provided that the two sides of the equation have the same point of view'. Let 'Tp' stand for 'p is true' and 'Bp' stand for 'p is believed'. Further, let us use numerical subscripts to identify points of view, the same number when repeated indicating the same point of view.[11] Then my formula is $T_1p = B_1p$ not, as Dr Oruka's comment suggests, $Tp = Bp$.[12]

A certain rider is in place here. The equation '$T_1p = B_1p$' is a contextual, rather than an absolute, equality. Although I maintain that every actual case of a truth is nothing more than a case of belief or opinion, it does not follow that the *concept* of truth itself is identical with the *concept* of belief. (A similar situation, it will be recalled, emerged with regard to knowledge and belief.) Truth has a certain excess of significance over belief. One way to see this is to reflect on the fact that we speak of truths as well as of Truth. We may say that by 'truths' we refer to the particular outcomes of rational inquiry, while by 'Truth' we allude to what all outcomes of rational inquiry have in common, namely, dependence on the processes of rational inquiry. Truth, then, is to be contrasted with belief in the way in which a method is contrasted with its outcome. Moreover, even when truth is conceived as the outcome of a rational inquiry, there is a subtle disparity between the concept of truth and the concept of belief. Truth, as noted earlier, is primarily a first person concept. Hence, *unless the context indicates otherwise*, reference to truth carries commitment in a way in which reference to belief does not. (It will, again, be recalled that we noted a similar difference between the concepts of knowledge and belief.) Thus when I say 'He believes that p', this does not commit me to p

---

[11] These are somewhat simplified formulations, but they will do for present purposes. On the formalisation of truth claims see J. E. Wiredu, 'Truth as a Logical Constant', *Philosophical Quarterly*, October 1975.

[12] I ought, perhaps, to point out that the individuation of points of view does not coincide with the individuation of persons. The same person can have different points of view at different times about the same matter.

whereas were I to say 'He is in possession of a truth', this would commit me to whatever proposition may be under consideration. As in the case of the concepts of knowledge and belief, so in this case too, the significance of these differences is purely semantic; it is neither epistemological nor ontological.

12

Truth: a dialogue

CRITIC: The view that truth is nothing but belief or opinion is open to so many objections that I hardly know where to start. But let me start with this one. On this view it is impossible for one person to contradict another or even himself of an earlier time. For if 'p is true' said by me means 'I believe that p', then if I say 'p is true' and another says '-p is true', what we would be saying would be jointly consistent, namely, on my part, that I have a certain belief p, and, on his part, that he has a certain belief -p.[1] There is, of course, nothing contradictory in different people having different beliefs or in the same person having different beliefs at different times.

PROPONENT: This objection is related to that concerning contradictory beliefs which I have discussed already. (See pp. 179–82.) It might be useful in answering it to start by dissolving a purely verbal appearance of paradox. When one person asserts p and another asserts -p there may indeed be no contradiction[2] by either person but there is a contra-dicting. The impression that where there is no contradiction there can be no contra-dicting must be due to nothing but the sound of words. To contradict somebody is simply to assert the negation, or something implying the negation, of what he asserts. This is without prejudice to the point that the fact of my asserting p is fully compatible with the fact of his asserting -p. That this is so has nothing specially to do with my view of truth. Presumably, then, what provides sustenance for the objection is the notion, lurking in the background, that when I say

[1] The sign '-' is used to mean 'not' in the sense of 'it is not the case that'.

[2] Of course, wherever there is a contradicting there is a possibility of a contradiction which would be actualised if some single point of view were to commit itself to both the affirmation and negation in an expression to some such effect as 'I believe that p and -p'.

'I believe that *p*', I am asserting, not that *p* is a fact but only that it is a fact that I believe that *p*. It is true, of course, that when I say 'I believe that *p*' I am asserting that I have a certain belief, but it is equally true that I am thereby claiming that something is so. It is because of this aspect of the semantic import of belief-statements that a man is apt to be dismayed if you announce to him: 'I believe that you are a fool.' He is most unlikely to take this merely as a phenomenal description of your state of mind. It is in virtue of this same aspect of belief-statements that one belief can contradict another.

CRITIC: Well, I will come back to what you have just said, but let me meanwhile put this objection to you. If truth is nothing but opinion, and, finally, nothing but my opinion, then the set of my opinions is co-extensive with the set of all true propositions. But this amounts to nothing short of epistemological megalomania. Any recognition of my own finitude should induce me to recognise that there is a multitude of true propositions that I do not know. Hence, truth must transcend opinion.

PROPONENT: Here again I think I have dealt with a basically similar objection in connection with knowledge and existence.[3] This objection is, however, important and deserves its own answer. Let me begin with an ontological caveat: There is more than a touch of metaphysical extravagance in the notion, which seems to underlie your objection, of a vast, or, rather, an infinite array of mind-independent abstract entities called propositions existing, or shall we say subsisting, in a rarefied realm of their own, endowed each with its own truth attribute. A proposition in my view is a mental content, a species of apprehension. When not being actually entertained, a proposition is but a possibility of apprehension. Provided that a mere possibility is not construed as a kind of entity[4] and the notion of a mental content is not assumed to presuppose an 'immaterial' substance in which it inheres,[5] this suggestion has the merit of bringing out the hypothetical character of a set such as the set of all true propositions. This set is open at

---

[3] See chapter 9, pp. 129–31.

[4] Philosophers have, in fact, sometimes spoken as if a mere possibility were a kind of entity as when, for example, Mill defines matter as the permanent possibility of sensation. See chapter 9, pp. 135–7.

[5] For a remark on the ontological status of such things as concepts and therefore of propositions since they are combinations of concepts, see p. 101, n. 3.

both ends. At any one time the propositions that I, or even the whole of mankind, actually entertain is only an infinitesimal fraction of the propositions that have actually been entertained in the past and might be entertained in the future. Now, if we conceive of a proposition on the model of a declarative sentence, then every proposition is a claim that something is, or may be, so or not so. There have been in the past and there will be in the future propositions that are not accessible to me. But I have excellent reasons to say at any one time that of those actual and potential propositions, a large number, *if studied*, will be found to be warranted, and others not. This is what can be meant by the remark that there are truths that are not known to me. Its import is hypothetical. Unless we note the hypothetical character of this remark, we would fall into profound difficulties: for, surely, it cannot be said that there is any proposition regarding which I could sensibly say 'This proposition is true but I do not know it.' Even when I believe a proposition to be true on the authority of others my reason for according them an authoritative status constitutes a reason for claiming knowledge. That, in fact, is how we acquire most of our knowledge. As for the comment that my view holds truth to be nothing but *my* opinion, this is misleading without the proviso that 'my' here is in the nature of a variable. There is a 'my' in any truth, but it may belong to anybody.

CRITIC: But you have shifted your ground. Your theory is that truth is nothing but opinion or belief. You have maintained that to be true is to be believed and *vice versa* (given an identical point of view). But the view you are now expounding is something like Dewey's, namely, that truth is warranted assertibility. Now, the two theories are not the same. An opinion may or may not be warranted; when it is not warranted it cannot be called true on Dewey's theory, but on yours it must be true.

PROPONENT: No, an opinion that is not warranted cannot be called true on my view. To say that an opinion is not warranted is to dissociate one's point of view from that opinion. To call an opinion true is to identify one's point of view with it. Thus to say of an opinion that it is both unwarranted and true would amount to saying something like 'I believe that p but p is not warranted', which is absurd.

CRITIC: I agree with you that it would be inappropriate to say 'I believe that p but p is not warranted'. Nevertheless, what is expressed in that sentence may actually be the case. The reason is simple: I may mistakenly believe a proposition which is not warranted. The same holds for a sentence like 'I believe that p but p is false'. Although it would be absurd for me to say a thing like this, still the substance of what is said may very well be true. It will be true when I believe something which is false. And this can, of course, happen to any fallible mortal. I should have thought that G. E. Moore made this sort of point clearly enough many years ago.[6]

PROPONENT: You have no qualms about saying that something can be both *absurd* and true?

CRITIC: Not in this case, certainly; for the explanation is simple. To adapt an example due to Moore (op. cit.), suppose I say 'I believe that Kwame has gone out, but it is false that he has'. The reason why this is absurd is simply that any warrant I might have for thinking that Kwame has gone out undermines any suggestion that he has not, and therefore destroys any warrant there might be for me to assert the conjunction.

PROPONENT: But doesn't this imply that the two components of the conjunction are mutually incompatible?

CRITIC: It does not. Suppose that at time t I believed that Kwame had gone out while, in fact, he had not, then quite clearly I can at a later time consistently and with propriety assert (1): 'At time t I believed that Kwame had gone out though he had not gone out'; and this surely entails (2): 'At time t I could truly (if not with propriety) have said "I believe that Kwame has gone out, but it is false that he has".'

PROPONENT: I deny the alleged entailment. In the first conjunction there are two different points of view involved, namely, the point of view of myself at time t and that of myself at a later time. That is why there is no self-contradiction, for although two incompatible statements from two different points of view contradict each other, they do not give rise to self-contradiction. On the other hand, in the second conjunction, which is supposed to be entailed by the first, the two incompatible components are embraced by one

---

[6] In his contribution to *The Philosophy of Bertrand Russell* (ed. Paul Schilpp, Library of Living Philosophers, Inc., 1944, p. 204). See also Norman Malcolm in *Philosophical Analysis* (ed. Max Black, Cornell University Press, 1950, pp. 259–60).

and the same point of view. That, of course, must result in a contradiction.

CRITIC: But you are begging the question. Whether the two components of the second conjunction are mutually incompatible is the question at issue, and yet you seem to take it for granted.

PROPONENT: That they are incompatible follows from the analysis I have already given, but I am willing to try again. Tell me, then, does not a man who says '. . . but it is false that Kwame has gone out' *assert* that it is false that Kwame has gone out?

CRITIC: That is obvious.

PROPONENT: And that implies asserting that Kwame has not gone out?

CRITIC: This too is obvious, but what is the point of these trivialities?

PROPONENT: The point is that since saying 'I believe that Kwame has gone out' entails asserting that Kwame has gone out, to say 'I believe that Kwame has gone out, but it is false that he has' entails asserting both that Kwame has gone out and that he has not gone out, which is self-contradictory.

CRITIC: This confirms my suspicion that you do not realise the distinction between the pragmatic and semantic ingredients of an utterance. I formed this suspicion when in your opening shot you suggested that a claim to the effect that something is so is an aspect of 'the semantic import' of an utterance of the form 'I believe that p'. In the present connection consider the utterance 'I believe Kwame has gone out'. What the sentence uttered *means* is that the speaker has a certain belief. This is the semantic ingredient. But besides this, there is what is globally conveyed or communicated by the utterance. This latter is the claim that Kwame has gone out. This is the pragmatic ingredient.

PROPONENT: And your contention is that although the utterance conveys the claim that Kwame has gone out, it does not *assert* it.

CRITIC: Yes.

PROPONENT: So that if Kwame has not gone out while the speaker actually believes that he has, then though what his utterance conveys is false, what it asserts is true.

CRITIC: Exactly. Moreover, that situation would render true his conjunctive utterance 'I believe that Kwame has gone out but it is false that he has', which should bring out clearly that fact that what an utterance conveys may negate what it asserts without self-contradiction.

PROPONENT: But suppose that Kwame has gone out, but the speaker does not, in fact, believe it?

CRITIC: Then, of course, what his utterance conveys is true but what it asserts is false.

PROPONENT: In a situation in which we are given that the speaker does not believe that Kwame has gone out how does he convey the claim that he has gone out?

CRITIC: It is not what he happens to believe that determines what his utterance conveys but the nature of what he utters.

PROPONENT: In other words, what an utterance conveys is determined on the basis of rules relating to the utterance.

CRITIC: Certainly.

PROPONENT: Very well; the point now is that these rules can only be rules of meaning, grammar and perhaps logic, and therefore the question of what an utterance 'conveys' is as much semantic as the question of what it asserts. Accordingly, I can see little rationale in your distinction between what an utterance conveys and what it asserts, at any rate, in relation to the disputed example. And it seems to me very much less problematic to recognise that when a man says 'I believe that p but p is false' he is asserting both that p, and that p is false. Besides, I don't think that even if your distinction were conceded you could avoid the contradiction in the conjunction, because you must admit that what a speaker asserts he also conveys, whether or not you accept the converse.

CRITIC: And what hangs on this?

PROPONENT: It follows from this fact that, on your own analysis, a speaker who utters 'I believe p but p is false' conveys a contradiction, even if he does not 'assert' one. And you then have on your hands the paradox of a consistent utterance which *by nature* conveys a contradiction.

CRITIC: You will have to balance this against the paradox in your opposing view. According to your analysis of belief-sentences an utterance such as 'X believes that p' asserts both that X believes that p, and that p. This implies that if p is false then 'X believes that p' is false even when X actually believes that p, which is patently absurd.

PROPONENT: This is a misunderstanding arising, I think, from inattention to the consequences of variations in point of view. What I maintain is that 'I believe that p' uttered by X entails the assertion of p by X. This is a remark about the first person point of view. It does not at all follow from it that 'X believes that p' entails 'p', for this would commit not just X but also a third person to p.

CRITIC: Forgive me if I misunderstood you. But you still have the problem of *explaining* how 'I believe p but p is false' can fail to be true if it turns out that the speaker, in fact, believes that p but p is false.

PROPONENT: If this were a problem for me, there would be a very similar problem for you. Consider the utterance 'I believe both that p and -p'. It is obviously a self-contradictory utterance. Now, suppose, the speaker actually believes p and it is not the case that p. On your showing, the utterance can be said to convey the message, on the part of the speaker, both that he believes that p and that it is not the case that p. May we, then, say that in the given circumstances he conveys something true?

CRITIC: Of course not.

PROPONENT: Why not?

CRITIC: Because we would be ignoring that part of the utterance which makes it inconsistent in what it conveys. That part is the claim that p, which clashes logically with the claim that -p, which is also conveyed in the same utterance.

PROPONENT: Observe, then, that anybody who is tempted to think that 'I believe that p but p is false' is true when it is true that the speaker believes that p but p is false is, in principle, doing the same thing. He is ignoring the fact that by his utterance the speaker commits himself to the claim that p, which is inconsistent with 'p is false' to which also he commits himself.

CRITIC: Suppose that you are right and that it is self-contradictory to say 'I believe that p but p is false'. Then how do you account for the fact that a person may mistakenly believe something false? You concede, don't you, that you yourself may believe something false by mistake?

PROPONENT: It is not just that I concede that I may mistakenly believe a false proposition; I have always insisted on the importance of recognising human fallibility in the theory of truth. (See, for example, pp. 66–7, 122–3, 177.)

CRITIC: It is not clear to me, though, that you are fully aware of the consequences of that acknowledgement. Let us examine your statement carefully. You say 'I may mistakenly believe something false'. Since this is to envisage a false belief from one and the same point of view, namely yours, does it not amount to conceding the possibility of your being right to say 'I believe p but p is false'?

PROPONENT: It quite certainly does not. What the statement under examination envisages is the possibility of a situation in which I might say 'I believed that p but p is false and I was mistaken'. Taken in connection with a current belief, it amounts to: 'I believe p but the time may come when I may be warranted in saying "p is false; I was mistaken".' There is here the idea of two distinct points of view, namely, the point of view of myself at one time and a possible antithetic point of view of myself at a later time.

CRITIC: And, presumably, you would give a similar interpretation to the possibility of other people entertaining false beliefs.

PROPONENT: Quite. To say that somebody might believe something false is simply to conceive of the situation in which one might be in a position to say 'X believes that p but p is false'. Such attributions of falsity always presuppose a corresponding third-person point of view.

CRITIC: If you would excuse my saying so, I find all this very unsatisfactory. When we talk of the possibility of false belief we cannot just be talking of the possibility of a third person believing the negation of the proposition in question; for whether the proposition is true or false does not depend on any point of view. Suppose a man believes that two plus two equals seven. Clearly, the falsity of this belief does not depend on what is believed from any third-person point of view. It is simply a mathematical truth, independent of me and you and anybody else, that two plus two equals four and not seven.

PROPONENT: Actually, it is not my suggestion that the truth or falsity of a proposition depends upon the point of view involved. That, as I have already pointed out, would amount to relativism, which, in my opinion, is an absurd doctrine. No; whether a proposition is true or false depends on the appraisal of ideas and situations and not on persons. The point, however, is that a truth always comes, and can only come, in the shape of a truth claim, and a truth claim *is* a point of view. Thus, that two plus two equals four *is* a point of view which is being opposed to the forlorn point of view to the effect that two plus two equals seven.

CRITIC: It is true that in saying, for example, that two plus two equals four I am making a claim. But it is not the claiming or believing that makes the belief true. It is the real state of affairs pertaining to the subject-matter in question that makes the claim true. I think there is a lot that we can learn from Tarski's theory of truth in this connection. His theory requires that any satisfactory definition of truth should be based on the principle that, to take our current example:

The sentence 'Two plus two equals four' is true if and only if two plus two equals four.

You will notice that while the first component of an equivalence of this sort represents a claim, the second one represents objective fact.

PROPONENT: The notion of what *makes* a proposition true is very obscure to me. I can understand the idea of reasons for saying that a proposition is true, but, presumably, that is not what is being talked about. However, since Tarski's principle has a certain formal clarity, I will let this pass and address myself to his conception. I believe that Tarski's semantic theory of truth in its full elaboration has some very deep difficulties which we do not need to go into since you are here only exploiting its initial, basic idea. But already your use of it highlights a certain feature of it which is of the utmost relevance to the issue between us. It is this: that in advancing the principle under discussion Tarski seems to have been motivated by the desire to accomplish the metaphysical *tour de force* of transforming a mere sentence, namely, the second component of the equivalence, into a manifestation of objective fact or reality. This, I think, is typical of all objectivistic theories of truth.

CRITIC: Now I, for my part, am totally mystified by your remark that Tarski's theory seeks to transform a sentence into a manifestation of reality. Perhaps, I might briefly explain the purport of the theory. Its aim is to give a precise and logically clear expression to what Tarski calls the classical Aristotelian conception of truth, which is formulated as follows in Aristotle's *Metaphysics*: 'To say of what is that it is not, or of what is not that it is, is false, while to say of what is that it is, or of what is not that it is not, is true.'[7] It is this classical intuition which he tries – successfully, one must add – to capture in the principle already mentioned. He calls it 'an equivalence of the form (*T*)'. In its generalised formulation it is to the following effect:

$$X \text{ is true if and only if } p$$

(where *p* stands for any sentence of the given language and *X* for the name of that sentence (*ibid.*, p. 55)). To take Tarski's own example, if *p* is taken to stand for 'snow is white' then the equivalence schema (*T*) becomes:

The sentence 'snow is white' is true if and only if snow is white.

PROPONENT: The trouble with all this is that . . .

CRITIC: Excuse me, but I really must say a little more about Tarski's theory, since otherwise one might get a misleading impression of it. It should be understood that Tarski does not regard the instituting of the schema (*T*) as itself providing a definition of truth; he takes it only as giving a necessary condition of a definition of truth or at best a partial definition of truth. It might seem that to obtain a full definition of truth all that need be done is to quantify the (*T*) sentence universally, but it turns out, according to Tarski, that this cannot be done. It turns out also, according to Tarski, that a satisfactory definition of truth cannot be formulated in a natural language but only in the kind of rigidly specified artificial 'languages' that are studied in modern logic, where the 'language' in which we might formulate the definition of the truth of a sentence is carefully distinguished from the 'language' to which the sentence itself primarily belongs, the former being called the *metalanguage* and the latter the *object language*. These two facts are responsible for the technical ramifications of Tarski's full definition of truth. Of his technical construction, which he presented to the world in 1931 in his epoch-making article entitled 'The Concept of Truth in Formalised Languages',[8] only an inkling is given in his marvellously simplified article 'The Semantic Conception of Truth'. But in as much as the basic ideas of the theory and its motivation are

---

[7] See Tarski, 'The Semantic Conception of Truth' in Feigl and Sellars (eds.), *Readings in Philosophical Analysis*, New York, Appleton-Century-Crofts, 1949, p. 54. The paper was originally published in *Philosophy and Phenomenological Research*, 1944.

[8] Alfred Tarski, *Logic, Semantics and Metamathematics*, Oxford, 1956, Ch. VIII.

fully presented there it may be regarded as an adequate basis for a philosophical discussion. One great merit of Tarski's approach is that in discussing the basis of his definition he replaces philosophically problematic terms like 'reality', 'states of affairs', 'correspondence with fact', which tend to figure in general formulations of the classical Aristotelian conception with such logically precise terms as *sentence* and *name* of a sentence. If he had defined truth in some such manner as 'The truth of a sentence consists in its agreement with (correspondence to) reality' or 'A sentence is true if and only if it designates an existing state of affairs', it would, perhaps, have been intelligible in an impressionistic, metaphorical, sort of way to say that he was trying to transform a sentence into 'a manifestation of reality'. But these are formulations which he specifically considers and rejects on account of their lack of logical precision. (See Feigl and Sellars, op. cit., p. 59.) This is why in trying to encapsulate the classical conception in a definition he started with his philosophically austere (*T*) sentence.[9]

[9] Tarski's semantic theory of truth is probably the most highly esteemed theory of truth among contemporary philosophical logicians. The reader who wants to pursue it cannot do better than start with Tarski's article 'The Semantic Conception of Truth' already referred to above. From this he can turn to another non-technical exposition of the theory, and of one consequence of it, by Tarski in his article on 'Truth and Proof' in *Scientific American*, June 1969. This article is reprinted in O. Hanfling (ed.), *Fundamental Problems of Philosophy*, Oxford, 1972. One of the most famous admirers of Tarski's theory of truth is Karl Popper who expresses his warm estimation of it in, for example, his *Objective Knowledge*, chapter 9. (The exposition on pp. 319–29 is non-technical. See also pp. 308–18.) Popper displays the same passionate enthusiasm for Tarski's theory in chapter 10 of his earlier work *Conjectures and Refutations*, London, Routledge and Kegan Paul, second edition, 1965, especially section 2. Popper here, incidentally, stigmatises a theory of truth such as the one defended by PROPONENT above as 'subjective'; he also on occasion calls it 'psychological', 'epistemic', 'epistemological'. It should be noted that, contrary to Tarski's own view of the limited applicability of his definition of truth, Popper maintains that the theory is applicable to natural languages as well. There is an approving, non-technical account of Tarski's theory by an outstanding mathematical logician in 'Truth and Provability' by Leon Henkin. This paper is included in *Philosophy of Science* edited by Sidney Morgenbesser (Basic Books, New York, 1967). Two well-known criticisms of the theory are to be found in Strawson, 'Truth', *Analysis*, 1949, reprinted in Margaret Macdonald (ed.), *Philosophy and Analysis*, Blackwell, 1954 and, in the same volume, Max Black, 'The Semantic Definition of Truth', *Analysis*, 1948, reprinted in the same author's *Language and Philosophy*, Cornell University Press, 1949. A recent criticism is in Part II chapter 1 of D. J. O'Connor's *The Correspondence Theory of Truth* (Hutchinson's University Library, London, 1975). Still more recent is Susan Haack's relatively more detached discussion of Tarski's theory in chapter 7 of her *Philosophy of Logics*, Cambridge University Press, 1978. The treatment in this last mentioned book is

PROPONENT: But exactly this is the trouble. Tarski is trying to capture a conception which construes truth as a certain relation between a sentence and reality. It is clear that in his schema (*T*) Tarski intends the sentences that replace *p* to be regarded in that position as *disclosing* states of affairs, reality. They are apparently to be taken as infallibly *representing*, nay, as *presenting*, reality. This is where the metamorphosis of sentences into manifestations of reality sets in. To see this more clearly, let us consider Tarski's own example of his equivalence schema (*T*) and raise one question about it. Choosing 'Snow is white' for *p* we get the following:

The sentence 'Snow is white' is true if and only if snow is white.

The quotation marks around the first 'Snow is white' in the equivalence is said by Tarski to convert it into the name of the sentence that snow is white. Not to talk of the highly puzzling use that is made here of the notion of the *name* of a sentence, let us ask: Is the equivalence merely saying that the sentence 'Snow is white' is true if and only if that sentence is *used* to make the assertion that snow is white? Obviously Tarski would say no. He would insist that the significance of the sentence which forms the second component of the equivalence is not just that of an assertion, a truth claim. This, in any case, is the status of the first component. Tarski's adherence to the classical Aristotelian conception requires that he should see the second component as having the status of an *exhibition* of the reality in virtue of which the sentence named is true. This is metaphysically mystifying, as it is virtually as if the sentence constituting the second component had the significance of a sentence which has coalesced with reality.

CRITIC: Whether these comments of yours are justified or not, I would like to point out that they do not affect the equivalence schema (*T*) itself. In the schema itself there is no mention of 'states of affairs' or of 'reality' or even of the notion of the name of a sentence. What we have in the equivalence is simply a sentence in quotes with a truth predicate attached, on one side, and, on the other, a sentence without quotes. Whether the quotation marks do

---

detailed and sophisticated. An additional usefulness of the exposition is that the author discusses the increasingly influential exploitation of Tarski's theory by Donald Davidson.

transform the sentence into a name or whether the second component of the equivalence is accorded a mysterious metaphysical
status is clearly independent of the question whether every
adequate definition of truth must imply all equivalences of the
form (*T*).

PROPONENT: That is a good point. People have not always
separated the logical status of the equivalence schema (*T*) from
Tarski's own (as it seems to me, metaphysical) interpretation of it.
Karl Popper is an eminent case in point. (See the references already
given.) The schema is, in fact, susceptible of an interpretation
which is radically different in spirit from Tarski's Aristotelian
preconceptions. In terms of my conception of truth the schema
receives a straightforward interpretation. I would say that its message is this: Given the availability of a declarative sentence con-
structed from an antecedent point of view, to say that it is true is
equivalent to corroborating it. To corroborate a sentence *p* or, what
is the same, to confirm it, is simply to assert that the sentence *p* is in
agreement with its previous assertion, actual or hypothetical. Thus
in the example in hand the 'Snow is white' on the right-hand side of
the (*T*) equivalence has the status of a confirmatory sentence. But a
confirmatory sentence is still an ordinary sentence; it is a representation of a human assertion, belief, opinion. It can be seen, thus,
that all equivalences of the form (*T*) are implied by my conception
of truth too.

CRITIC: Notice that you are, after all, corroborating Tarski's
remark that 'we may accept the semantic conception of truth
without giving up any epistemological attitude we may have had'
(Feigl and Sellars, op. cit., p. 71).

PROPONENT: To Tarski, though, this particular type of corroboration is bound to be unexpected, to say the least. Incidentally, in
order not to spoil the corroboration, you must substitute 'the
schema (*T*)' for 'the semantic conception of truth' in the remark
just quoted from Tarski.

CRITIC: This has been a long, though very worthwhile, excur-
sion away from my original objection which was that your conception of truth is open to an objection to which Dewey's definition of
truth as warranted assertibility is not open. But I suspect that you
would want to say that believing a proposition is the same as
holding it to be warranted. Am I right?

PROPONENT: Yes, it is one and the same thing to believe a proposition and to hold it to be warranted.

CRITIC: The difficulty is that examples of beliefs that are *avowedly* unsupported by any reasons are not far to seek. A woman convinced that her husband has been unfaithful often does not care admitting that she has no proof or even circumstantial evidence. She says she just knows. Or, if this is not an ideal example, take the more elevated case of Tertullian.[10] When that divine says 'the Son of God dies; just because it is absurd, it is to be believed' is he not actually taking pride in the lack of a rational justification for his belief? Besides, you have to reckon with the mystics who are famously given to spurning reason in giving expression to their convictions.[11] Are these not obvious counter-examples to your position?

PROPONENT: I think that a certain distinction is being smothered under your objection. Being warranted is not *definitionally* the same as being *rationally* warranted. Surely the woman would not admit that she has no warrant for her protestations. She has a certain feeling, and she takes that feeling to provide her with enough warrant. Tertullian, for his part, obviously believes that his self-confessed 'absurdities' are warranted, only he would claim that human logic is not the only possible warrant for belief. Nor can we suppose that the mystic would take kindly to the suggestion that he has no warrant for his beliefs. What he would say – what he actually does say – is that his deliverances are warranted by his special kind of experience which is beyond the reach of logic and the principles of rational evidence in general.

CRITIC: Here then is a definite difference between your view and Dewey's. When Dewey defines truth as warranted assertibility what he obviously has in mind is *rationally* warranted assertibility.

PROPONENT: I agree. I part company with Dewey on this point. To define truth as rationally warranted assertibility is to invite counter-examples such as you presented a moment ago. On this definition, you would have to say, not just that a person who asserts a proposition to be true while avowing a complete lack of rational warrant is wrong, which is fair, but also, that he is misusing the

---

[10] See page 180 on Tertullian.
[11] Some attention was given to mystical talk in relation to logic in chapter 7.

word 'true'. That would sound rather like a cavalier piece of linguistic legislation.

CRITIC: Yet, if there is anything at all that is attractive about Dewey's view of truth, it is his linking of truth with rational inquiry. Your view, by contrast, seems to trivialise truth. Anybody makes an assertion, and, on your theory, there is a truth – truth from his point of view. Another person asserts exactly the opposite, and, there and then, there arises another truth – a truth from the new point of view. There is then, apparently, no stable truth. Are you not merely confusing the notions of a claim to truth and a truth, one with the other? I think that if you consider the matter carefully you will find that what your view of truth is concerned with is not really truth but only claims to truth. You will then realise how unremarkable your thesis is: It comes to merely this: A truth claim is nothing but an opinion.

PROPONENT: Let me start from the phrase 'a truth from a given point of view'. This phrase does not quite do justice to my idea, though I have occasionally used cognate phrases for convenience. It would be nearer what I have in mind to employ a phrase like 'truth as a point of view'. Truth, as I believe I have stressed more than once, cannot be said to *depend* on a point of view – that gives the impression of relativism; a truth *is* a point of view. But reference to a truth is not just a reference to a point of view, for the following reason. Reference to a truth carries a commitment which a mere reference to a point of view does not carry. To talk of a truth is to commit yourself to whatever proposition may be in question. On the other hand, one can talk detachedly about a point of view, merely noting its existence, for example. A truth claim is obviously the same as a point of view. We may therefore say that the difference between talking of a truth claim and talking of a truth lies in this, that the former does not necessarily involve commitment while the latter involves a commitment on the part of the one who does the talking. In the matter of what a truth has over and above a truth claim I would say that a truth is a truth claim with a contemporaneous commitment.

CRITIC: But this only rescues your view from triviality at the price of total implausibility. First, on your view two people cannot ever be said to disagree as to the truth; for, of course, there can be no such thing as the truth over and above their differing commitments. Any arguing between them is pointless in that case, and I cannot see the point of your occasional jibes at relativism. Secondly, how can we make sense of the human fallibility on which you yourself have seemed to place so much emphasis?[12] Admitting my fallibility can only consist in acknowledging that it is possible that what I believe is false, but if the truth is nothing but what I believe, then does that not amount to saying that it is possible for the truth to be false, contrary to the principle of non-contradiction? Thirdly, since a man's opinions or beliefs or commitments change over a period of time, you are committed to the absurdity that truth can change. Fourthly . . .

PROPONENT: Excuse me for breaking in, but you have already advanced more than enough objections to occupy me for the time being. First, as to disagreement: To speak of people disagreeing as to the truth is only an idiomatic abbreviation. What people disagree about are *issues*. They may disagree, for example, as to whether human civilisation can survive a third world war. One man opines that it can, another, that it cannot. If we ask what is the truth of the matter, we can only be asking for the opinion of him to whom the question is addressed.

CRITIC: I am afraid it is my turn to butt in. I cannot forbear remarking that the truth of the matter must exist irrespective of a third point of view, or of any point of view, for that matter. It is simply a fact of logic that any proposition is either true or false. Thus given any proposition and its contradictory, it is logically necessary that one of them must be true whether or not we know which one it is. To borrow a nice example from Bertrand Russell, we have no evidence as to whether the proposition 'It snowed on Manhattan Island on the first of January in the year 1 A.D.' is true or false, 'but,' to quote Russell's words, 'it seems preposterous to maintain that it is neither'.[13]

PROPONENT: You are referring to the principle of excluded middle, one of the so-called 'Laws of Thought'?

CRITIC: Yes; the principle which states that every proposition is

---

[12] See, for example, chapter 8, page 122.

[13] Bertrand Russell, *My Philosophical Development*, George Allen and Unwin, London, 1959, p. 111. On the principle of excluded middle generally see also Russell, *An Inquiry into Meaning and Truth*, chapter xx where the Manhattan example is more amply discussed on p. 227.

either true or false. And I may add that, as Carnap remarked in his article 'Truth and Confirmation',[14] any view of truth, such as yours, which implicitly denies the distinction between truth and knowledge of truth, is incompatible with this law of logic. In this matter, incidentally, Dewey is as vulnerable as you are.

PROPONENT: I fear that we are in danger of being launched on a long journey into the philosophy of logic. I will here merely say that the principle which you call excluded middle is more appropriately called by some other name, say, bivalence, as Lukasiewicz suggests.[15] The principle in question amounts to saying that there are only two truth values, namely, truth and falsity, and every proposition has one or the other. It seems more natural to call this the principle of two values (bivalence) than the principle of excluded middle.

CRITIC: But in saying that there are only two values and each proposition has one or other we are excluding any middle ground between truth and falsity.

PROPONENT: Very well, then, let us say that what you call excluded middle involves, or perhaps we might say presupposes, bivalence. Lukasiewicz, on the other hand, recommended reserving the name '*excluded middle*' for the principle that two contradictory propositions cannot both be false. This obviously does not imply bivalence since if there are more than two values the fact that a proposition has not got the value *falsity* would not itself imply that it has the value *truth* rather than some other value.

CRITIC: Obviously what Lukasiewicz calls excluded middle says rather less than what I, and, be it noted, most other logicians and philosophers call by that name. But I would agree that it serves the purpose of clarity to know exactly what is involved in the customary principle of excluded middle. I would prefer to give the name 'bivalence' to the principle which says simply that there are only two truth values, truth and falsity. If you combine this with the principle that every proposition has at least one truth value, you then obtain the principle which generally goes by the name of excluded middle.

[14] In Feigl and Sellars, op. cit.
[15] See 'On Determinism' in Lukasiewicz, *Selected Works*, ed. L Borkowski, North-Holland Pub. Co., 1970. Also reprinted in *Polish Logic*, ed. Storrs McCall, Oxford, 1967.

PROPONENT: I must say that I rather like your way of formulating the matter. It gives us a more general way of stating the laws of thought than one encounters in logical texts and, if we were employing symbolic formulations, I would be inclined to make the most of it. In terms of your formulation, I think, we could give a highly generalised version of the principle of non-contradiction as follows: No proposition can have more than one truth value. This is neutral as to whether one is operating in a *two-valued* logic, that is, one which recognises only two truth values, as in your case, or in a *many-valued* logic, that is, one which recognises more than two values.

CRITIC: That is correct.

PROPONENT: Furthermore, your formulation of the excluded middle brings out the bone of contention between us with the greatest clarity.

CRITIC: What is it?

PROPONENT: It is the claim which you advance in the context of your two-valued logic that every proposition has at least one truth value.

CRITIC: What is your objection to it?

PROPONENT: It makes it look as if truth values are properties which 'propositions' have antecedently to inquiry whereas they are properties – if we must call them properties – which *we* assign to them in inquiry.

CRITIC: This is becoming obscure, and, in any case, why are you suddenly putting the word 'propositions' in quotation marks?

PROPONENT: I am putting 'propositions' into quotes because I think that the ordinary way of talking about propositions whereby a proposition is conceived as what is expressed by a declarative sentence becomes inapplicable when we come to consider seriously what it is that can be the bearer of a truth value.

CRITIC: Why inapplicable?

PROPONENT: The point is that a *declarative* sentence declares something to be so or not so. Now, obviously, you cannot start an inquiry with a declaration. What you start with is a question, a problem. A declarative sentence is an outcome of inquiry, standardly, that is. It represents a solution to a problem. To solve a problem is to determine an issue affirmatively or negatively. Either way constitutes assigning a primary truth value[16] to what I have previously called an *ideational content.*[17]

CRITIC: How do you mean?

PROPONENT: Perhaps, the matter will become more clear with an example. Suppose we are considering the question of the survival or non-survival of human civilisation after a third world war. Then 'the survival of human civilisation after a third world war' is the ideational content of our problem, and what we add to this content at the close of inquiry so as to obtain the affirmative judgment 'Human civilisation can survive a third world war' or the negative judgment 'Human civilisation cannot survive a third world war' is what I am calling a primary truth value.

CRITIC: If I understand you correctly, you are saying something like this: Assigning a primary truth value to an ideational content is like answering yes or no to a yes-or-no question.

PROPONENT: Exactly. And I wish to point out, further, that if in talking of propositions we are thinking of the bearers of truth values, i.e. the elements of discourse to which truth values are added, then a proposition is something less than what is expressed by a declarative sentence; it is something in the nature of what I have called an ideational content.[18]

CRITIC: But don't we sometimes predicate truth or falsity of a proposition in the sense of what is expressed by a declarative sentence? For example, when a person says 'Human civilisation can survive a third world war' and another comments: 'That is false', falsity is clearly predicated of a declarative sentence.

PROPONENT: We do, indeed. In fact, normally, that is how the concepts of truth and falsity are used.[19] That kind of truth value predication is what I call 'comparative' and the resulting judgment

---

[16] See chapter 8, p. 121, n. 6.

[17] See chapter 10, pp. 156–8.

[18] It corresponds, in fact, to what is called a *truth function* in truth functional logic. See my 'Truth as a Logical Constant, with an Application to the Principle of Excluded Middle', *Philosophical Quarterly*, October 1975. C. I. Lewis and John Dewey are among the philosophers who have held this 'participial' conception of propositions. See Lewis, *Analysis of Knowledge and Valuation* (La Salle, 1946), p. 49; and Dewey, 'Propositions, Warranted Assertibility and Truth', *Journal of Philosophy*, 1941, reprinted in Dewey, *Problems of Men* (Philosophical Library, New York, 1946); see also Dewey, *Logic: The Theory of Inquiry* (Holt, Rinehart and Winston, New York, 1938), ch. xv, especially p. 287.

[19] See chapter 8, p. 121.

is what I call, in a rather specialised usage, a comparative judgment. But notice that when the second person, responding to the first, says 'That is false', what he says is equivalent to 'Human civilisation cannot survive a third world war'. This, as we have seen, involves assigning a primary truth value to the corresponding ideational content.[20] In terms of question and answer it involves answering no to the question or problem: 'Can human civilisation survive a third world war?' Thus the truth value *falsity* in the primary sense corresponds to a negative answer and the truth value *truth* in the primary sense corresponds to an affirmative answer. The point now is that it is obvious that every comparative truth value assignment presupposes a primary truth value assignment. It follows that, fundamentally speaking, the bearers of truth values are not propositions conceived in the image of declarative sentences but ideational contents which in the context of inquiry have the significance of questions or problems.

CRITIC: All this is interesting, but what is its relevance to the principle of excluded middle?

PROPONENT: It is this. If truth and falsity are *primarily* affirmative and negative answers to questions or problems, then to say that every proposition has at least one of these truth values implies that every problem has been solved, which is to go a bit too far.

CRITIC: Even on your own conceptions this is taking things too literally. As you yourself pointed out a while ago, a class such as the class of all propositions is open-ended. There is an infinity of propositions that have not been considered. What may justly be said to be presupposed by excluded middle is not that every problem has been solved but only that every problem is solvable.

PROPONENT: Granted. But is this claim, that every problem is solvable, a logical truth?

CRITIC: Well, it is, at least, an indispensable presupposition of logic.

PROPONENT: I doubt it. Suppose we do not know any method at all for solving a certain problem. Then to insist that it is solvable is not much more than to express a pious hope. In such a case your excluded middle would lead to needless dogmatism.

[20] Frege says what amounts to much the same thing in his *Begriffsschrift*. See *Translations from the Philosophical Writings of Gottlob Frege*, edited by Peter Geach and Max Black, Oxford, 1952, p. 2.

CRITIC: Let '*P?*' represent a problem. I should say that were '*P?*' to be shown even to be unsolvable in principle, still the corresponding declarative sentence '*P*' would be intelligible as a sentence and, hence, conceivably true.

PROPONENT: '*P*' would be intelligible only formally, only as conforming to the syntactical category of a declarative sentence. In other words '*P*' or '*P* is true' or '*P* is false' would have the form of a declarative sentence without its substance.

CRITIC: You are talking like an intuitionist logician.[21]

PROPONENT: I have some sympathy for intuitionism, but I am not a full-blown intuitionist. All that I am saying is that the assumption that every problem is solvable is not a safe claim to make in logic. This is, however, without prejudice to its utility as a hypothetical assumption in formulating the law of excluded middle.

CRITIC: I am afraid I do not understand your last sentence.

PROPONENT: What I mean is that we can incorporate a hypothetical solvability clause into the informal statement of the law of excluded middle in some such fashion as: Given that a problem is solvable, the corresponding proposition is either true or false. In terms of my own conceptions this becomes something like: Given that a problem is solvable, it is either solvable affirmatively or negatively; and of course, solving a problem presupposes a point of view.

CRITIC: How do you apply this interpretation to Russell's example?

PROPONENT: It is specifically because we believe that the problem of whether it rained on Manhattan Island on the first of January is solvable in principle in spite of the fact that we do not have the relevant evidence that we feel so certain that it either rained or did not rain at that time and place. Note, moreover, that although we do not have the evidence, we have an idea of what sort of evidence would be relevant.[22]

---

[21] Intuitionist logic is a logic based, among other things, on the rejection of excluded middle as formulated by CRITIC above. The first chapter of *Intuitionism: An Introduction* by A. Heyting (North Holland Publishing Co., Amsterdam, 2nd revised edition 1966) gives something of the flavour of the thinking underlying intuitionism. The elementary portions of intuitionist logic are represented in ch. VII, pp. 97–105.

[22] See Russell, op. cit., p. 278.

CRITIC: By the way, can you tell me how you would represent this 'hypothetical solvability clause', which you make an integral part of excluded middle, in the context of an actual symbolic logic?

PROPONENT: Actually the hypothetical assumption need not be part of any one symbolic formula. The assumption, for example, that every proposition has at least one truth value, which is common to two-valued logic and to the many-valued varieties – the notion of truth value is used in such a broad sense in many-valued contexts that a proposition's being 'undetermined' as to truth or falsity may be reckoned as indicating a truth value – this assumption is not one that you incorporate into any one symbolic formula; it is a prior assumption. The same applies to the solvability assumption. In the presence of the assumption that every proposition has at least one truth value, the principle of bivalence becomes a basic assumption of solvability. What it means, then, to say that your logic is a two-valued logic is that you are dealing with solvable problems. I would now like to return to your three-fold objection. I had not even finished answering the first of the three when the question of excluded middle cropped up. I believe I have already shown that, rightly interpreted, the principle of excluded middle is not incompatible with my view of truth.

CRITIC: Return by all means to those objections. I have no wish to force you into the technicalities of the philosophy of logic.

PROPONENT: Taking the first of the objections, then, let me say that I can see why you think that my view of truth has the consequence that when people disagree there is no point in their arguing. You seem to think that I am committed to the notion that beliefs are manifestations of arbitrary psychological impulses. Nothing is further from my conception. Belief, as I have said elsewhere, is, *standardly*, the outcome of rational inquiry. Whether a belief is rationally supportable or not is an *objective* issue, that is, an issue whose determination does not depend on the psychological peculiarities of any given person.[23] There are inter-personally specifiable criteria of rationally warranted assertibility. The existence of such criteria is made possible by the fact that human beings have certain similarities of basic physiological and mental make-up. This is what lies at the back of the possibility of human community – the possibility, that is, of the use of language and logic among

[23] See chapter 4, pp. 56–8 on objectivity and subjectivity.

men, the possibility of agreement as also of disagreement, the possibility of moral relations, and so on. The purpose of arguing when there is disagreement among persons is to bring it about by non-arbitrary means that they are of one opinion, that is to say, one rationally warranted opinion.

CRITIC: Well, then, we are back to Dewey. Truth, for you, after all, is, by and large, warranted assertibility. I wonder what, then, has happened to the difference between your view and Dewey's.

PROPONENT: I am glad that the similarity between Dewey's view of truth and mine strikes you so forcibly. I believe that the similarity is worth emphasising more than the difference. But if only for the sake of setting the record straight, I will explain the difference. For Dewey the relation between truth and rationally warranted assertibility is one of analytic identity. For me it is a synthetic relation, since not all points of view are rational. In my view the claim that truth is rationally warranted assertibility holds only in the case of normal belief. This relation between truth and rationality arises not from the formal significance of truth but from the substantive nature of belief.

CRITIC: Would you care to explain your distinction between the formal significance of truth and the substantive nature of belief?

PROPONENT: The distinction is a rather important one. The theory of truth consists, or ought to consist, of a formal or analytical part and a substantive part. The formal or analytical part, which I suspect is often taken to be the whole, seeks to clarify the relations between the concept of truth and such concepts as fact, reality, assertion, belief, proposition, statement, belief, opinion, knowledge, reason, verification, justification, etc.[24] But when this has been achieved it still remains to give an account of the vital importance of truth. This can only be done by a substantive exposition of the concepts in terms of which the formal definition of truth is fashioned. By a substantive exposition of a concept I mean an account that is not principally concerned with disclosing its conceptual relations but with its very possibility[25] and with its functions in human life. Having defined truth as warranted

---

[24] See ch. 10, p. 162.
[25] Inquiries about the possibility of concepts and modes of knowledge are called by Kant *transcendental*. Given a more empirical orientation than Kant's one might call them genetic. See chapter 10, pp. 162–71, especially pp. 162–70.

assertibility, it still remains to pursue questions such as: What are its canons? What is the fundamental basis of those canons and what role do they play in the interactions and transactions of human beings with their environment and with their own kind? Questions of this sort belong to what I call the substantive, as distinct from the formal, analytical, part of the theory of truth.

CRITIC: Could you illustrate this distinction in terms of the actual work of any philosophers?

PROPONENT: Tarski's semantic theory of truth is a paradigm of the formal,[26] analytical, theory of truth, while Dewey's leaned (in, for example, *Logic, The Theory of Inquiry*) more in the direction of the substantive theory of truth.

CRITIC: I hope it is not your suggestion that the distinction in question is a rigid one.

PROPONENT: The distinction itself is a conceptually clear one, but in the matter of exposition there is no need to separate the two parts of the theory of truth into two watertight compartments. Thus while still primarily occupied with the formal theory of truth one can take note of the fact that belief is normally the outcome of a rational effort. And this should lead us to anticipate that the substantive theory of truth would be a theory of rationality.

CRITIC: Would it not also be a theory of irrationality, since not all belief, even on your own showing, is rational?

PROPONENT: The theory of a category of thought or behaviour has to be a theory of the normal case (though defining the notion of the *normal* case can itself be quite a substantive problem, particularly in a matter like belief). Once the normal case has been clarified, the deviant or degenerate case can easily be seen for what it is. In the theory of belief the degenerate case turns out to be of a psychological rather than epistemological interest.

CRITIC: I cannot wait any longer to press an objection which is, I think, quite fatal to your view and to Dewey's. Truth is rational belief, you say. But it is specifically because we want our beliefs to be true that we bother at all to pay heed to the canons of rational inquiry. Thus by rational belief we mean a belief that is more likely than not to be true. Let us express this by saying that a rational

[26] Tarski's theory might be held to be formal in the further sense of being, in its fully elaborated form, cast in the framework of a formalised system. But this is not the aspect of it that is under consideration here.

belief is a truth-inclined belief. Then your definition as well as Dewey's involves saying that truth is truth-inclined belief. The circularity in this cannot escape any schoolboy.

PROPONENT: Actually, there would be no circularity if an independent account of truth-inclination is available. But, in any case, I have very serious reservations about the whole talk of our wanting our beliefs to be true.[27] It is apt to encourage a shopper's model of belief formation. It is as if there was a store room full of ready-made beliefs, and one went round to inspect them to find out those endowed with the truth attribute. No, the truth enterprise starts with problems, not with beliefs on hangers, and what we seek to do is not to make selections but to *solve* problems. We should not take the notion of searching for truth too literally. Searching for truth means trying to solve problems.

CRITIC: But, surely, we want our solutions to apply to the world, to be *true*, in other words, of the actual world.

PROPONENT: That is putting the cart before the horse. The message of a solution is of the form: 'The conceptual content X applies to the world'.[28] It makes doubtful sense to require that when one makes such a claim one should also entertain the idea that this too applies to the world. I fancy that in Twi, the language of the Akans of Ghana, there would be little temptation to make such a requirement, for the following reason. In this language we do not express the notion of truth as a cognitive concept with a single word. We do, indeed, have the word '*nokware*' which may be translated as 'truth', but this translation would be acceptable only as a translation of the moral rather than the cognitive, concept of truth. Thus, more strictly, '*nokware*' conveys the notion of truthfulness or veracity. We render the cognitive concept of truth by some such phrase as '*nea ate saa*', *that which is so*.[29] It would, I think, be quite natural, if one wanted a single word for truth in the cognitive sense when doing epistemology in Twi to coin some such word as '*asem – te saa*'. Strictly, the nearest equivalent of this in English would be 'true proposition'. But with or without the

---

[27] See chapter 8, pp. 119–20.

[28] If the proposition is a necessary proposition the claim is extended to all possible worlds. On the above analysis of judgment see, further, chapter 10, pp. 156–8.

[29] In chapter 8, p. 116, the bearing of this fact on the desirability of avoiding a confusion between the moral and the cognitive concepts in question was commented on.

coinage, it is obvious that such a language gives little encourage-
ment to the suggestion that a claim to the effect that something is
so ('*asem no te saa*') should be proffered as itself being so ('*te saa*').

CRITIC: Are you sure that other Akan philosophers will agree
with you?

PROPONENT: Every philosopher is welcome to his own interpretations of his language.

CRITIC: Well, it seems to me that if what you have been saying is
correct then we cannot so much as talk of true beliefs. If it is
inappropriate to say that we want our beliefs to be true, it can
hardly be appropriate to say that our beliefs are true!

PROPONENT: When we talk of the truth (or falsity) of a belief we
ipso facto convert the belief into an ideational content. Syntactically, this is indicated by the fact that what we predicate truth of is –
to take a specific example – *that* snow is white. Alternatively, we
put the sentence which expresses the belief into quotes. Both
syntactical expedients have the effect of suspending the assertoric
force of the sentence and transforming it into an ideational content.
This assertoric force is, of course, brought into play again, from the
relevant point of view, by the truth predication. This is what
happens when we speak, exploiting quotes, of the truth of the
sentence 'Snow is white'. In this process we *mention* the sentence as
distinct from *using* it in its belief-advancing role. Note, incidentally, that my account of the effect of quotation is radically different
from Tarski's, according to whom, you will recall, quotation trans-
forms a sentence into a name.[30] The upshot of these remarks is,
once again, that we should not take phrases like 'true belief' too
literally. There is, of course, nothing wrong about talking of 'true
belief', but it is important to bear in mind that this involves a
syntactical transference of commitment from the 'belief' part of the
phrase to its 'truth' part.

CRITIC: I know that you are anxious to confront the issue of
relativism but may I put one last objection before that. You ought,
I think, to show how you think you can get over obvious counter-
examples to your claim that truth is rationally justified belief. As

---

[30] Quine too insists on the name-creating powers of quotation. See, for example,
W. V. Quine, *Mathematical Logic*, Harper Torchbooks, 1962, pp. 23–33. Quine
gives here a clear account of the corresponding view of the distinction between the
use and *mention* of expressions. My suggestion above hints at a different account.

you must know, the American philosopher Edmund Gettier has given a perfect counter-example to the view that a justified belief is necessarily a true belief. In a short article entitled 'Is Justified True Belief Knowledge?',[31] where his direct concern is to refute the view that justified true belief is the same as knowledge, which he does with admirable ingenuity, he manages, in the process, to construct a simple example of a rationally justified belief which is false.

PROPONENT: I am often besieged with such supposed counter-examples.

CRITIC: But I think you will find that this one has a special simplicity and clarity. I will quote his own words as they are so precise. 'Let us suppose,' he writes, 'that Smith has strong evidence for the following proposition: "Jones owns a Ford". Smith's evidence might be that Jones has at all times in the past within Smith's memory owned a car, and always a Ford, and that Jones has just offered Smith a ride while driving a Ford ... But now imagine that ... Jones does *not* own a Ford, but is at present driving a rented car' (p. 146). Surely, here is as perfect a counter-case as there conceivably can be to your claim that truth is the same as justified belief.

PROPONENT: No, it isn't, for the following simple reason. The finding that Smith's justified belief is false is made, and can only be made, from a point of view other than Smith's; it is made from the point of view of the story teller whose company we are privileged to join. This latter point of view is obviously more richly furnished with evidence, and, by hypothesis, the evidence supports not the proposition that Jones owns a Ford but its negation. In speaking of Smith's *justified* belief, we are temporarily putting ourselves, so to speak, in his epistemological shoes. In our own shoes, we would not be justified to entertain that belief. Hence the counter-example fails. I suspect that you have forgotten the crucial role of the notion of point of view in my thesis.

CRITIC: I will not bother to bring up the converse of the counter-example just discussed, namely, the case in which a belief that is not justified is nevertheless true, since it is obvious that you would treat it in analogous fashion by reference to differences in point of view. One might almost say that the notion of point of view

---

[31] Originally published in *Analysis*, vol. 23, 1963, and reprinted in A. Phillips Griffiths (ed.), *Knowledge and Belief*, Oxford, 1967, pp. 144–6.

has become a protective talisman in your hands. But I don't want to delay you any further from your promised assault on relativism. I am myself extremely interested to see that operation, for you have said various things that I cannot distinguish from relativism. Not only have you spoken against the notion of absolute truth[32] but also you have actually said things like 'there are as many truths as there are points of view',[33] and 'truth is personal'.[34] If this is not relativism, I fail to see why.

PROPONENT: Let us then try to specify what relativism is. It is usual for relativism to be defined as 'the view that truth lacks objectivity and absoluteness – that all truth is a matter of personal opinion'.

CRITIC: That sounds exactly like your view of truth.

PROPONENT: Except that at least the part about truth lacking objectivity ruins the similarity. On my view truth is both personal and objective.

CRITIC: How is that possible? What is personal is subjective. Consequently, in identifying truth with personal opinion you have reduced it to something subjective.

PROPONENT: The trouble is that you seem to be employing an objective/subjective distinction which is defective. It is wrong to think that anything which involves essential reference to a person is subjective. As I have explained elsewhere, something is subjective only if it is connected in an unlawlike manner with the peculiarities of a person.[35]

CRITIC: Though I do not want to turn this into a dispute about words, I ought to point out to you that as a matter of idiom to say that something is personal is to say that it is private, and that certainly suggests subjectivity.

PROPONENT: Idiom is a very tricky guide. The connotations of both the words 'personal' and 'private' are heavily dependent on context. You might say, for example, that a person's sex life is a personal affair and mean by this that it is private in the sense that it ought not to be the subject of public comment or a legal inquiry.

---

[32] See, for example, chapter 5, pp. 63–7.

[33] In chapter 8, p. 115.

[34] In chapter 4, p. 55.

[35] See chapter 4, p. 57. See further my 'Logic and Ontology: IV: Meanings, Referents and Objects', *Second Order, An African Philosophical Journal*, vol. IV, no. 1, January 1975, pp. 31–3.

And you would be right, though only within obvious limits. But in the same sense you might also say that a person's metaphysical opinions are his own personal affair. In this case there surely would be no implication that a man's metaphysical opinions are irrational and capricious or immune from public criticism.

CRITIC: Your point seems to be this: something can be both personal and rational; and what is rational is *ipso facto* objective. Is that right?

PROPONENT: That is right. Rationality is absolutely crucial in this matter. I maintain that, as a psycho-epistemological fact, a basic sensitivity to the demands of rational inquiry is part of the mental make-up of any creature that can be called a human being. This, as I have pointed out already, is why there are inter-personal criteria of rational belief. The existence of inter-personal criteria is the test of objectivity. Through this what is personal can also be inter-personal. I hope you can now see that my view that truth is opinion does not imply that truth is a subjective matter.

CRITIC: Well, what you have just said seems to point away from the direction of subjectivism and relativism but I cannot forget the other things you have said about truth which seem to me to bear the stamp of subjectivism.

PROPONENT: I see that you associate relativism with subjectivism without any apparent qualification.

CRITIC: But isn't the connection obvious from the definition you cited?

PROPONENT: Yes, indeed. But I think that for the sake of greater accuracy we will have to note that there are at least two forms of relativism. There is an individualistic one, which is the sort that is articulated in the definition I started with, and there is, what one might call, a cultural type which relativises truth not to what individuals think but what various groups think.

CRITIC: You would have, I think, to interpret the term 'cultural' in the broadest manner in order to comprehend, for example, the kind of *class* relativism which the pronouncements of some Marxists on morals suggest. There is also a certain kind of relativism which revolves around the classes of believers and unbelievers.

PROPONENT: That is true. Your remark shows also that we ought to distinguish between epistemological and moral relativism.

It is obvious that in this discussion we are concerned only with epistemological relativism, though I dare say that our treatment of the moral version, which unfortunately we cannot undertake here, would be importantly analogous.

CRITIC: As regards epistemological relativism, we might quite fairly say that both of its forms involve subjectivism; the first involves individualistic subjectivism and the second, cultural subjectivism.

PROPONENT: Again, I agree; and I would say that both are afflicted with the same logical defect. But before I come to that let me deal with the remark you quoted from me to the effect that there are as many truths as there are points of view. Isn't it this remark which is bothering you the most?

CRITIC: Yes.

PROPONENT: I grant you that you can instantly reduce my view to relativism, i.e. to absurdity, by taking that remark in a certain unimaginatively literal way. On that reading, it becomes equivalent to saying that all points of view, and therefore, by and large, all propositions, are true. I have, however, previously pointed out that the remark was meant in a meta-theoretic spirit.[36] It was an attempt to put oneself into everybody's epistemological shoes for a moment. That can be done only imaginatively.

CRITIC: And, you ought to add, hypothetically.

PROPONENT: Granted. But at the moment I want to stress the following aspect of the matter. Points of view are not windowless monads, incapable of interaction. They do interact through the medium of rational discussion. Points of view can frequently be, and are, regulated by the canons of rational thinking. So in addition to taking the remark of mine under discussion imaginatively and hypothetically, you have to place it in the light of this last reflection that points of view are, to adapt a phrase of Peirce's, subject to rational self-control.

CRITIC: I must say, nevertheless, that from what you seem to have had in mind when you said that there are as many truths as there are points of view you chose a remarkably misleading phraseology.

PROPONENT: In view of the ease with which critics have been misled, you may be right.

[36] See pp. 185–6.

CRITIC: One of the main reasons why I have found your view of truth so unsatisfactory is that it seems to cut off that regulative pull which the idea of objective truth exercises on human thinking. When one person asserts something and another person asserts its negation, we who believe in an objective, absolute, truth find discussion between them worthwhile only because there is something which they both are striving to attain, namely, objective truth. But if truth is nothing but opinion it is hard to see what is the purpose of any further ado about divergent opinions. But now it begins to appear that your proposal is to substitute rationality or, shall we perhaps say, reason for truth in this office.

PROPONENT: Although, I would not phrase the matter exactly as you have, I concede that there is something in your presentation of my proposal. I think that there are various advantages in not seeing truth as something over and above reason. This, however, is not the place to pursue this matter. My immediate interest is to separate my view from relativism. When the relativist says that truth is personal – let us for convenience restrict our considerations to individualistic relativism – he means that each individual's opinions are true in their own private ways. In other words, there are no inter-personal criteria for regulating beliefs and opinions. So, if a man asserts something and another asserts its contradictory, each assertion is true in its own way and there is an end of the matter. Now, this is a highly illogical thing to say, for two mutually contradictory propositions cannot both be true in any sort of way at all.

CRITIC: Far be it from me to want to defend relativism, but you seem to dispose of it too easily. It might be said that when the relativist says that two mutually contradictory propositions may be true *each in its own way* he is not committing himself to the truth of both of them in any way. The relativist might argue that he is merely saying that the one proposition is true for a particular person and its negation is true for another.

PROPONENT: But now suppose we were to ask him whether the two propositions are both true. He would be bound, on pain of self-contradiction, to say no. And that would mean that the conjunction '*P* and not-*P*' is false *simpliciter*, contrary to his relativism.

CRITIC: On the contrary. He need not accept that he is committed to saying that the conjunction is false *simpliciter*, but only *for him*.

PROPONENT: That won't do, for what can be the significance of the phrase 'for him' in this context? It can only be construed as a hint at the possibility of the conjunction being true for another person. But in this case where the conjunction is false for our man what can 'true *for* another person' possibly mean beyond 'held to be true by another person'? Precisely nothing. The relativist just cannot make out any difference between 'true for him' and 'held to be true by him'.

CRITIC: You are saying then that it is against the relativist that the charge of confusing the notion of truth with that of a truth claim which I made against you earlier on can be made to stick.

PROPONENT: Very much so. It is only through confusion that the relativist can come to think that in using phrases like 'true for him' he is propounding a doctrine about truth as opposed to purveying trivialities about truth claims.

CRITIC: Remember I hold no brief for the relativist, but this sounds to me rather harsh. However, I would like to ask you whether you would say the same thing about the phrase 'true for me'.

PROPONENT: Well, 'true for me' and 'held to be true by me' are even more obviously equivalent. But there is an important asymmetry in the ego-centric case. Whereas 'true for him' in being shown to be equivalent to 'held to be true by him' is thereby revealed to be an allusion to nothing more than a truth claim, in the case of 'true for me', the fact that it is equivalent to 'held to be true by me' clearly brings out the redundancy of the 'for me' component.

CRITIC: You mean that 'P is true for me' is equivalent to 'P is held to be true by me' which, since the passive voice is equivalent to the active, is in turn equivalent to 'I hold P to be true' which, finally, is equivalent to asserting in the first person that P is true.

PROPONENT: That is nicely put. I would only add the following summary: The phrase 'for me' in 'P is true for me' is logically otiose, while 'true for him' is merely a deceptive way of taking note of somebody's truth claim.

CRITIC: This, presumably, is why you have been at pains to point out that it is no part of your thesis that '*P* is true' means '*P* is true from my point of view'.

PROPONENT: Yes. That would be a pointless redundancy.

CRITIC: Come to think of it, you could have made more of the case of the inconsistent conjunction. You could have asked the relativist what he would think of a man's sense of logic if he were to say quite serenely of the conjunction in question: 'It is contradictory but it is true *for me*'. Unless he himself had a poor sense of logic he would be bound to say that such a person had a poor sense of logic. And whether or not he went through the relativist ceremony of affixing 'for me' to that animadversion, it would constitute a straightforward criticism: He would be saying in essence that *no one* in his right logical senses ought to say a thing like that.

PROPONENT: Interesting! We are now being equally severe on the relativist. Seriously, I think that in so clearly demonstrating the unavoidability of criticism you have exposed the Achilles heel of relativism. The whole point of the trafficking in phrases like 'true for me', 'true for him' in relativist quarters is to protect truth claims from rational criticism.

CRITIC: That, I might say, is why I felt a moment ago that you were being rather harsh on the relativist. The real meat of the relativist doctrine is the thesis that truth claims are inaccessible to rational criticism. That, certainly, is not a triviality about truth claims. It is true that resorting to phrases like 'true for me' and 'true for him' is logically futile, but when one has shown this, one still has to deal with the question of rational criticism.

PROPONENT: But the argument you gave a moment ago killed the two birds with one stone. The logical futility of such phrases consists in the fact that they are of no avail in warding off rational criticism of truth claims.

CRITIC: But that argument dealt with contradictory assertions, which are a rather special class.

PROPONENT: I am afraid you underestimate the strength of your own argument. The question of contradictory assertions arises for the relativist in connection with every truth claim, for the following simple reason. Given any assertion, however internally consistent, one can always confront the relativist with the question whether the conjunction of this with its contradictory *could* be true *for* anybody.

And, as it emerges in your argument, he would have to say no.

CRITIC: But still this only compels him to criticise contradictory assertions.

PROPONENT: No. There is more to it. If the conjunction '*P* and not-*P*' cannot be true for anybody then this implies that when I assert that *P* is true I am committed to saying that anybody who asserts that not-*P* is true is wrong – wrong *simpliciter*, and this holds for any proposition whatever.

CRITIC: Although this is a valid criticism of relativism it sounds rather formal and, to that extent, superficial. Given that the use of the concepts of truth and falsity implies that all assertions are, in principle, open to criticism, that, by itself, does not show that criticism is always humanly feasible.

PROPONENT: Here I think that what you are saying really is that more moderate forms of relativism are not immediately vulnerable to the criticisms so far deployed. Such forms of relativism do not contend that all truth claims are immune to rational criticism, they assert only that some truth claims, perhaps a large class of them, have this immunity, for particular reasons. But the point is that any protection that such a doctrine might be thought to have from our criticisms derives specifically from its departure from the full-blooded doctrine of relativism.

CRITIC: Even so I think that a truly convincing refutation of relativism must give reasons against it which go deeper than mere formal arguments.

PROPONENT: Formal arguments are not 'mere', but I agree with the spirit of your comment. The deeper reason against relativism is, as is already apparent in my earlier remarks, that it falsely denies the existence of inter-personal criteria of rationality. That is what the denial of objectivity amounts to. Unless at least the basic canons of rational thinking were common to men they could not even communicate among themselves. Thus in seeking to foreclose rational discussion the relativist view is in effect seeking to undermine the foundations of human community.

CRITIC: In all this it would be interesting to know in what way you think your view of truth contributes to the refutation of relativism.

PROPONENT: In this way. In identifying the principle of the

objectivity of truth with the principle of rational belief it makes it possible to see in the most direct manner not only that relativism is logically and epistemologically objectionable but also that it is morally unacceptable.

CRITIC: The logical aspect is clear enough from the discussion above. It follows closely from the discussion also that no claim to *knowledge* can be immune from criticism. But how does the moral aspect arise?

PROPONENT: All three aspects are united in the principle, which I believe to be of the most overriding importance, that from the fact that a given person believes a certain proposition, it does not follow that the proposition is true.

CRITIC: Pardon me, but I should have thought that one of the most persistent criticisms of your view was exactly that it involves the denial of this principle.

PROPONENT: Well, I am sure that anybody who has followed our discussion from the start will understand that this criticism is incorrect. But it is relevant here to give the meaning of the principle in terms of my conception of truth. It comes to this: From the fact that a given person believes a certain proposition it does not follow that others will, or ought to, believe that proposition. Seen in this light, the moral dimension of the principle is unmistakable. It is obviously implied in our formulation that no one has a moral right to impose his beliefs on others and that every person has the moral right to form his own opinions. Incidentally, in the context in which I made the remark that truth is personal this is the considera-tion that was in the foreground.[37]

CRITIC: In what way does the position differ in what you call the objectivist theory of truth?

PROPONENT: The position is that this moral principle is not an internal principle of the objectivist theory of truth, but is held, if it is held, by the adherents of that theory as a separate moral princi-ple.

CRITIC: Are you not conflating the cognitive concept of truth with the moral concept of truth, contrary to a distinction which you yourself have insisted on in the course of our discussion as well as elsewhere?

PROPONENT: No; what I am maintaining is that my theory of

[37] See chapter 4 pp. 54–5.

the cognitive concept of truth contains the moral principle mentioned as an intrinsic part.

CRITIC: I wonder, though, what your moral principle is going to be worth in practice if, as your view implies, truth is not absolute, eternal, but can change with changes in commitment.

PROPONENT: This was the third part of your three-fold objection. Of course, to say that truth can change is nonsensical; it is self-contradictory. But my view has no such implication. Let us see in more precise terms what a change of commitment might mean. Suppose I believe that P at time t_1 and at time t_2 I find good reasons to jettison it and assert its contradictory. This is a change of opinion; it indicates a change in commitment, ordinarily speaking.

CRITIC: Which, on your view, must entail, even strictly speaking, that truth can change, contrary to the law of non-contradiction.

PROPONENT: Let us be more cautious.

CRITIC: Even about so obvious a point?

PROPONENT: It may become less obvious the more closely you look. Let me ask you this. Is the situation just described not one in which one commitment is succeeded by another?

CRITIC: Of course it is.

PROPONENT: Has any change occurred in the first or the second commitment?

CRITIC: There has not been any change in any one of the two commitments considered in itself. But you ought, I think, to note that when we talk of a change in commitment it is always in relation to a person.

PROPONENT: So that it is in the person that the change has occurred not in the commitments.

CRITIC: I can see what you are driving at. You are going to say that, *strictly speaking*, we cannot say that commitments actually change. And your argument is that since commitments do not really change the question of the corresponding changeability of truth does not arise.

PROPONENT: I am bound to concur, and I would add that this point about commitment illustrates the frequent need to take ordinary language locutions with a philosophical pinch of salt.

CRITIC: But there is a difficulty. If the first commitment has not changed, then presumably the corresponding truth remains in force. The same obviously applies to the second commitment. Hence we are compelled to say that both P and not-P remain in force as truths, disregarding non-contradiction utterly! So whether we say that commitments change or do not change we are, or, more literally, you are, entangled in a contradiction.

PROPONENT: There is a simple mistake in your reasoning. You say that if the first commitment has not changed then it remains in force as a truth. But this is contrary to our hypothesis. We have abandoned it and so it is no longer *our* commitment. It remains a commitment, historically a commitment, but not a contemporary one. Truth, notwithstanding such appearances as are fostered by phrases like 'it used to be true', 'it was true', 'it will be true', is *contemporary* commitment; it is ongoing commitment. Take the contemporaneity away and what you have left is only a truth claim.

CRITIC: A fresh dilemma awaits you. You maintain that it is nonsensical to say that truth can change. I, of course, applaud. But if so, then truth is changeless, Eternal and Absolute. And yet you have inveighed against these notions.

PROPONENT: When I say that truth does not change I am doing no more than repeating the principle of non-contradiction, which says that no proposition can be true together with its contradictory, or reaffirming its equivalent, the principle of identity which says that if a proposition is true, then it is true. If saying that truth is eternal and absolute means simply that when a proposition is true, it is true, then I have no quarrel with it. But I doubt that it is this tautology that so much excites the enthusiasm of the devotees of Eternal and Absolute truth. I see in these notions a reification of truth; truth is conceived by them as an independent entity. That is naïve metaphysics. I see in it, furthermore, a certain tendency to claim infallibility. The process is somewhat as follows. Infallibility is, first, modestly attributed to Absolute truth, something independent of us mortals. But in due course the devotee comes to see himself as being in possession of the truth about some highly important matter. There is then a smooth, almost imperceptible, transference of the infallibility of the independent, abstract entity Truth to a concrete inhabitant of this earth. I have often commented on the practical dangers that might arise from this habit of thought.[38] I believe that a measure of fallibilism is morally benefi-cial.[39]

CRITIC: Before you get too expansive, perhaps you should note that you cannot begin to talk of fallibilism until you have made sense of the notion of fallibility in the context of your view of truth.

PROPONENT: Fallibility was the subject of the second of your three-part objection. Given all that we have said already I think that this notion can here be treated quite briefly. To say that a proposition I now believe may be false is simply to withdraw my commitment from it hypothetically, and contemplate, equally hypothetically, a negative issue to the corresponding problem.

CRITIC: I don't quite follow you. If my saying 'P is true' means the same as 'I believe P', then if I hypothetically contemplate the falsity of P, I am envisaging the possibility of a true proposition being also false.

PROPONENT: Your difficulty is founded on a mistaken identity. It is not my belief, as my belief, that becomes the object of my hypothetical contemplation; it is only the conceptual residue left after the hypothetical subtraction of my commitment that now becomes the object to which falsity is ascribed. Indeed, irrespec-tive of the theory of truth that may be in the background, any statement of the form 'P is true but it may be false' will have to construe the 'it' as referring to something devoid of a truth assign-ment.

CRITIC: I can see that this takes us back to your earlier remarks about the bearers of truth value.

PROPONENT: Yes, those remarks are very relevant here.

CRITIC: Talking of the bearers of truth value, I have noticed that in the context of what you call comparative truth-value assignment you speak indiscriminately of the truth of propositions, sentences, statements, etc., without compunction. Yet something quite weighty hangs on whether it is propositions rather than sentences that can be spoken of as true or false. As you must know, one of the principal objections that has been urged against Tarski's semantic theory of truth, for example, is that we don't predicate truth (or falsity) of a mere sentence, which is just a sequence of physical

---

[38] In chapters 4 (p. 54), 5 (pp. 66–7), 6 (p. 96) and 8 (p. 122).

[39] See in addition to the references in the immediately preceding footnote, chapter 8, p. 123.

marks or sounds. According to this view, that which may intelligibly be said to be either true or false is the statement which a sentence may be used to convey.[40]

PROPONENT: I am afraid Tarski himself is partially to blame, for he invites this criticism by speaking sometimes as if a sentence is, to quote his own words, 'certain physical objects, namely, linguistic expressions' or, more strictly, 'classes of inscriptions of similar form (thus not individual physical things, but classes of such things)'. Yet Tarski in the same place[41] says 'By "sentence", we understand here what is usually meant in grammar by "declarative sentence".' But in grammar a sentence is a group of words expressing a complete thought and a declarative sentence is one expressing a declaratory thought. In this sense a sentence is not just a class of physical objects but a class of that sort taken in association with a thought. Hence the notion of a sentence in this sense – there is no other applicable sense when talking of the truth or falsity of sentences – is more complex than that of, say, a proposition because a proposition, a declarative thought, turns out to be an aspect, namely, the signification, of a declarative sentence. Accordingly, I find nothing wrong with talking of the truth or falsity of sentences, properly so conceived, alongside propositions, statements, assertions, beliefs, and so forth.[42]

CRITIC: Every little point threatens to take us into the deep waters of the philosophy of logic. I hope my next objection does not lead us into complications. You remember you cut me short in the process of advancing a fourth objection some time ago.

---

[40] See, for example, Strawson in Margaret MacDonald (ed.), *Philosophy and Analysis* (Blackwell, 1954). Popper (*Objective Knowledge*) dismisses this kind of objection contemptuously and, unfortunately, rather hastily.

[41] Feigl and Sellars, op. cit., p. 53.

[42] See further my 'Logic and Ontology, Part III: Abstract Entities and the Analysis of Designation', *Second Order, An African Journal of Philosophy*, vol. III, no. 2, July 1974, pp. 48–52. There are, to be sure, certain fine points about sentences, propositions and statements such as are brought out in Lemmon's 'Sentences, Statements and Propositions' in Williams and Montifiore (eds.), *British Analytical Philosophy* (Routledge and Kegan Paul, 1966). Indexical sentences, such as 'I am happy', are particularly worthy of note. The significational aspect of an indexical sentence, taken on its own, is an incomplete proposition which requires further specification before becoming susceptible of ascriptions of truth or falsity. Given adequate specification, the corresponding sentence, of course, also becomes susceptible of truth value. All this is without prejudice to the fact that for formal purposes sentences may be viewed from a purely structural point of view.

PROPONENT: Let us hear it by all means. What is it about?

CRITIC: It concerns necessary truth. As you know, a necessary truth is a proposition that cannot possibly be false. Since you admit, even insist, that any belief or opinion may be false it follows that a necessary truth cannot be just a belief or an opinion. Hence your theory breaks down when applied to necessary truth.

PROPONENT: Not so. This one, I think, can be disposed of quite simply. Your point about necessary truth can be reformulated as follows: If a proposition is a necessary truth, then its negation is impossible, that is, necessarily false.

CRITIC: I would accept that. Yes.

PROPONENT: And given any proposition whatever, the claim that it is a necessary truth may be true or false.

CRITIC: Right.

PROPONENT: Therefore, the statement that a necessary truth or, what amounts to the same thing, a necessary proposition, cannot be false is a remark about the logical character rather than the epistemological status of such propositions. As far as knowing is concerned, we are as fallible with regard to our claims of necessary truth as we are in our claims of contingent truth.

CRITIC: That seems plausible.

PROPONENT: Therefore, a necessary truth is just as much a matter of belief as a contingent truth.

CRITIC: Is this, perhaps, what was at the back of Quine's mind when he claimed in his famous essay 'Two Dogmas of Empiricism'[43] that even logical principles are ultimately open to revision?

PROPONENT: Something of this sort is certainly relevant to Quine's position, but I would not speculate as to what was at the back of his mind at the time. Note, however, that his position is more radical, for he does not accept that the alleged difference in logical character between necessary and contingent propositions is irreducible.[44] On this point my position is, of course, different.

CRITIC: Be that as it may, I must say that I still find your view

[43] In W. V. Quine, *From a Logical Point of View*, Harper Torchbooks, New York, 1953.

[44] See also Quine's beautiful essay on 'Necessary Truth' in Sidney Morgenbesser's collection *Philosophy of Science* (Basic Books, New York, 1967). The essay is also reprinted in Quine's own *The Ways of Paradox*, revised and enlarged edition, Harvard, 1976.

that truth is nothing but opinion highly implausible, particularly in relation to necessary truth. For example, we talk of necessary truths, as we have been doing lately, without any sense of incongruity, but who can talk of necessary opinions with an easy linguistic conscience?

PROPONENT: Actually my linguistic conscience is not as easy as yours seems to be in talking of necessary truth. 'Necessary' is a relative term. It does not make sense to say that a thing is necessary in itself. Something is necessary only for a purpose. The philosophical idiom of 'necessary truth' may, thus, be no more than a linguistic impropriety that has gained dignity through long usage.

CRITIC: But this does not mean that there is any impropriety about what the phrase 'necessary truth' refers to.

PROPONENT: Then why may we not say the same about the phrase 'necessary opinion'?

CRITIC: Supposing you could get over this particular objection, what about other obvious incongruities?

PROPONENT: Such as?

CRITIC: Such as that we speak of learning new truths but not of learning new opinions.

PROPONENT: But we form new opinions, solve new problems, acquire new beliefs, in the course of rational inquiry. And what I am saying is that this is the sort of thing we are referring to when we talk of learning new truths. The linguistic circumstance you mention has no tendency to show that this is not so.

CRITIC: I was also going to point out as another example of incongruity that if you take a statement like 'It is an unfortunate fact that might sometimes prevails over right', a translation in terms of your thesis produces an absurdity. It becomes something like: 'It is my unfortunate opinion that might sometimes prevails over right.'

PROPONENT: Are you surprised that a mechanical translation leads to an absurdity?

CRITIC: You are saying, then, that a more correct translation is possible?

PROPONENT: Definitely. We might begin by noting that the statement could be rendered simply as 'Might, unfortunately, sometimes prevails over right.'

CRITIC: An admission that reference to belief or opinion cannot be accommodated in the translation?

PROPONENT: No. We might also give the following translation: 'It is my belief (opinion) that, unfortunately, might sometimes prevails over right.' I should observe that, in general, the production of translations such as you have mentioned cannot be of any real consequence unless it can be shown that no normalising translation is possible.

CRITIC: May I make a confession?

PROPONENT: Go ahead, if it is a philosophical confession.

CRITIC: I feel an uneasiness about our treatment of relativism. I have the suspicion that in the criticism of relativism, in which we have more or less co-operated, we may perhaps have been, both of us, aiming at a straw man. One effect of this uncertainty is that I am not sure that your own view has been shown to be really different from relativism.

PROPONENT: You suspect that we have unfairly saddled the relativist with absurd tenets?

CRITIC: It occurs to me that a relativist might retort that he does not have to think that our belief is immune to rational criticism nor deny the existence of inter-personal criteria of rationality.

PROPONENT: Then why would he call himself a relativist?

CRITIC: Because he does not accept the objectivity of truth. The point is that the existence of inter-personal criteria of rational belief may show the objectivity of rational belief; it does not show the objectivity of truth, if, as you maintain, truth is logically distinct from rational belief.

PROPONENT: Apropos your last clause let me explain one thing. Though I contend that the concept of truth is not analytically identical with that of rational belief, still, on my view, given that a belief is rationally warranted, it follows logically that it is true.

CRITIC: Nevertheless, you are bound to deny that given that a belief is true, it follows logically that it is rationally warranted, otherwise truth and rational belief would not be logically separable. Here, incidentally, is a respect in which your departure from Dewey creates difficulties for you. Dewey can claim that truth is objective on his view because rational belief is objective, and truth is identical with rational belief. This line of argument is not open to you, though you sometimes – especially, when trying to secure objectivity – talk as if your view were the same as Dewey's. Your view simply identifies truth with belief, and this is what makes it, unlike Dewey's, relativistic and subjectivistic.

PROPONENT: You seem to ignore one of my premises. I hold that normal belief is rational belief. To recognise that a proposition is not rationally warranted and yet to claim it to be true, that is, to commit oneself to it, is, as I have said elsewhere, to manifest an abnormality of the mind.[45] No one who espouses this view of belief can consistently admit that a proposition is not rationally warranted and yet commit himself to it by calling it true. From this point of view, then, one can say that a belief is true if and only if it is rationally warranted.

CRITIC: So that in your view too there is an equivalence between truth and rational belief?

PROPONENT: Yes, but the point is that the equivalence is a relative one; it is relative to the conception of belief mentioned.

CRITIC: If I understand you right, your argument is that the conception of belief in question does not follow logically from your view of truth as opinion. Thus a person may conceivably combine this formal theory of truth with a conception of belief according to which in some cases, such as in the phenomenon of religious faith, belief need not be based on a rational warrant. For such a person the equivalence will not hold.

PROPONENT: Exactly. The irrationalist who says things like '*P* is true but it is not rationally warranted' is not contradicting himself. He is wrong; more tragically, he is something of a mental case, but he is not necessarily misusing the concept of truth.

CRITIC: May I take it, then, that your position is that your conception of truth might be said to be relatively objective, relative, that is, to your conception of belief? And, presumably, you would distinguish between your view and relativism by describing the latter as absolutely subjective.

PROPONENT: As regards my view, it is not quite accurate to put the matter in this way. I would say that my view is objective, pure and simple. There are two points to note in this connection. First, the question of the objectivity of truth is, strictly, a question about the nature of belief, not about the formal definition of truth. It is a judgment of truth or falsity that is either objective or subjective,

---

[45] See pp. 117–18, pp. 179–80.

not the concept itself of truth.[46] Second, relativism itself is a theory of belief and communication, not a formal theory of truth. In fact, relativism is compatible with any formal theory of truth. Take the theory that truth is correspondence with reality. Suppose this is so, still the relativist can say: 'But whether any given proposition corresponds with reality is a matter of individual belief not decidable on inter-personal criteria.' (If he is a 'cultural' relativist, he would, of course, say it is a matter of cultural-group belief not decidable on cross-cultural criteria. The objection against both forms of relativism is essentially the same.)

CRITIC: But you are repeating the claim that the relativist is committed to denying the existence of inter-personal criteria of rational belief, which is in dispute.

PROPONENT: If belief is what relativism is about, there is nothing else for it to be committed to. A relativist who believes in the existence of inter-personal criteria of rationality among the human species, who grants that disagreements are, in principle, resolvable by rational argument, is a relativist only in name. Historically, that is the opposite of what the relativist has maintained.

CRITIC: Well, I have found this conversation on truth interesting. I am afraid I cannot say that you have persuaded me, but you are going to keep me thinking.

PROPONENT: Fair enough. The question 'What is truth?' looks simple, but it is now obvious that its answer, even when given in one word: 'opinion', is by no means simple. In such matters there is no excuse for dogmatism, and I too will continue to reflect on them. Goodbye and thank you.

---

[46] Explanations of the objective/subjective distinction are to be found on pp. 56–8, and pp. 121–2.

Origins of the essays

Except for chapter 12 ('Truth: a dialogue'), which is new, all the chapters of this volume were first published in the places indicated below. They have been revised and, in some cases, expanded.

1 Philosophy and an African culture:
Fellow's Inaugural Address delivered to the Ghana Academy of Arts and Sciences, Accra, October 1976.

2 On an African orientation in philosophy:
Second Order: An African Journal of Philosophy, University of Ife Press, Ile-Ife, Nigeria, July 1972.

3 How not to compare African traditional thought with Western thought:
Ch'indaba, Accra, July/December 1976.

4 What can philosophy do for Africa?:
Paper presented at the International Council for Philosophy and Humanistic Studies Colloquium on 'The Place and Role of the Humanities in Africa Today' in April 1975 at Accra.

5 Marxism, philosophy and ideology:
Abridged version of a paper published as a Supplement of *The Legon Observer*, Accra, 1966.

6 In praise of utopianism: *Thought and Practice: Journal of the Philosophical Association of Kenya*, vol. 2, no. 2, 1975.

7 Philosophy, mysticism and rationality: *Universitas: An Inter-Faculty Journal*, University of Ghana, Legon, Ghana, March 1972.

8 Truth as opinion: *Universitas*, Legon, March 1973.

9 To be is to be known: *Legon Journal of the Humanities*, University of Ghana, vol. 1, 1974.

10 What is philosophy?:   *Universitas*, Legon, March 1974.

11 In defence of opinion (originally 'On behalf of opinion: a rejoinder'):   *Universitas*, Legon, May/November 1976.

Index